Volume 3, Numbers 3 & 4, Fall & Winter 1997

Women's Health:
Research on Gender, Behavior, and Policy

SPECIAL ISSUE:
Black Women's Health
Hope Landrine and Elizabeth A. Klonoff, Guest Editors

Guest Editors

Hope Landrine is a Black clinical and health psychologist. She received her PhD in clinical psychology from the University of Rhode Island, postdoctoral training in social psychology at Stanford University, and postdoctoral training in cancer prevention as a National Cancer Institute Fellow in the Department of Preventive Medicine, University of Southern California Medical School. A Senior Research Scientist at the Public Health Foundation (Los Angeles County), her research focuses on the health of women and of ethnic-cultural minorities. Her outstanding research in both areas has gained her Fellow status in APA Divisions 35 (Psychology of Women) and 45 (Psychology of Ethnic Minorities), more than $1 million in grants, the 1996 Association of Women in Psychology Distinguished Publication Award, and numerous other awards. Her books include *Bringing Cultural Diversity to Feminist Psychology: Theory, Research, Practice* (APA, 1995), and with Elizabeth Klonoff, *African American Acculturation: Deconstructing Race and Reviving Culture* (Sage, 1996), *Preventing Misdiagnosis of Women: A Guide to Physical Disorders That Have Psychiatric Symptoms* (Sage, 1997), and *Discrimination Against Women: Prevalence, Consequences, Remedies* (Sage, 1997).

Elizabeth A. Klonoff is a clinical and health psychologist who received her PhD from the University of Oregon. She was a faculty member at Duke University Medical School (Obstetrics/Gynecology, Psychiatry, and Pediatrics) and then at Case Western Reserve University Medical School (Psychiatry, Psychology, Neurology, and Pediatrics) where she was also the Director of the Behavioral Medicine Clinic and of the Chronic Pain Unit (University Hospitals of Cleveland) from 1979 to 1988. She joined the faculty of California State University–San Bernardino (CSUSB) in 1988 and is currently a professor of psychology and Executive Director of The Behavioral Health Institute at CSUSB. Her research focuses on the health of women, ethnic-cultural minorities, and children. Her outstanding research on these topics has gained her Fellow status in APA Division 45 (Psychology of Ethnic Minorities) and more than $2 million in grants. Her books, with Hope Landrine, include *African American Acculturation: Deconstructing Race and Reviving Culture* (Sage, 1996), *Preventing Misdiagnosis of Women: A Guide to Physical Disorders That Have Psychiatric Symptoms* (Sage, 1997), and *Discrimination Against Women: Prevalence, Consequences, Remedies* (Sage, 1997).

WOMEN'S HEALTH: RESEARCH ON GENDER, BEHAVIOR, AND POLICY, 3(3&4), 165–181

Introduction: The State of Research on Black Women in Health Psychology and Behavioral Medicine

Elizabeth A. Klonoff

Behavioral Health Institute
California State University–San Bernardino

Hope Landrine

Public Health Foundation
City of Industry, CA

Delia L. Lang

Behavioral Health Institute
California State University–San Bernardino

In this article we briefly review data on the poor state of Black women's health and then analyze the nature of research on their health in health psychology and behavioral medicine. We demonstrate that health psychology and behavioral medicine not only exclude Black women as participants in empirical studies, but also fail to thoroughly investigate the problems that are most prevalent among and accountable for the poor health of Black women. We conclude that this special issue devoted to Black women's health is crucial and long overdue.

Key words: Black women, health status, health psychology, behavioral medicine

In this article we briefly review the most recent (1996) data from the National Center for Health Statistics (NCHS) to provide an overview of the current state of Black American women's health. This review reveals two findings:

Correspondence concerning this article should be addressed to Elizabeth Klonoff, Department of Psychology, California State University, San Bernardino, 5500 University Parkway, San Bernardino, CA 92407. E-mail: eklonoff@wiley.csusb.edu.

1. The health of Black women is significantly poorer than that of White women in terms of morbidity (prevalence of diseases), mortality (death rates from diseases), or both.
2. Black women have a higher morbidity and mortality from certain diseases (e.g., diabetes) and health problems (e.g., obesity) than other groups of women.

With Black women's poor health status and their prevalent diseases and health problems highlighted, we then examine the extent to which research in health psychology and behavioral medicine has addressed these in an effort to decrease Black women's morbidity and mortality. Specifically, we review all empirical articles published in the two leading health psychology journals (*Health Psychology* and *Journal of Behavioral Medicine*) from 1982 to 1996, and ask two related but different questions: (a) Does research in these journals focus on the diseases and health problems that are most prevalent among and problematic for Black women? (b) To the extent that there are articles on these topics, do those—and articles on other topics as well—include Black women as participants, so that statements about the correlates of Black women's health and ways to improve it can be made? The results of this analysis of journal articles provide the rationale for this special issue, and so we conclude this article with a discussion of its content.

THE STATE OF BLACK WOMEN'S HEALTH

NCHS publishes annual reports on the health status of Americans by age, gender, disease, and ethnicity, using data from surveys, death records, interviews, and physician reports on a random, stratified, representative sample. To provide a brief overview of the state of Black women's health relative to that of White women, we summarized some of the data from the NCHS (1996) report in Tables 1 to 4.

As shown in Table 1, the 1993 death rate for Black women (per 100,000 in the population) from all causes was 1.57 times higher than that for White women. Death from heart disease, cerebrovascular disease, diabetes, kidney disease, AIDS, homicide, and cancer contributed to these ethnic differences among women. Specifically, Black women's death rate from heart disease was 1.67 times higher, and from cerebrovascular disease was 1.76 times higher, than that for White women; and Black women's death rate from cerebrovascular disease also was higher than that for White men. For diabetes, Black women's death rate was 2.69 times higher than that for White women, and for kidney disease it was 2.88 times higher. Black women also were more likely than White men to die from diabetes and kidney disease. For AIDS, Black women's death rate was 9.11 times that for White women. Similarly, Black women's death rate due to homicide was 4.47 times that for White women, and was higher than that for White men as well. For deaths from cancers,

Black women's death rates exceeded those for White women for all cancers except respiratory cancers.

As shown in Table 2, Black women's 5-year survival rate of cancers also was poorer than the survival rates for their White cohorts: 59% of White but only 47% of Black women cancer patients (all sites) survived 5 years after diagnosis. These differences in cancer survival rate held for a variety of types of cancer (e.g., colon, lung, and bronchus), and were large for breast cancer: Whereas 84.4% of White women with breast cancer survived 5 years postdiagnosis, only 69% of Black women did. Similarly (Table 3), 49.6% of all Black women were overweight or obese (as measured by physicians rather than self-reported) compared to 32.6% of White women; and 31% of Black women were diagnosed with hypertension (based on physician measures) compared to 18.3% of White women. Likewise, Black women were 16.5 times more likely than White women to be diagnosed with AIDS:

TABLE 1
Age-Adjusted Death Rates (Per 100,000) From Selected Causes by Race and Gender, 1993

	Men		Women	
Cause of Death	White	Black	White	Black
All causes	627.5	1052.2	367.7	578.8
Heart disease	190.3	267.9	99.2	165.3
Cerebrovascular disease	26.8	51.9	22.7	39.9
Diabetes	12.2	26.3	10.0	26.9
Kidney disease	4.9	12.4	3.2	9.2
AIDS	19.0	70.0	1.9	17.3
Homicide	8.9	70.7	3.0	13.4
Cancer deaths: All sites	156.4	238.9	110.1	135.3
Colorectal	15.4	20.7	10.5	15.2
Respiratory	56.3	86.0	27.6	27.3
Breast	—	—	21.2	27.1

TABLE 2
Five-Year Survival Rates From Cancer: Percentage of Patients, 1986–1991

	Men		Women	
Cause of Death	White	Black	White	Black
All sites	48.8	38.2	59.0	47.2
Colon	63.7	51.3	61.4	53.6
Lung and bronchus	12.1	10.7	15.9	11.1
Breast	—	—	84.4	69.0

From June 1994 to June 1995, 61.2 Black women, compared to 3.7 White women (per 100,000 in the population) received the diagnosis. Finally, in 1993 the number of years of life lost before age 65 (because of deaths before that age) for Black women was 2.23 times that for White women: Black women lost 7,182.4 years compared to 3,218.8 years for White women.

These data represent only a small portion of those available from such national surveys, but indicate clearly that the current status of Black women's health is poor relative to that of White women. Other data from the NCHS indicate that Black women's health is poor relative to that of Hispanic, Native American, and Asian and Pacific Islander women, despite the fact that some of these ethnic groups of women have rates of poverty and low education similar to those of Black women (NCHS, 1996). For example, as indicated in Table 4, Black women's death rates from heart disease, cerebrovascular disease, and breast cancer exceeded those of all American women—White, Latino, Native American, and Asian and Pacific Islander alike.

TABLE 3
Other Health Data

Cause of Death	Men		Women	
	White	Black	White	Black
Percentage of population over-weight, 1988–1991	32.2	32.9	32.6	49.6
Percentage of population with hyper-tension, 1988–1991	25.1	37.4	18.3	31.0
Number of cases of AIDS diagnosed, 1994–1995	36.1	199.5	3.7	61.2
Years of potential life lost before age 65, 1993: All causes	6,291.1	14,344.0	3,218.8	7,182.4

TABLE 4
Age-Adjusted Death Rates (Per 100,000) From Selected Causes: Women by Ethnicity, 1991–1993

Cause of Death	White	Black	Native American	Asian	Latino
Heart disease	99.3	164.4	73.5	55.8	70.3
Cerebrovascular disease	22.7	40.3	19.0	21.7	17.3
Breast cancer	21.8	27.2	9.7	10.0	12.9

Thus, from such data, it is reasonable to conclude that the state of Black women's health is poor relative to that of all other American women (particularly relative to that of White women), and that this difference is due in part to Black women's higher morbidity and mortality from eight sources: diabetes, hypertension, obesity, cardiovascular disease, AIDS, cerebrovascular disease, homicide, and cancer. Likewise, because these eight diseases, health problems, and threats to health are prevalent among Black women, it is appropriate to conceptualize these as Black women's health problems. Finally, it is reasonable to conclude that research on Black women's health, and particularly on these eight diseases and problems, is needed to decrease Black women's morbidity and mortality.

THE STATE OF RESEARCH IN HEALTH PSYCHOLOGY AND BEHAVIORAL MEDICINE

With the health problems and diseases that are prevalent among Black women outlined, we assess the current state of research in health psychology and behavioral medicine on Black women's health and pose these two questions:

1. Do empirical investigations in health psychology and behavioral medicine include Black women as research participants, so that statements and suggestions for improving Black women's health can be made?
2. Do empirical investigations in health psychology and behavioral medicine focus on the previously mentioned diseases and health problems that are prevalent and problematic for Black women, and thereby highlight ways to decrease Black women's morbidity and mortality?

METHOD

Journals Selected

To answer these questions, we reviewed all empirical articles published in *Health Psychology* and in the *Journal of Behavioral Medicine*, 1982 through 1996, and coded each article for ethnicity and gender of participants, and for topic. We selected *Health Psychology* because it is the official journal of APA Division 38 (Division of Health Psychology), and as such, largely represents the focus, interests, and direction of health psychology as a discipline. Thus, articles on health published in other APA journals (e.g., *Journal of Consulting and Clinical Psychology* or *Journal of Personality and Social Psychology*) are similar to those in *Health Psychology* in their focus. Likewise, we selected the *Journal of Behavioral Medicine* because it is a well-known, long-established, and respected health psychology journal that also is representative of the focus, concerns, and direction of the field. It is then reasonable to select these two journals as prototypical of health psychology and behavioral medicine, and to argue that their treatment of Black women's health is mirrored in other journals as well. We treat these separately here because one is the official journal of an APA division, whereas the other is not, and then we also analyze them together.

Coding Gender and Ethnicity

Where the gender of participants was concerned, articles were coded in six categories. The first three categories were (a) All Women, if all of the participants were women; (b) Mostly Women, if more than 56% of the participants were women; and (c) Equally Split, if 45% to 55% of the participants were women. These three categories were analyzed separately and then summed into the additional category (d) Total That Included Women to yield information on the number of studies that had a reasonable percentage of women participants. Remaining categories were (e) All or Mostly Men, in which 56% to 100% of the participants were men; and (f) Gender Unspecified, in which the gender of the participants was never specified in the article.

Likewise, where the ethnicity of the participants was concerned, articles were coded in eight categories. The first two categories were (a) All or Mostly Black, in which 80% to 100% of the participants were Black; and (b) Black Versus Other Ethnic Group, in which Blacks were included in sufficient number to compare them to some other ethnic group, and hence make comments about Black health (at least 30% of the participants were Black in these cases). These two categories were analyzed separately and then summed into a third category (c) Total That Included Blacks, to yield information on the number of studies that could speak to Black health. Other categories were (d) All or Mostly White, in which 80% to 100% of the participants were White; (e) White Versus Other Ethnic Group, in which Whites were compared to some other ethnic group (not Blacks) who were present in sufficient number for such analyses; (f) All or Mostly Other Minority, in which 80% to 100% of the participants were a minority group (e.g., Latinos, Asians); and (g) Multiple Ethnic Groups, in which there were at least three ethnic groups. Some of the articles in the latter category included Blacks as participants but did not analyze Blacks separately or compare Blacks to the other ethnic groups, and hence could not make any statements about Black health (these articles seemed to be striving for representative samples). A final category was (h) Ethnicity Unspecified, in which the ethnicity of the participants was not described anywhere in the article.

Coding Topics

The diverse topics in health psychology and behavioral medicine were collapsed into eight categories reflecting the health problems that are most prevalent among Black women, and were coded as: (a) Diabetes, (b) Obesity and Exercise, (c) Breast

Cancer, (d) Other Cancer, (e) Cardiovascular Disease, (f) Hypertension, and (g) AIDS and HIV. All other articles, although on important topics, did not address these health problems known to pose the greatest threats to Black women where morbidity and mortality are concerned, and so were all categorized together as (h) Other Topics.

RESULTS

Gender and Ethnicity in *Health Psychology*

Table 5 displays the results of analyses for the gender and ethnicity of participants for both journals. As shown (top of table), there were 570 empirical articles with human participants (the seven articles with animal subjects are omitted) published in *Health Psychology* between 1982 and 1996. Of these 570, 248 (43.5%) focused primarily on women (56%–100% of the participants were women), and the majority (373 or 65.4%) included women as at least 45% of the participants (shaded row, top of Table 5). Only 149 (26.1%) focused primarily on men, and 48 (8.4%) failed to ever specify the gender of the participants. Thus, 65.4% of the studies in *Health Psychology* could speak to women's health insofar as women constituted 45% to 100% of the participants. The story for Blacks was quite different.

As shown (Table 5 top, shaded column), only 45 of the 570 studies (7.9%) published in *Health Psychology* included Black participants (women, men, or both) in sufficient numbers to analyze for and make statements about Black health, and only 8 studies (1.4%) focused on Blacks (80%–100% of the participants were Black). In 53.0% of the studies (302 of 570), the ethnicity of the participants was never described anywhere in the article, and in an additional 25.4% ($n = 145$) of the studies, all or almost all of the participants were White.

Finally, analyzing the intersection of gender and ethnicity (intersection of shaded row and shaded column, top of Table 5) reveals that only 35 of the 570 studies (6.1%) included Black women as participants in a manner that made it possible to analyze for and make statements about Black women's health. Stated differently, the majority of the studies (373 or 65.4% of all studies published) included a large sample of women, but Black women were among them in only 35 articles (9.4%).

Gender and Ethnicity in *Journal of Behavioral Medicine*

Results for the *Journal of Behavioral Medicine* were similar. As shown (bottom of Table 5), 560 articles with human participants were published in the journal between 1982 and 1996. Of these 560, 223 (39.8%) focused primarily on women (56%–100% of the participants were women), and the majority (368 or 65.7%) included women as at least 45% of the participants (shaded row, bottom of Table 5). Only 127 (22.7%) focused primarily on men, and 65 (11.6%) failed to mention

TABLE 5
Ethnicity and Gender of the Participants in Health Psychology Research, 1982–1996

| | 1 | 2 | 3 | 4 | (3 + 4) | | | | |
Journal	Ethnicity Unspecified	All or > 80% White	All or > 80% Black	Black vs. Other Ethnic Group	Total That Included Blacks	White vs. Other Ethnic Group	All or > 80% Other Minority	Multiple Ethnic Groups	Total
Health Psychology									
Total articles	302	145	8	37	45	4	8	66	570
1. All women	39	31	4	10	14	0	2	9	95
2. Mostly women	81	40	1	6	7	4	1	20	153
3. Equally split	61	27	1	13	14	0	2	21	125
Total that included women (1 + 2 + 3)	181	98	6	29	35	4	5	50	373
All or mostly men	82	44	1	7	8	0	3	12	149
Gender unspecified	39	3	1	1	2	0	0	4	48
Journal of Behavioral Medicine									
Total articles	366	118	13	10	23	3	3	47	560
1. All women	46	23	1	0	1	0	0	7	77
2. Mostly women	95	33	6	1	7	1	0	10	146
3. Equally split	95	24	1	5	6	1	1	18	145
Total that included women (1 + 2 + 3)	236	80	8	6	14	2	1	35	368
All or mostly men	84	29	4	2	6	0	2	6	127
Gender unspecified	46	9	1	2	3	1	0	6	65

Note. Total articles, both journals = 1,130. Total including women = 741 (65.6%); Blacks = 68 (6.02%); Black women = 49 (4.3%). Total with unspecified gender = 113 (10%); unspecified ethnicity = 668 (59.1%); both gender and ethnicity unspecified = 85 (7.5%).

the gender of the participants. Thus, 65.7% of studies in *Journal of Behavioral Medicine* (like 65.4% of articles in *Health Psychology*) could speak to women's health insofar as women constituted 45%–100% of the participants. The story for Blacks again was quite different.

As shown (Table 5 bottom, shaded column), only 23 of the 560 studies (4.1%) published in *Journal of Behavioral Medicine* included Black participants (women, men, or both) in sufficient numbers to analyze for and make statements about Black health and only 13 studies (2.3%) focused on Blacks (80%–100% of the participants were Black). In 65.4% of the studies (366 of 560), the ethnicity of the participants was never mentioned anywhere in the article, and in an additional 21.1% ($n = 118$) of the studies, all or almost all of the participants were White.

Finally, analyzing the intersection of gender and ethnicity (intersection of shaded row and column, bottom of Table 5) reveals that only 14 of the 560 studies (2.5%) included Black women as participants in a manner that made it possible to analyze for and make statements about Black women's health. Stated differently, the majority of the studies (368 or 65.7% of all studies published) included a large sample of women, but Black women were among them in only 14 articles (3.8%).

This review indicates remarkable similarity in neglect between the two journals. Although they are independent and are not associated with each other, both journals contained articles that included women as participants about 65% of the time, all-White participants about 25% of the time, Black participants 4% to 8% of the time, and Black women participants 2% to 6% of the time. Such similarities justify combining the articles from the journals to arrive at an overall view of research in health psychology and behavioral medicine. This analysis (notes at bottom of Table 5) revealed the following: From 1982 to 1996, 1,130 articles were published in these two leading health psychology journals, and although 741 (65.6%) of those included women among the participants in a manner that made it possible to analyze for gender differences and make statements about women's health, only 68 (6%) studies included Black women, men, or both, in a manner that made it possible to analyze for ethnic differences and speak to Black health. Likewise, only 49 of the 1,130 articles (4.3%) included Black women. Finally, the gender of the participants was never mentioned in 10% of the studies ($n = 113$), the ethnicity of the participants never described in 59.1% ($n = 668$) of them, and neither the gender nor ethnicity of the participants was described in 85 (7.5%) of the articles. From this it is accurate to conclude that contemporary empirical research in health psychology and behavioral medicine excludes Blacks and Black women from participation in research and is characterized by the view that race and ethnicity is irrelevant to health.

Topics of Focus in Both Journals

As noted earlier here, certain diseases (e.g., diabetes, hypertension), health problems (obesity), and poor health outcomes (e.g., survival rates from breast and other cancers) are far more prevalent among Black women than among other women, and are problematic for Black women. Thus, after our review of articles in the two journals, we analyzed the extent to which published studies focused on Black women's health problems as opposed to focusing on other health topics and problems that, although important, are not the major variables that contribute to Black women's differential morbidity and mortality. In addition, we examined the extent to which studies on these major threats to health that Black women face (to whatever degree such studies exist) included Blacks and Black women as participants such that statements about and suggestions for improving Black women's health could be made. For this analysis, we excluded all studies that focused on multiple ethnic groups or on other American minority groups, or compared other minority groups to Whites; we focused only on the representation of Blacks and of Whites in the articles. Hence, the total number of articles analyzed (999) is slightly less than (a subset of) the 1,130 reviewed previously. Likewise, for this analysis, we combined articles in the two journals. Results of this analysis of ethnicity, gender, and topics are displayed in Table 6. We cover the findings by specific topics first and then overall across topics.

As noted earlier, diabetes is a major health threat for Black women. Nonetheless, as shown in Table 6, only 43 of the 999 articles (4.3%) published in the two leading health psychology journals focused on diabetes. The majority of these (37 of 43, or 86%) focused on women, but only 2 of the 43 studies (4.6%) included Black women as participants; hence, diabetes among Black women was the focus in 2 of 999 (0.2%) articles published in the journals in the past 14 years. Similarly, as noted earlier, about 49% of Black women are obese. Nonetheless, only 60 of the 999 articles (6%) focused on obesity or on exercise. Although the majority of these studies (47 of 60, or 78%) focused on women, only 1 included Black women as participants; obesity among Black women was the focus of 1 of 999 (0.1%) studies published in the journals in the past 14 years. Likewise, although Black women have a higher death rate from most cancers than do White women, and cancers are a threat to the health of all women, cancer was not often a topic of published articles. Breast cancer was the topic of only 25 of the 999 studies (2.5%), and Black women were included in only 3 of those studies. Similarly, there were only 33 studies of other cancers (3.3% of all studies published), and Blacks (women or men) were not included as participants in any of them.

Cardiovascular disease and hypertension are prevalent problems for Black men and women but these were not frequent research topics. Only 47 of the 999 studies (4.7%) focused on cardiovascular disease, and only 74 of the 999 (7.4%) focused on hypertension. Blacks were included in only 4 (8.5%) of the studies of cardiovascular disease and Black women in only 2 (4.3%) of those studies. In the 74 studies on hypertension on the other hand, Blacks were included in 23 (31.1%) and Black women in 12 (16.2%) of the studies. Finally, AIDS likewise poses a major threat to Black women's health, as well as to the health of all Americans, but only

TABLE 6
Analysis of Studies by Selected Topics

Study Type	1 Diabetes	2 Obesity/ Exercise	3 Breast Cancer	4 Other Cancers	5 Cardiovasc- ular Disease	6 Hyperten- sion	7 AIDS	8 Other Topics	Total
Studies of 50% to 100% women									
All or > 80% Black	0	0	1	0	0	4	4	5	14
Black vs. other ethnic group	2	1	2	0	2	8	2	18	35
Total Blacks	2	1	3	0	2	12	6	23	49
All or > 80% White	9	9	12	9	8	3	4	124	178
Ethnicity unspecified	26	37	10	16	14	12	4	298	417
Σ	37	47	25	25	24	27	14	445	644
Studies of all or mostly men									
All or > 80% Black	0	0	0	0	0	3	0	2	5
Black vs. other ethnic group	0	0	0	0	0	8	0	1	9
Total Blacks	0	0	0	0	0	11	0	3	14
All or > 80% White	1	1	0	3	4	13	9	42	73
Ethnicity unspecified	4	5	0	1	14	18	1	123	166
Σ	5	6	0	4	18	42	10	168	253
Studies with no gender specified									
All or > 80% Black	0	0	0	0	0	0	1	1	2
Black vs. other ethnic group	0	0	0	0	2	0	0	1	3
Total Blacks	0	0	0	0	2	0	1	2	5
All or > 80% White	0	0	0	1	0	1	0	10	12
Ethnicity unspecified	1	7	0	3	3	4	1	66	85
Σ	1	7	0	4	5	5	2	78	102
Grand totals by topic	43	60	25	33	47	74	26	691	999
Grand total Blacks	2 (4.7%)	1 (1.7%)	3 (12%)	0 (0%)	4 (8.5%)	23 (31.1%)	7 (26.9%)	28 (4%)	68 (6.8%)
Grand total Black women	2 (4.7%)	1 (1.7%)	3 (12%)	0 (0%)	2 (4.3%)	12 (16.2%)	6 (23.1%)	23 (3.3%)	49 (4.9%)

26 of the 999 articles (2.6%) focused on AIDS and HIV; Blacks were included as participants in 7 (26.9%) of the studies, and Black women were included in 6 of those (23.1%).

Thus, although hypertension (7.4% of articles) and AIDS (2.6% of articles) were not frequently the focus of research, articles on these topics alone included Black women and men frequently and in large enough numbers to permit analyses of and statements about either Blacks' or Black women's health. However, this apparent inclusion (vs. general exclusion) of Blacks and Black women must be viewed in the larger context of research in the journals. For example, although (summing across both journals) seven studies of AIDS included Blacks (and six included Black women), seven studies published in *Health Psychology* alone during this period had rats as subjects.

Summing columns 1 through 7 to arrive at the number of studies that focused on the major threats to Black women's health reveals that 308 (30.8%) of the 999 articles focused on these topics and that the majority of the articles (691 or 69.2%) focused on other topics. Of the 308 articles on major issues related to Black women's health, Black women were included as participants in only 26 (8.4%) of them; that is, even when the topic was a disorder (e.g., diabetes) or a problem (e.g., obesity) that is highly prevalent among Black women, Black women were rarely included in the study.

As noted, most of the articles (69.2%) were on topics other than the eight major threats to Black women's health and so were coded as Other. These topics included health behaviors (e.g., consumption of fruits and vegetables, salt, fatty food), personality types, coping styles, health schema, pain, smoking, arthritis, stress, compliance with treatment, interactions with physicians, preparation for procedures, surgery, and the like. Although these topics are important, a focus on them while ignoring the problems in columns 1 through 7 is unlikely to reduce Black women's morbidity and mortality. Furthermore, Black women were rarely included in these Other studies; Black women were participants in 23 (3.3%) of the 691 articles coded as Other, with both Black men and women participating in only 28 (4%) of the Other articles. Hence, although one could justifiably argue that studying stress or the tendency to consume a diet high in fat and salt and low in fruits and vegetables is relevant to Black women's morbidity and mortality (because these factors play a role in hypertension, cardiovascular disease, and obesity), the fact remains that Black women were rarely included in these Other studies.

Looking at all of the topics and articles as a whole (Table 6) reveals that of 999 empirical studies, Blacks were participants in 68 (6.8%) of them, and Black women in 49 (4.9%). It is then not an exaggeration to conclude that Blacks and Black women are excluded from empirical investigations in health psychology and behavioral medicine. In addition, given that 64.5% (644 of the 999) of the studies included women in their samples (top of Table 6), the exclusion of Black women cannot represent a bias against women in health psychology and behavioral medicine research.

DISCUSSION

Reid and Kelly (1994) analyzed the race and ethnicity of participants in psychology of women research by reviewing empirical studies published in *Sex Roles* and in *Psychology of Women Quarterly* from 1986 to 1991. They found that "80% of the research articles ... focused primarily or exclusively on white populations, with the vast majority of authors neglecting not only the mention of race or ethnicity, but also failing to consider the implications of their omissions" (p. 480). Reid and Kelly characterized this failure to include minority women in studies as a "vacuum" in the psychology of women literature, and noted that "one would have to dig quite furiously" (p. 481) to find empirical articles on Black women. Likewise, Graham (1992) analyzed the race of participants in empirical studies in psychology by reviewing articles published between 1970 and 1989 in six major APA journals: *Developmental Psychology, Journal of Applied Psychology, Journal of Consulting and Clinical Psychology, Journal of Counseling Psychology, Journal of Educational Psychology,* and *Journal of Personality and Social Psychology.* Graham found that only 3.6% of studies in clinical, social, developmental, counseling, and other areas of psychology included Blacks as participants. Like Reid and Kelly, Graham similarly concluded that "there has been a growing exclusion of ... African Americans" (p. 629) from psychological studies, because the 3.6% represented a drop from prior years (see also Hall, 1997).

In this review, we conducted a similar analysis of the representation of Blacks and of Black women in empirical studies in health psychology (by using studies published from 1982–1996 in the two leading health psychology journals) and we found similar results: Only 6% of the 1,130 studies published in the two journals for the past 14 years included Blacks (women, men, or both), only 4.3% included Black women, and there were more studies of white rats ($n = 7$) than there were of diabetes, obesity, and breast cancer, combined, among Black women ($n = 6$). Like the conclusions that have been drawn about clinical, developmental, social, educational, counseling, and feminist psychology, we conclude from our review that health psychology and behavioral medicine similarly can be characterized as excluding and neglecting Blacks and Black women. Indeed, we conclude—as Reid and Kelly (1994) did—that one would "have to dig quite furiously" to find empirical studies of Blacks or of Black women in health psychology and behavioral medicine despite the fact that the health of Black women and men is significantly poorer than that of their White counterparts (NCHS, 1996). In addition, our review indicates that Black women's exclusion from participation in health psychology and behavioral medicine research does not reflect the exclusion of all women, but instead reflects the exclusion of Black women specifically.

In addition to excluding Black women as participants in research, the specific diseases and health problems that pose the greatest threats to Black women's health also are not frequent topics of research. For example, only 2.6% of all studies focused on AIDS, only 6% focused on obesity and exercise, only 4.7% addressed cardiovascular disease, and only 7.4% addressed hypertension. Furthermore, Black women tended to be excluded from studies on these specific problems as well. For example, approximately 16 million Americans, 60% of whom are women, have non-insulin-dependent diabetes, and the majority of those women are Black (McNabb, Quinn & Tobian, this issue). Nonetheless, only 43 of 999 articles (4.3%; Table 6) published were on diabetes, and Black women were participants in only 2 of these. The exclusion of Black women from health psychology and behavioral medicine research is undeniable and the dearth of studies of Black women's most prevalent health problems also is clear. The neglect of Black women's health in health psychology and behavioral medicine is mirrored by research in the psychology of women and feminist psychology. For example, we reviewed all studies published in *Psychology of Women Quarterly* (the official journal of APA Division 35, Psychology of Women) from 1980 to 1996 as well. We found that, of the 568 empirical articles published in that period, only 44 focused on women's health (7.7%). Given the neglect of women's health by psychology of women, we did not include a table here analyzing those 44 articles in detail. However, we did find that the majority of the 44 studies focused on the gynecological issues (e.g., menstruation, menopause, pregnancy, abortion, fertility) that dominate traditional women's health research because they reflect the concerns of White women of privileged class status (Klonoff, Landrine, & Scott, 1995). In addition, although nearly 50% of those 44 women's health articles ($n = 21$) did indeed include minority women (of various ethnic groups), only two included Black women. Hence, minority women were well represented in women's health studies published in *Psychology of Women Quarterly,* but Black women were not. Similarly, a recent highly acclaimed, "comprehensive" book on women's health, *Women's Health Care: A Comprehensive Textbook* (Fogel & Woods, 1995), rarely mentions Black women in its 744 pages, and devotes the majority of its attention to the health issues of White, middle-class and upper class women alone. For example, Fogel and Woods (1995) devoted 10 pages to lesbian health issues but only 2 to diabetes, 9 pages to feminism but only 1 to heart disease, and 16 pages to infertility but only 5 to obesity. Thus, feminist psychology and psychology of women (represented by articles in *Psychology of Women Quarterly*), and traditional women's health research (represented by Fogel & Woods) also exclude Black women and have done little empirical work where the most prevalent health problems of Black women are concerned.

In summary, research on Black women and on Black women's most prevalent health problems is largely absent in health psychology and behavioral medicine and in feminist psychology and traditional women's health as well, such that the need is clear for this special issue devoted to the health of Black women.

CONTENT OF THIS SPECIAL ISSUE

In this special issue on Black women's health (the first of its kind to be published by any psychology journal), we focus on just a few of the many previously mentioned major health threats to Black women—diabetes, obesity, cancer, violence, and AIDS—and we also include an article on Black women's notorious underutilization of health services because such underutilization plays an obvious role in their morbidity and mortality. Although this special issue certainly does not redress the blatant neglect of these topics and of Black women as participants in health psychology and behavioral medicine, it is a long-overdue step in that direction.

In the first article, Hoffman-Goetz and Mills of the National Cancer Institute examine cultural barriers to cancer screening among low-income Black women by reviewing the qualitative studies in the literature; their meticulous review of qualitative studies that permit Black women to speak openly about health issues reveals that Black women's cultural beliefs (e.g., that domestic violence causes breast cancer) play a significant role in their utilization of cancer-screening services. In the second article, Paskett and her colleagues at Bowman Gray Medical School similarly analyze cancer screening among low-income Black women, but do so through a review of the quantitative studies in the literature, and through an empirical investigation of the beliefs and behaviors of women in their Forsyth County, North Carolina, Cancer Screening Project. Together, these two articles examine the often-neglected qualitative studies, the quantitative studies, and include an empirical investigation, thereby providing a complete picture of the nature of cancer screening among low-income Black women. In the next article, Bowen and her colleagues at the Fred Hutchinson Cancer Research Center provide an empirical investigation of the breast cancer-related risk perceptions of affluent Black women. Their findings differ from those of the prior two articles and thereby highlight the role of education and socioeconomic status in Black women's cancer-related beliefs and behaviors.

In the fourth article, Allison and his colleagues at the Obesity Research Center (Columbia University Medical School) provide a review of both the qualitative and quantitative literature on obesity among Black women; note the cultural and social factors involved; and emphasize the relations among obesity, cancer, hypertension, diabetes, and socioeconomic status. Next, in the fifth article, McNabb and his colleagues at the Chicago Diabetes Research Center (University of Chicago Medical School) provide an equally thorough review of the qualitative and quantitative studies on non-insulin-dependent diabetes mellitus (NIDDM) among Black women, and highlight the cultural, social, and socioeconomic status variables of relevance, as well as the ties between NIDDM and obesity. Together, these five articles explicate the roles of cultural and social-contextual variables in Black women's health.

In the sixth article, Snowden and his colleagues at the University of California–Berkeley Center for Mental Health Services Research review the literature on Black women's underutilization of screening and other health care services more generally, and then provide an empirical investigation of more than 18,000 women to test the extent to which Black women's cultural beliefs do or do not predict their actual utilization of such services. In the seventh article, Russo (Arizona State University), Koss (University of Arizona), Keita (APA Office on Women), and their colleagues provide an extensive review of the literature and an empirical investigation of the role of intimate violence in Black women's health. Although violence and other aspects of Black women's social context rarely are examined empirically in a discipline dominated by an individual-lifestyle paradigm, violence against Black women plays a role in their beliefs about and utilization of screening for breast cancer (Hoffman-Goetz & Mills, this issue), as well as in their morbidity and mortality as evidenced by the NCHS data presented in Table 1. Russo and her colleagues highlight violence against women as an important social–contextual variable in Black women's morbidity and mortality. Likewise, in the eighth article, Sikkema, Heckman, and Kelly of the Center for AIDS Intervention Research (Medical College of Wisconsin) present an empirical investigation that examines the role of other contextual variables in the HIV risk of low-income Black women. Their study reveals that contextual factors such as community cohesiveness and dangerousness figure prominently in Black women's risk for HIV and AIDS.

Finally, in the concluding article, we analyze the nature and direction of research on Black women's health and highlight the dangers of continued neglect on the one hand, and of a focus on individual and cultural lifestyles on the other. In our view, Black women's health can be understood only by examining the social, structural, and contextual variables related to their status as a socially defined race (as "Blacks") on the one hand, and by examining the cultural variables related to their status as an ethnic cultural group (as "African Americans") on the other. In the concluding article, we highlight the victim-blaming dangers inherent in regarding Black women solely as an ethnic group (whose cultural beliefs and practices figure in their mortality and morbidity), while ignoring their status as a race that suffers economic, institutional, and structural deprivation, exploitation, and racism as a consequence of their racial status (Landrine & Klonoff, 1996). Because one can focus, however, on either the ethnic–cultural or the racial status of Black women, it is acceptable to refer to them as Black (emphasizing race) or as African American (emphasizing culture and ethnicity), and hence both terms are used in and vary from article to article here.

ACKNOWLEDGMENT

This work was supported by Grant R03–MH54672 from the National Institute of Mental Health.

REFERENCES

Fogel, C. I., & Woods, N. F. (Eds.). (1995). *Women's health care: A comprehensive handbook.* Thousand Oaks, CA: Sage.

Graham, S. (1992). "Most of the subjects were white and middle class": Trends in published research on selected APA journals 1970–1989. *American Psychologist, 47,* 629–639.

Hall, C. C. I. (1997). Cultural malpractice: The growing obsolescence of psychology with the changing U.S. population. *American Psychologist, 52,* 642–651.

Klonoff, E. A., Landrine, H., & Scott, J. (1995). Double jeopardy: Ethnicity and gender in health research. In H. Landrine (Ed.), *Bringing cultural diversity to feminist psychology: Theory, research, practice* (pp. 335–360). Washington, DC: American Psychological Association.

Landrine, H., & Klonoff, E. A. (1996). *African American acculturation: Deconstructing race and reviving culture.* Thousand Oaks, CA: Sage.

National Center for Health Statistics. (1996). *Health United States, 1995.* Hyattsville, MD: U.S. Public Health Service.

Reid, P. T., & Kelly, E. (1994). Research on women of color: From ignorance to awareness. *Psychology of Women Quarterly, 18,* 477–486.

WOMEN'S HEALTH: RESEARCH ON GENDER, BEHAVIOR, AND POLICY, 3(3&4), 183–201

Cultural Barriers to Cancer Screening Among African American Women: A Critical Review of the Qualitative Literature

Laurie Hoffman-Goetz and Sherry L. Mills

Division of Cancer Prevention and Control, National Cancer Institute
National Institutes of Health, Bethesda, MD

There have been numerous studies demonstrating the enormous cancer burden for African American women and the impact of structural barriers in the dissemination of cancer control interventions. Few of these studies have dealt with the influence of cultural factors in the success or failure of intervention research. The purpose of this review is to provide a critical appraisal of qualitative studies that inform on social–cultural factors in cancer screening programs for African American women, and to evaluate the extent to which general methodologic criteria have been used in these studies. The article discusses the theoretical underpinnings of social science qualitative methodologies, including ethnography, hermeneutics, ethnomethodology, and symbolic interactionism. Published qualitative studies from 1980 to 1996 on cancer screening among African American women are critically reviewed. Among the themes identified were bruises as contributory to breast cancer development; the low priority women placed on personal preventive screening behaviors in the context of other family health priorities; and the importance of female friends, relatives, and social networks in the flow of cancer information. The importance of qualitative approaches to cancer prevention and control programs and policies is threefold: (a) collection of greater depth of information, (b) identification of processes and relations among behaviors, and (c) framing of variables and hypotheses for quantitative research. Greater emphasis on methodologic rigor will be necessary, however, if

---

Correspondence concerning this article should be addressed to Sherry L. Mills, National Cancer Institute, National Institutes of Health, Executive Plaza North, Room 232, 6130 Executive Boulevard, Bethesda, MD 20892–7332. E-mail: Sherry_Mills@nih.gov.

qualitative studies of cancer screening are to effectively inform the development of research, programs, and policies.

Key words: cancer screening, cancer control, African American women, qualitative research, cultural factors

Breast cancer, colorectal cancer, and cancer of the cervix uteri were the first, second, and fifth leading incident cancers among African American women from 1987 to 1991 (Harras, Edwards, Blot, & Ries, 1996). These are also cancers for which effective screening tests are widely available (Boyes, 1981; Fletcher, Black, Harris, Rimer, & Shapiro, 1993; National Cancer Institute, 1987; Olesen, 1988; Schiffman, Brinton, Devasa, & Fraumeni, 1996; Shapiro, Venet, Strax, Venet, & Roesner, 1982; Sox, 1994) and for which U.S. national objectives for screening have been articulated (U.S. Department of Health and Human Services, 1990, 1995). Despite the proven efficacy of clinical breast exam, mammography, Pap smears, fecal occult blood tests, and sigmoidoscopy in the reduction of premature cancer morbidity and mortality, many African American women do not practice regular breast, cervical, or colon health-screening behaviors. Factors that have been identified as barriers to optimal screening utilization by African American and other minority women include a variety of complex and interacting variables, including individual psychological barriers (Lauver, 1992, 1994; Price, Desmond, Wallace, Smith, & Stewart, 1988), fear of pain and radiation (Dignan, Michielutte, Wells, & Bahnson, 1994), cancer fatalism (Powe, 1995, 1996), lack of cancer knowledge (Nemcek, 1989), lack of self-efficacy and skills to perform breast self-exam (Jacob, Penn, Kulik, & Spieth, 1992), failure of physicians to recommend screening (Burns et al., 1996; Caplan, Wells, & Haynes, 1992; Gemson, Elinson, & Messeri, 1988), access barriers due to high cost and lack of insurance coverage among the poor (Dignan et al., 1994; Freeman, Muth, & Kerner, 1995), and discrimination (Greenberg & Schneider, 1995). Several excellent recent reviews are available on psychological, economic, and structural barriers to cancer screening among African American women (Long, 1992; Mansfield, 1996; Moormeier, 1996; Rimer, 1994); however, the influence of social–cultural variables has not been systematically addressed in such reviews.

That cultural factors can influence screening and other preventive health behaviors is evidenced by disparate rates of breast and cervical cancer screening utilization across different ethnic, racial, or cultural groups; see, for example, the reviews on the Pathways projects (Engelstad, Bedeian, Schorr, & Stewart, 1996; Pasick, D'Onofrio, & Otero-Sabogal, 1996). We use culture to mean the *Zeitgeist,* outlook, or worldview adopted by a community, a group, or a social class. Culture encompasses the shared norms, values, and meanings held by a group and embedded in the language, symbols, signs, and relations. Spector (1996) identified the elemental features of culture as including "an interlinked web of symbols, a device for creating and limiting human choices, and the medium of personhood and social relationships" (p. 68). Analysis of cultural factors is important for cancer screening behavior because, as Triandis (1972) described,

> We may be able to do two kinds of study of great social significance: we may study what causes the particular perceptions of the environment and also learn about the precise consequences of these perceptions. [Further, if we can understand the consequences of perceptions of barriers to cancer screening] ... we may be able to design organizations, societies, and other social systems so that cultural influences will help rather than hinder the members of these social systems to reach their goals. (p. 6)

To capture the nature and impact of cultural factors in the context of cancer screening requires qualitative research approaches that emphasize in-depth information about women's internal and external experiences, using thick description (Gertz, 1973). Qualitative approaches that document cultural context are important because they provide fuller accounts about individual attitudes, appraisals, behaviors, and knowledge about cancer and cancer control. Although quantitative approaches provide necessary standardization and are useful for prediction of patterns, trends, and relations among variables in cancer control science, the information captured about any individual is fragmentary and incomplete. Weiss (1994) noted research questions and aims that are conducive to a qualitative approach include developing detailed descriptions, integrating multiple perspectives, describing process rather than outcome, developing holistic descriptions, learning how events are interpreted, and bridging intersubjectivities. Furthermore, qualitative research methods are of considerable utility in identifying variables and framing hypotheses for quantitative research.

The purpose of this article is to describe the insights and perspectives about sociocultural barriers to breast and cervical cancer screening for African American women that can be gleaned from studies using qualitative research strategies. A second objective of this article is to examine the extent to which general methodologic criteria have been used in qualitative research on breast and cervical cancer control among African American women. Although lung and colorectal cancer are leading causes of mortality and of significant public health concern for African American women, there are no published reports, using predominantly qualitative data, to inform either the prevention or the control of lung and colorectal cancers. Therefore, this review summarizes the qualitative studies focusing on breast and cervical cancer in African American women, and discusses the general methodologic concerns and utility of qualitative studies to inform on the design, development, and implementation of cancer prevention and control programs and policies. After a brief overview of cancer epidemiology in African American women, we address the scope and theoretical assumptions of qualitative studies, the search methodology used to conduct the review of the qualitative literature, the specific qualitative findings on sociocultural barriers to breast and cervical cancer screening for African American women, and the extent to which the current qualitative research in cancer control can (or cannot) inform programs and policies.

CANCER EPIDEMIOLOGY IN AFRICAN AMERICAN WOMEN

The high cancer incidence and mortality among African Americans remains a large concern for both the public health and medical communities. Although cancer incidence has declined in the U.S. population over the past several years, among African American women in the United States cancer incidence remained steady during the period from 1987 to 1991. Although the breast cancer incidence rate was lower among African American (94.0 per 100,000) than among white American (113.2 per 100,000) women during this time period, the mortality rate from breast cancer was higher for African American women, 31.2 per 100,000, compared with the rate of 27.2 per 100,000 in white American women (Harras et al., 1996). Cancer of the colon and rectum has both a higher incidence (46.7 per 100,000 vs. 39.9 per 100,000) and a higher mortality rate (20.6 per 100,000 vs. 15.6 per 100,000) among African American compared with white American women. Cervical cancer similarly has higher incidence (14.0 per 100,000) and mortality (6.7 per 100,000) rates relative to the patterns observed in white American women (i.e., incidence rate of 7.8 per 100,000 and mortality rate of less than 2.8 per 100,000 for the period 1987–1991). Cancer of the lung and bronchus, which has a higher incidence rate among African American women (44.5 per 100,000) than among white American women (41.3 per 100,000), has only a marginally lower death rate in African American women (30.4 per 100,000) compared with white American women (30.9 per 100,000). These incidence and mortality rates point to a significant and disproportionate cancer burden among African American women, a burden that has profound implications for women, families, communities, and the nation. Many factors contribute to these differential rates; as access barriers do not fully explain these differences, social–cultural variables may better help us to understand them.

SCOPE AND THEORETICAL ASSUMPTIONS OF QUALITATIVE STUDIES

Qualitative studies are those that emphasize a phenomenological approach to understanding human behavior and that typically use qualitative research techniques. Cook and Reichardt (1979) summarized the attributes of qualitative research paradigms as process-oriented, descriptive, inductive, and concerned with understanding behavior from the women's own frame of reference. Qualitative methods are useful in addressing those aspects of behavior not easily explained by quantitative analysis. For example, qualitative methods could address questions such as why some educated women fail to participate in screening tests or why some women view screening tests as opportunities for health, whereas other women view these same tests as barriers. Black (1994) commented that qualitative approaches are most valuable when the variables of greatest concern are unclear or cannot be precisely delineated. Qualitative studies provide insight into the cultural dynamics of a given setting, clarify the meanings of patterns elucidated through quantitative research, and serve as an opportunity to recast, reframe, and reconceptualize basic assumptions, questions, and problems in new ways (Needleman & Needleman, 1996).

There are several well-established theoretical traditions in qualitative inquiry that draw from different social science and nursing perspectives. These include ethnography (anthropology), hermeneutics (nursing), ethnomethodology (sociology), and symbolic interactionism (social psychology). Although there are other theoretical frameworks in qualitative research (e.g., heuristics, phenomenology), these derive largely from philosophical or humanistic traditions rather than from social or nursing sciences (Patton, 1990).

Ethnography is guided by the assumption of multiple realities that are socially constructed, rather than the belief in a single, objective reality. Integral to the ethnographic approach is the concept of culture—that collection of behaviors and beliefs that form the basis of "[shared] standards for deciding what is, what can be, how one feels about it, what to do about it, and how to go about doing it" (Goodenough, 1971, pp. 21–22). Hermeneutics investigates the individual woman's experience of cancer by description and interpretation of that experience, sometimes called the "lived experience" (Anderson, 1991; Jorgensen, 1989; Patton, 1990). This approach presents cancer not simply as a disease but as a series of experiences that profoundly affect the person who has cancer and the individuals (e.g., family, friends, medical personnel) who share in that experience and as having direct relevance for quality of life issues in cancer.

Other important qualitative perspectives include ethnomethodology, symbolic interactionism, and grounded theory. Ethnomethodology is a qualitative perspective that focuses on how members of a group make sense of their social world, such as when people are thrust into new or unexpected situations. This conceptual model attempts to understand a group's tacit knowledge and beliefs that are forced to the surface during critical or transitional incidents (Patton, 1990; Taylor & Bogdan, 1997). An ethnomethodological approach would be appropriate for understanding how African American women make sense of unexpected, problematic situations such as being informed of a high genetic risk for breast cancer. Finally, symbolic interactionism is a qualitative approach that emphasizes the direct importance of symbols and how those symbols acquire meaning for women through social interactions (Patton, 1990). Cutting across many of these qualitative perspectives is grounded theory, which "is a general methodology for developing theory that is grounded in data systematically gathered and analyzed. Theory evolves during actual research" (Strauss & Corbin, 1990, p. 273). The critical aspect of grounded theory is to identify emergent categories (e.g., of cancer causation) from empirical data, to build theory and frameworks from the ground up. The assumptions underlying a qualitative approach are (a) a woman's behavior is firmly linked with the meaning that the situation has for the woman; (b) a woman's understanding and, hence, behavior change as interactions with others occur; (c) within any given situation there will normally be different perspectives; and (d) a woman's behavior and beliefs can only be fully understood within the larger context of social organization or culture (Mackenzie, 1994).

Qualitative research techniques include focus groups, semistructured interviews, key informant interviews, case studies, case histories, participant observation, observation without participation, and ethnography. These research methods incorporate the concept of naturalistic inquiry or constructionism (Guba & Lincoln, 1989; Schwandt, 1994) and assume that women, individually and collectively, interpret the stimuli around them and that these interpretations, which are continually being revised as the events unfold, shape attitudes and behaviors. At the heart of qualitative research is a description of events, situations, or behaviors that is at best independent of the investigator's own culturally derived and arbitrary imposition on complex phenomena, but at the very least acknowledges the cultural biases of the researcher.

METHOD

The method used was the literature review, and a search was conducted through CancerLine, Cumulative Index to Nursing and Allied Health Literature (CINAHL), PsychInfo, and Sociological Abstracts. The search was conducted for the time period January 1980 through August 1996, and used the following index terms: African American, woman or female, underserved, cancer or neoplasm, social science, and culture. The term qualitative research method was also used in searching the CINAHL database. The following areas were covered in this search: (a) the relation between sociocultural variables and barriers to cancer screening in African American women, and (b) the use of qualitative research methods or a qualitative social science paradigm to study these relations. Cultural variables were assumed, for this review, to include factors such as ethnicity, culture, urbanization, language, acculturation, social support, role of women in the context of family and community, and individual and group normative beliefs about disease and cancer causation.

There were 300 citations recovered from CancerLine, 8 from PsychInfo, 29 from CINAHL, and 13 from Sociological Abstracts, using the search terms already identified. Of these citations, 12 studies were identified that exclusively or primarily used qualitative research methods to investigate sociocultural variables and cancer among African American women. Six of the studies focused on breast cancer, four addressed issues in cervical cancer screening, and the remaining two studies did not focus on any specific cancer site. There were no qualitative studies on colorectal cancer screening among African American women identified by the literature search. Studies that used survey research methods and standard instruments, but in which the questionnaires were delivered face-to-face by trained interviewers, were not considered qualitative studies (e.g., Mandelblatt et al., 1992; Powe, 1995). Studies that used peer role models or outreach workers as part of a cancer education survey and intervention were also excluded from the review (e.g., Suarez, Nichols, & Brady, 1993; Whitman et al., 1994). Studies that used qualitative methods to develop survey instruments but that did not detail the scope or approach of qualitative methodologies were also excluded from this study. The qualitative studies are examined with respect to the purpose of the study, the qualitative research method used, limitations or important methodological weaknesses, whether a specific qualitative research paradigm or theory guided the interpretation of the findings, and the main findings of the study.

INSIGHTS FROM QUALITATIVE STUDIES

A summary of the research approaches, limitations, and findings for the qualitative studies is presented in Table 1. Each of the 12 studies included in this review is individually described here.

Mathews, Lannin, and Mitchell (1994) collected in-depth narratives of 26 African American women between 39 and 83 years old and living in rural North Carolina, who delayed seeking treatment for breast cancer and presented with late-stage, advanced breast cancer (Stage 3 or later). The purpose of the study was to elicit reasons for delay in seeking treatment for breast cancer. The authors wanted to inform "the processes involved in adapting personal experience to preexistent cultural models" (p. 789). Of the 26 women who participated in the study, 14 told their personal story prior to confirmation of breast biopsy results and 12 told their personal story retrospectively (after treatment, during treatment, or after refusal of treatment for breast cancer). The data collection technique was in-depth conversational interviews using standard procedures (team of trained interviewers matched by race and sex to the participants; interviews lasting 1 hr, tape-recorded). Although the authors addressed the issue of data quality (validity) by interviewing the women at least twice, the methods of data analysis (e.g., content analysis to determine recurring themes) and the specific qualitative social science paradigm (e.g., hermeneutics, ethnography) driving the research were not identified in the study. The key findings about cancer that emerged from these case histories included the idea that painless lumps were unrelated to cancer, having a painless lump tested was just looking for trouble, exposing a lump to air (opening up the lump by surgery or biopsy) stimulated growth, and that impurities in blood can surface in the form of

TABLE 1
Summary of Qualitative Studies Reviewed

Cancer Site	Participants	Stated Research Paradigm	Is Paradigm Qualitative	Qualitative Methods Used	Key Findings	Reference
Breast	26 African American women: rural North Carolina	None stated	NA	In-depth conversational interviews (60 min duration)	Model of breast health emphasizing balance in blood	Mathews et al. (1994)
Breast; cervix	89 African American women: urban Atlanta	Anthropology literature—explanatory models	Not determined from available information	Semistructured ethnographic interviews (30–60 min duration)	Screening tests as heralds of fatal disease	Gregg & Curry (1994)
Breast	50 African American women: urban Atlanta	Ethnography	Yes	Semistructured interviews (30–90 min duration)	Association of cancer (knots in breast) with domestic violence	Wardlow & Curry (1996)
Breast	132 African American women, 14 social networks: rural North Carolina	Lay helping conceptual model	Yes	Focus groups	Cancer screening for medical problem, not prevention; importance of female social networks	Tessaro et al. (1994)
Cervix	29 African American women: urban New York City	Self-regulation theory	No	Focused, semistructured interviews (10–20 min duration)	Pervasive fear about cervical health, apprehension, and poor knowledge about colposcopy	Tomaino-Brunner et al. (1996)

Cancer site	Sample	Theory/model	Research paradigm stated	Method	Finding	Reference
Breast	19 African American women: urban-suburban Florida ($n = 281$ for parallel quantitative survey)	Social learning theory, Health Belief model, PRECEDE	No	Focus groups	Need for clear physician–patient communication about screening	Danigelis et al. (1995)
Cervix	60 African American women: rural North Carolina	None stated	NA	Focus groups and workshops for pretesting education program	Confusion whether Pap test necessary for all women	Dignan et al. (1990)
Cervix	39 African American women: rural North Carolina	None stated	NA	4 focus groups (90 min duration)	Fear and fatalism reactions to cancer	Dignan et al. (1990)
Cervix	103 African American community leaders (men and women): rural North Carolina	PRECEDE framework	No	Semistructured interviews	Process evaluation for identification of community leaders	Michielutte et al. (1990)
Breast	171 African American women: rural North Carolina	Social change model	Yes	14 focus groups	Importance of female social networks for advice about cancer	Eng (1993)
No site identified	African Americans: rural North Carolina (number, gender not identified)	Ethnography	Yes	Ethnography; archival documents	Blood impurities boil out of body causing cancer, skin eruptions, sores, rashes, fevers	Mathews (1987)
No site identified	African Americans, Puerto Ricans, Cubans, Bahamians, Haitians (number, gender, location not identified)	Ethnography	Yes	Ethnography; archival (folklore) documents	Blood impurities leading to fever, skin eruptions, skin cancer	Snow (1983)

Note. NA = not applicable; research paradigm is not stated.

"risens" or lumps. These findings suggest that the cultural norm was to interact with medical personnel for treatment of cancer but not for prevention of cancer. Bruises or blows to painless lumps, impurities in blood that feed the lump, and exposure of the lump to air were articulated as being in the causal chain in breast cancer. "Because cancer is a powerful and virtually unstoppable disease once it is activated, women need to be careful not to stir it up" (p. 795).

Gregg and Curry (1994) used semistructured ethnographic interview methods from 89 women attending two low-income medical clinics in Atlanta to frame explanatory models of breast and cervical cancer causation and the role of screening. The investigators established criteria for inclusion in the study (over 40 years of age, African American) and used a standardized method for collection of ethnographic information (interviews lasting 30–60 min, tape-recorded for later transcription). Methods of data analysis were not specified in the article. No conceptual model or theory is explicitly stated as guiding the study, although the authors refer to the anthropological literature on explanatory models. The method used to check for validity of information (e.g., triangulation of data) was not specified in the study. A number of themes emerged from these ethnographies, including the belief that cancer originates as a bruise, blow, or sore; that surgery worsens cancer prognosis (and hence many of the women rejected surgery as a viable treatment option); and that once a lump is labeled cancerous it is invariably fatal. Mammograms and Pap smears were tests to be used to diagnose cancer, not as tests used for early detection and prevention of cancer. Other themes that were identified included the impact of cancer on a woman's mental health (the mental distress of cancer was seen as worse than the physical distress), and the knowledge of having cancer speeds the disease progression (and hence the reluctance of women to follow through with screening).

In a follow-up investigation, Wardlow and Curry (1996) collected ethnoetiologies from 50 African American women from the same medical clinics in Atlanta using a semistructured interview technique. None of the participants had been involved in the earlier study. Although the purpose of the study was clearly identified (i.e., reexamination of some of the initial findings, investigation of beliefs about breast cancer and mammography), how the focused ethnographies were analyzed and what the theoretical paradigm for this study were not explicitly stated. One of the main themes that was explored in this study was the idea that bruises to the breast could turn into malignant knots (i.e., breast cancer). The relation between knots and physical violence against women or objectionable sexual practices was identified by many of the participants; based on the participants' interviews, not only can physical violence to the breast lead to breast cancer, but earlier injuries can also be internalized and made latent until some future time. Wardlow and Curry suggested that the connections between breast cancer, feelings of physical vulnerability, male–female discord, and ambivalence about how to respond to domestic violence have important implications for breast cancer education and screening programs. Another important finding was the role of mother–daughter social networks for the flow of health-related information and for the responsibility of each other's health. Thus, African American women may participate in mammography screening in part because their more knowledgeable female relatives or friends urge them to do so. This qualitative information not only broadens the channels or opportunities for reaching African American women, but also speaks to the importance of women's social networks in designing effective programs.

Tessaro, Eng, and Smith (1994) conducted 14 focus-group interviews, comprising a total of 132 African American men and women (35 years and older) from North Carolina, to explore the meanings of breast cancer held by older African American women and to uncover the impact of their social networks on health and cancer beliefs, expectations, and behaviors. Focus group methodology is derived from marketing research. Focus group interviewing is a technique to stimulate discussion and probe expressions of differing opinions within a small group of unrelated individuals on a set of questions or topical issues (Krueger, 1988; Marshall & Rossman, 1995). The participant composition of the 14 focus groups was clearly described (i.e., church women, sons and husbands, social workers, nurses) and the number of participants in each focus group was listed. Several of the focus groups (e.g., nurses, business women) were likely too small (more than 5 individuals) for productive discussion or too large (more than 15 individuals) for effective management by the focus group moderator. Data collection was standardized (e.g., clearly identified focus group moderator and notetaker, development of a pretested interview guide using 17 open-ended questions). Transcribed responses from the focus group sessions were analyzed using a qualitative research software package (Ethnograph), and content categories were grounded in an emic approach (naturalistic and incorporating culturally specific conceptualization and categorization of phenomena) rather than in etic approach (structured and reflecting pancultural conceptualizations and categorization of phenomena). The reader is referred to Pike (1967) for the original usage of the concepts emic and etic. The investigators identified the lay helping conceptual model as the conceptual framework to guide data collection and analysis. Several important themes about perceptions of breast cancer and screening for breast cancer among older African American women emerged from these focus group interviews: (a) Breast cancer was not a major health concern relative to other health issues; (b) family health was of higher priority than the woman's personal health; (c) prevention was not a cultural norm for the women; (d) the social and physical consequences of breast cancer treatment on relationships with sexual partners, friends, and family was a source of fear among the women; and (e) female relatives (daughters, daughters-in-law, other female relatives) and friends were the most important sources of social support and advice concerning health and breast cancer issues.

Eng (1993) described recruitment of lay health advisors to the Save Our Sisters Project, a pilot project to increase mammography screening among African American women from 50 to 74 years old living in North Hanover, North Carolina. Focus groups were conducted, as described in Tessaro et al. (1994), and from the dynamics within each focus group certain women were identified as "natural helpers." There were no other qualitative methods used or further description in this study once the focus groups were concluded.

Danigelis et al. (1995) used qualitative (focus groups) and quantitative (household survey) methods to study relations between behaviors and levels of breast cancer screening (mammography, clinical breast exam, breast self-exam) among African American women over the age of 40 living in a Florida community. The PRECEDE framework (Green & Kreuter, 1991) to identify predisposing, reinforcing, and enabling factors was used to guide data collection in the qualitative and quantitative components of the study. Focus group methodology was employed although details of the participant composition of the three focus groups was not given (other than fulfilling two criteria of low income and limited education). Data collection was standardized (e.g., use of a trained African American female moderator and an independent recorder), but no details are given about the development and pretesting of the discussion guide. One of the three focus groups may have been too small ($n = 5$) for productive group discourse (Stewart & Shamdasani, 1990). Details about the specific qualitative analysis of the data are not provided in the article. The main findings from the focus groups were that (a) there was a discrepancy between what women said about mammography in the survey questionnaire and what women actually understood about mammography; (b) despite knowledge about breast self-examination, self-efficacy to perform breast self-examination was low; (c) cancer screening was a low-priority health issue (in contrast to the survey results); and (d) women felt afraid to ask questions of their health care provider about breast screening. The emic bruise theory of cancer causation was also described by some participants in the focus groups.

Dignan, Michielutte, et al. (1990) conducted four focus group interviews, comprising a total of 39 African American women from North Carolina, to develop a conceptual framework for producing health education material about Pap smears and cervical cancer as part of the Forsyth County Project. The participant composition of the groups was homogenous with respect to age groups (younger than 49; older than 49) and education (less than Grade 12 education; at least Grade 12 education). Efforts to avoid bias in the conduct of the focus groups were addressed by using a single moderator for all focus group interviews, videotaping the group interviews for analysis, and predefining clear issues (e.g., perceived value of Pap smears or perceptions about quality of medical care) for discussion and probing of participants. The authors did not describe the method of qualitative data analysis or the underlying conceptual model and assumptions used to interpret the results from the focus groups. The main findings of this study were that health (including cervical health) was valued only insofar as it was linked to the woman's ability to carry out duties for the family, that all cancers were viewed as inevitably fatal, that interaction with the medical system occurs for treatment and not for prevention, and that physicians were the bearers of bad news.

In a related study, focus group interviews and workshops for 60 African American women were conducted to pretest direct educational materials about cervix cancer (Dignan, Beal, et al., 1990). Details about the participants, the composition of the focus groups, and methods of data analysis were not provided. An etic perspective was used in organizing the data, as the investigators "classified the reactions into seven categories" (p. 219). The central issues that emerged were (a) a general fear and fatalistic view about cancer; (b) familiarity with the phrase "Pap smear," but uncertainty and confusion about the purpose, accuracy, and frequency of testing; and (c) widespread belief that a woman would unambiguously "know" if she had cervix cancer because of clear symptomatology.

Michielutte and Beal (1990) used semistructured interviews of leaders in the African American community in Forsyth County, North Carolina, to determine what factors and characteristics in community leadership are necessary to sustain a cervical cancer screening program. Hence, the purpose of this study was only indirectly related to ascertaining barriers to cancer screening. The investigators used a modified snowball technique beginning with a nonrandom sample of 10 recognized leaders in the community to identify 589 individuals recognized as community leaders. No data were provided about attitudes and beliefs of the community leaders about cervical cancer or the use of Pap tests.

Tomaino-Brunner, Feda, and Runowicz (1996) presented data on knowledge level, attitudes, and concerns among urban women scheduled for colposcopy, using a qualitative, exploratory design. Focused, semistructured, individual interviews were conducted with 29 women from 17 to 59 years old, drawn from an academic medical center's division of gynecologic oncology. More than half of the participants were African American ($n = 19$) and most women had at least a 12th-grade education ($n = 24$). Data collection was standardized by using a single nurse practitioner to conduct the interview. Seven open-ended questions (e.g., "Do you know what an abnormal Pap test means?") were asked during the 10- to 20-min interviews, which were audiotaped and transcribed. Validity of the interview data was determined when no new answers were elicited by interviewees. Data were analyzed using a content analytic approach, and accuracy of the thematic categories was independently checked by the three authors. The conceptual framework that guided the interview data collection and analysis was stated as self-regulation theory. Four common themes emerged from the data: fear about their health (14 of the 29 women used the term *cancer* in describing their health fears), apprehension about colposcopy due to limited knowledge, uncertainty about the meaning of the Pap test, and pervasive lack of knowledge about the referral process. Another finding from this study was that many of the women did not tell their partners about the colposcopic referral and this was suggested to have been due to fear of being rejected or of an unfavorable response by the sexual partner when a cancer diagnosis was a potential outcome of the screening test. Differentiation of themes by ethnicity or race was not described in the study. The authors concluded with the suggestion that the results have implications for nursing practice, such as expanding patient education to include colposcopy and enhancing patient–provider communication to reduce anticipatory anxiety.

Two older studies (Mathews, 1987; Snow, 1983) used an ethnomedical approach to (a) understand health and cancer beliefs, (b) delineate the logic underlying patterns of pluralistic treatment choice, and (c) identify the impact of folk beliefs on symptom presentation and treatment compliance in clinical settings. Snow (1983) summarized data drawn from archival sources (Center for the Study of Comparative Folklore at the University of California at Berkeley) and from sociological, anthropological, and ethnographic studies (Health Ecology Project of the University of Miami) of lower socioeconomic status African Americans from rural and urban areas. Mathews, drawing from a variety of archival and ethnographic sources, described a coherent and persistent system of traditional medical beliefs called *rootwork,* which is found in some areas in the rural South. Both ethnomedical analyses described cancer as being related to impurities in blood, lumps, or skin eruptions, or "something in the body trying to come out" (Snow, 1983, p. 139). Neither study detailed the qualitative methods used to collect and analyze the data, how many individuals were interviewed, or the underlying theoretical framework that guided the ethnomedical analysis.

SUMMARY AND CONCLUSIONS

The qualitative studies reviewed here point to several common themes, including a set of core beliefs that place a low priority on cancer prevention in the women's everyday lives, the perceived association of (breast) cancer and physical injury (with implications for gender relations), and a cultural perspective that values women-to-women social networks for support and encouragement about health issues. These studies demonstrate that cultural issues are not trivial and play a key role in women's attitudes, behaviors, and values about cancer and participation in screening.

This review has considered the literature on qualitative approaches in understanding cultural issues and barriers to cancer prevention and control among African American women. Among the themes identified in these studies of poor African American women in the South was that of a cultural value system that equates biopsy with exposure of the tumor to air and a poorer prognosis. This value system informs barriers to cancer screening that may not be evident in quantitative surveys of cancer knowledge and attitudes. Another important finding that emerged from this review was the belief that blood "impurities" or "toxins" have an etiological role in breast cancer. Indeed, the toxins-in-blood folk etiology has a widespread basis in African American ethnomedicine as a cause of many illnesses, not just cancer (Landrine & Klonoff, in press).

It was also clear that the richness of information that could potentially be obtained through qualitative methods was either lacking, inconsistent, or not fully detailed in these reports. This points to the observation that qualitative studies will only be useful for informing cancer education and screening interventions if methodological rigor is applied. Although the criteria for achieving rigor or trustworthiness of the findings will differ from traditional quantitative criteria (i.e., internal validity, external validity, reliability, and objectivity), the application of criteria, agreed on a priori, is essential to conducting sound qualitative research. Several investigators have developed criteria to judge research soundness in qualitative studies. For example, Marshall and Rossman (1995) identified 20 standards for judging qualitative reports (e.g., detailed methods, assumptions stated, value judgments avoided). Lincoln and Guba (1985) proposed four criteria to assess soundness of qualitative studies (credibility, transferability, dependability, confirmability). Triangulation, which is the use of more than one source of data to inform, elaborate, or illuminate a point, could also be used to judge soundness of qualitative research results.

Qualitative approaches can inform the cultural dimensions in the dissemination of cancer policy, programs, and interventions to serve minority women. Qualitative methods provide information that can complement information obtained from quantitative methods. For example, if the questions are "What is the impact of managed care on mammography utilization by African American women over the last 5 years?" or, "How much of the variance in Pap test screening rates between African American and white women are due to differences in social class?", then quantitative approaches are most informative. Questions framed in this manner are useful in identifying linkages and relations among phenomena (e.g., the contribution of low socioeconomic status to delays in breast cancer screening) and in comparing specific screening behaviors of different groups (e.g., the frequency of mammography utilization, by insurance coverage, between African American women in different geographic regions of the country). If, however, the questions are of the type "Why do some African American women who have been informed about abnormal screening results to fail to follow through?", or "Why does a woman choose to participate in cervical cancer screening but not colorectal cancer screening tests? ", then qualitative studies are useful to address these types of questions. Questions framed in this manner are helpful in describing processes antecedent to outcomes (e.g., the extent to which African American women feel they have control over cancer risks and outcomes). A schematic representation of the role of qualitative research in elucidating cultural context relevant to cancer control is shown in Figure 1.

Qualitative approaches clarify social complexity and contribute to the understanding of beliefs and rules of behavior that are part of any cultural group. By

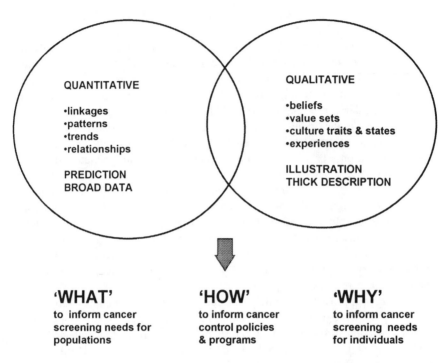

'WHAT'
to inform cancer
screening needs for
populations

'HOW'
to inform cancer
control policies
& programs

'WHY'
to inform cancer
screening needs
for individuals

FIGURE 1   Application of quantitative and qualitative approaches to cancer screening.

identifying the dynamic traits or elements of culture, qualitative research has the potential to contribute to the design of successful cancer prevention and control interventions, programs, and policies for African American women. Qualitative approaches to cancer prevention and control may be especially useful in articulating the cultural context for behavior, for probing meanings and values, and for illuminating broad attitudes or detailing behavioral subtleties. J. W. Tukey commented "far better an approximate answer to the right question ... than an exact answer to the wrong question" (cited in Black, 1994, p. 426). We believe that the strength of qualitative methodologies to the design of cancer control research is in the contribution to the understanding of what are culturally meaningful questions to ask. Qualitative research is farther reaching than simply an academic exercise. Application of qualitative information has the potential to inform on medical and structural barriers (Holman, 1993), such as physician recommendation, insurance coverage, and access, and in reducing systemic barriers in cancer control. However, for qualitative studies to have relevance for cancer control program dissemination and policy development, greater attention to methodologic criteria will be necessary.

ACKNOWLEDGMENTS

Laurie Hoffman-Goetz is currently a professor in the Department of Health Studies and Gerontology, University of Waterloo, Waterloo, Ontario, Canada. We gratefully acknowledge the helpful suggestions and comments on this article by Helen Meissner, Nancy Breen, Tom Glynn, Karen Gerlach, and Douglas Weed.

REFERENCES

Anderson, J. M. (1991). The phenomenological perspective. In J. M. Morse (Ed.), *Qualitative nursing research: A contemporary dialogue* (pp. 25–38). Newbury Park, CA: Sage.

Black, N. (1994). Why we need qualitative research. *Journal of Epidemiology and Community Health, 48,* 425–426.

Boyes, D. A. (1981). The value of a Pap smear program and suggestions for its implementation. *Cancer, 48,* 613–621.

Burns, R. B., McCarthy, E. P., Freund, K. M., Marwill, S. L., Shwartz, M., Ash, A., & Moskowitz, M. A. (1996). Black women receive less mammography even with similar use of primary care. *Annals of Internal Medicine, 125,* 173–182.

Caplan, L. S., Wells, B. L., & Haynes, S. (1992). Breast cancer screening among older racial/ethnic minorities and whites: Barriers to early detection. *Journal of Gerontology, 47,* 101–110.

Cook, T. D., & Reichardt, C. S. (1979). *Qualitative and quantitative methods in evaluation research.* Beverly Hills, CA: Sage.

Danigelis, N. L., Roberson, N. L., Worden, J. K., Flynn, B. S., Dorwaldt, A. L., Ashley, J. A., Skelly, J. M., & Mickey, R. M. (1995). Breast screening by African-American women: Insights from a household survey and focus groups. *American Journal of Preventive Medicine, 11,* 311–317.

Dignan, M. B., Beal, P. E., Michielutte, R., Sharp, P. C., Daniels, L. A., & Young, L. D. (1990). Development of a direct education workshop for cervical cancer prevention in high risk women: The Forsyth County Project. *Journal of Cancer Education, 5,* 217–233.

Dignan, M., Michielutte, R., Sharp, P., Bahnson, J., Young, L., & Beal, P. (1990). The role of focus groups in health education for cervical cancer among minority women. *Journal of Community Health, 15,* 369–375.

Dignan, M., Michielutte, R., Wells, H. B., & Bahnson, J. (1994). The Forsyth County cervical cancer prevention project: I. Cervical cancer screening for black women. *Health Education Research, 9,* 411–420.

Eng, E. (1993). The Save our Sisters Project. *Cancer Supplement, 72,* 1071–1077.

Engelstad, L., Bedeian, K., Schorr, K., & Stewart, S. (1996). Pathways to early detection of cervical cancer for a multiethnic, indigent, emergency department population. *Health Education Quarterly, 23*(Suppl.), S89–S104.

Fletcher, S. W., Black, W., Harris, R., Rimer, B. K., & Shapiro, S. (1993). Report of the international workshop on screening for breast cancer. *Journal of the National Cancer Institute, 85,* 1644–1656.

Freeman, H. P., Muth, B. J., & Kerner, J. F. (1995). Expanding access to cancer screening and clinical follow-up among the medically underserved. *Cancer Practice, 3*(1), 19–30.

Gemson, D. H., Elinson, J., & Messeri, P. (1988). Differences in physician prevention practice patterns for white and minority patients. *Journal of Community Health, 13,* 53–64.

Gertz, C. (1973). *Interpretation of cultures.* New York: Basic Books.

Goodenough, W. (1971). *Culture, language, and society.* Reading, MA: Addison-Wesley.

Green, L. W., & Kreuter, M. W. (1991). *Health promotion planning: An educational and environmental approach.* Mountain View, CA: Mayfield.

Greenberg, M., & Schneider, D. (1995). The cancer burden of southern-born African Americans: Analysis of a social-geographic legacy. *The Milbank Quarterly, 73,* 599–620.

Gregg, J., & Curry, R. H. (1994). Explanatory models for cancer among African-American women at two Atlanta neighborhood health centers: The implications for a cancer screening program. *Social Science & Medicine, 39,* 519–526.

Guba, E. G., & Lincoln, Y. S. (1989). *Fourth generation evaluation.* Newbury Park, CA: Sage.

Harras, A., Edwards, B. K., Blot, W. J., & Ries, L. A. G. (1996). *Cancer: Risks and rates* (4th ed.). Washington, DC: Department of Health and Human Services.

Holman, H. R. (1993). Qualitative inquiry in medical research. *Journal of Clinical Epidemiology, 46,* 29–36.

Jacob, T. C., Penn, N. E., Kulik, J. A., & Spieth, L. E. (1992). Effects of cognitive style and maintenance strategies on breast self-examination (bse) practice by African American Women. *Journal of Behavioral Medicine, 15,* 589–609.

Jorgensen, D. L. (1989). *Participant observation: A methodology for human studies.* Newbury Park, CA: Sage.

Krueger, R. A. (1988). *Focus groups: A practical guide for applied research.* Newbury Park, CA: Sage.

Landrine, H., & Klonoff, E. A. (in press). Cultural diversity in health psychology. In A. Baum, T. Revenson, & J. Singer (Eds.), *Handbook of health psychology.* Mahwah, NJ: Lawrence Erlbaum Associates, Inc.

Lauver, D. (1992). Psychosocial variables, race, and intention to seek care for breast cancer symptoms. *Nursing Research, 41,* 236–241.

Lauver, D. (1994). Care-seeking behavior with breast cancer symptoms in Caucasian and African-American women. *Research in Nursing & Health, 17,* 421–431.

Lincoln, Y. S., & Guba, E. G. (1985). *Naturalistic inquiry.* Beverly Hills, CA: Sage.

Long, E. (1992). Breast cancer in African-American women. *Cancer Nursing, 16,* 1–24.

Mackenzie, A. E. (1994). Evaluating ethnography: Consideration for analysis. *Journal of Advanced Nursing, 19,* 774–781.

Mandelblatt, J., Traxler, M., Lakin, P., Kanetsky, P., Kao, R., & Harlem Health Team. (1992). Mammography and Papanicolaou smear use by elderly poor black women. *Journal of the American Geriatrics Society, 40,* 1001–1007.

Mansfield, C. M. (1996). Cancer in the African American. *Journal of the National Medical Association, 84,* 638–641.

Marshall, C., & Rossman, G. B. (1995). *Designing qualitative research.* Thousand Oaks, CA: Sage.

Mathews, H. F. (1987). Rootwork: Description of an ethnomedical system in the American South. *Southern Medical Journal, 80,* 885–891.

Mathews, H. F., Lannin, D. R., & Mitchell, J. P. (1994). Coming to terms with advanced breast cancer: Black women's narratives from eastern North Carolina. *Social Science and Medicine, 38,* 789–800.

Michielutte, R., & Beal, P. (1990). Identification of community leadership in the development of public health education programs. *Journal of Community Health, 15,* 59–68.

Moormeier, J. (1996). Breast cancer in Black women. *Annals of Internal Medicine, 124,* 897–905.

National Cancer Institute. (1987). *Working guidelines for early cancer detection: Rationale and supporting evidence to decrease mortality.* Washington, DC: Author.

Needleman, C., & Needleman, M. L. (1996). Qualitative methods for intervention research. *American Journal of Industrial Medicine, 29,* 329–337.

Nemcek, M. A. (1989). Factors influencing black women's breast self-examination practice. *Cancer Nursing, 12,* 339–343.

Olesen, F. (1988). A case-control study of cervical cytology before diagnosis of cervical cancer in Denmark. *International Journal of Epidemiology, 17,* 501–508.

Pasick, R. J., D'Onofrio, C. N., & Otero-Sabogal, R. (1996). Similarities and differences across cultures: Questions to inform a third generation for health promotion research. *Health Education Quarterly, 23*(Suppl.), S142–S161.

Patton, M. Q. (1990). *Qualitative evaluation and research methods.* Newbury Park, CA: Sage.

Pike, K. (1967). *Language in relation to a unified theory of the structure of human behavior.* The Hague, Netherlands: Mouton.

Powe, B. D. (1995). Fatalism among elderly African Americans. *Cancer Nursing, 18,* 385–392.

Powe, B. D. (1996). Cancer fatalism among African-Americans: A review of the literature. *Nursing Outlook, 44,* 18–21.

Price, J. H., Desmond, S. M., Wallace, M., Smith, D., & Stewart, P. W. (1988). Black Americans' perceptions of cancer. *Journal of the National Medical Association, 80,* 1297–1304.

Rimer, B. K. (1994). Interventions to increase breast screening. *Cancer Supplement, 74,* 323–328.

Schiffman, M. H., Brinton, L. A., Devasa, S. S., & Fraumeni, J. F., Jr. (1996). Cervical cancer. In D. Schottenfeld & J. F. Fraumeni, Jr. (Eds.), *Cancer epidemiology and prevention* (pp. 1090–1116). New York: Oxford University Press.

Schwandt, T. A. (1994). Constructivist, interpretivist approaches to human inquiry. In N. K. Denzin & Y. S. Lincoln (Eds.), *Handbook of qualitative research* (pp. 118–137). Thousand Oaks, CA: Sage.

Shapiro, S., Venet, W., Strax, P., Venet, L., & Roesner, R. (1982). Ten to fourteen year effect of screening on breast cancer mortality. *Journal of the National Cancer Institute, 69,* 349–355.

Snow, L. F. (1983). Traditional health beliefs and practices among lower class black Americans. *Western Journal of Medicine, 139,* 820–828.

Sox, H. C., Jr. (1994). Preventive health services in adults. *New England Journal of Medicine, 330,* 1589–1595.

Spector, R. E. (1996). *Cultural diversity in health and illness.* Stamford, CT: Appleton & Lange.

Stewart, D. W., & Shamdasani, P. N. (1990). *Focus groups: Theory and practice.* Newbury Park, CA: Sage.

Strauss, A. L., & Corbin, J. (1990). *Basics of qualitative research: Grounded theory procedures and techniques.* Newbury Park, CA: Sage.

Suarez, L., Nichols, D. C., & Brady, C. A. (1993). Use of peer role models to increase pap smear and mammogram screening in Mexican-American and black women. *American Journal of Preventive Medicine, 9,* 290–296.

Taylor, S. J., & Bogdan, R. (1997). *Introduction to qualitative research methods: The search for meaning.* New York: Wiley.

Tessaro, I., Eng, E., & Smith, J. (1994). Breast cancer screening in older African-American women: Qualitative research findings. *American Journal of Health Promotion, 8,* 286–293.

Tomaino-Brunner, C., Freda, M. C., & Runowicz, C. D. (1996). "I hope I don't have cancer": Colposcopy and minority women. *Oncology Nursing Forum, 23,* 39–44.

Triandis, H. C. (1972). *The analysis of subjective culture.* New York: Wiley-Interscience.

U.S. Department of Health and Human Services and U.S. Public Health Service. (1990). *Healthy people 2000: National health promotion and disease prevention objectives.* Washington, DC: U.S. Government Printing Office.

U.S. Department of Health and Human Services and U.S. Public Health Service. (1995). *Healthy people 2000 midcourse review and 1995 revisions.* Washington, DC: U.S. Government Printing Office.

Wardlow, H., & Curry, R. H. (1996). "Sympathy for my body": Breast cancer and mammography at two Atlanta clinics. *Medical Anthropology, 16,* 319–340.

Weiss, R. S. (1994). *Learning from strangers: The art and methods of qualitative interview studies.* New York: Free Press.

Whitman, S., Lacey, L., Ansell, D., Dell, J., Chen, E., & Phillips, C. W. (1994). An intervention to increase breast and cervical cancer screening in low-income African-American women. *Family and Community Health, 17,* 56–63.

WOMEN'S HEALTH: RESEARCH ON GENDER, BEHAVIOR, AND POLICY, 3(3&4), 203–226

Cancer Screening Behaviors of Low-Income Women: The Impact of Race

Electra D. Paskett, Julia Rushing, Ralph D'Agostino, Jr., and Cathy Tatum

Department of Public Health Services
Bowman Gray School of Medicine

Ramon Velez

Department of General Internal Medicine and Gerontology
Bowman Gray School of Medicine

Cancer mortality rates are greater for African Americans than for whites. Reasons for this are due in part to the disproportionate number of the poor who are African American. Of particular concern are breast, cervical, and colorectal cancer, as screening exams, when used regularly, can reduce mortality. As part of an National Cancer Institute-funded study to improve breast and cervical cancer screening among low-income, predominately African American women, a survey was done to collect data on knowledge, attitudes, and practices related to breast, cervical, and colorectal cancer. A total of 300 women, African American and white residents of low-income housing communities, completed the survey. More African American women than white women had a mammogram within guidelines (52% vs. 40%), a clinical breast exam within the last year (60% vs. 56%), a Pap smear within the last 3 years (80% vs. 59%), and a Fecal Occult Blood Test within the last year (21% vs. 17%). Slightly more white women had a flexible sigmoidoscopy (FS) exam within the last 5 years (31% vs. 24%). When adjusted for age differences in the two populations, the differences in receiving regular screening exams were not statistically significant. Variables related to receiving these tests for all women included receiving regular check-ups (breast cancer); beliefs (breast and colorectal cancer screening), and

Correspondence concerning this article should be addressed to Electra D. Paskett, Department of Public Health Sciences, Bowman Gray School of Medicine, Medical Center Boulevard, Winston-Salem, NC 27157–1063. E-mail: epaskett@rc.phs.bgsm.edu.

knowledge (cervical cancer). Among African American women, barriers to screening were important for breast screening and regular checkups were related to Pap smear screening (odds ratio [OR] = 13.9, $p < .01$). High perceived risk of colorectal cancer was related to recent FS only for white women (OR = 47.9, $p = .012$). Women in this homogenous income group had similar rates of screening and had similar barriers to receiving recommended screening tests; thus, interventions should address beliefs and knowledge of risk targeted to all low-income women.

Key words: cancer screening, African American, breast cancer, cervical cancer, colon screening, fecal occult blood tests, flexible sigmoidoscopy

Approximately 1 million persons in the United States are diagnosed, and over one-half million die of cancer each year (Parker, Tong, Bolden, & Wingo, 1996). A disproportionately greater number of incident cases and deaths are among the socioeconomically disadvantaged (Freeman, 1989). Freeman characterized poverty as increasing the chances of getting cancer and diminishing the chances of survival because it creates an inadequate physical and social environment, discourages the acquisition of information and knowledge, encourages risk-promoting lifestyles, and reduces access to health care. As a disproportionate percentage of the poor are members of minority groups, their status is reflected in higher cancer incidence and poorer survival rates. The disparity is particularly large in African American populations.

Although African Americans comprise only 12% of the total population, they represent about one third of the poor. African Americans have the highest overall age-adjusted cancer incidence and mortality rates of any population group in the United States (Baquet, Clayton, & Robinson, 1986). African Americans also have 5-year cancer survival rates 12 percentage points lower than that of whites (Baquet et al., 1986). In addition, cancer incidence rates for African Americans have increased by 27% over the last several decades, whereas the rates for whites have increased by 12%. Cancer mortality rates during this same period increased by 40% in African Americans and 10% in whites (Miller et al., 1993). African Americans are also more likely than whites to have their cancer diagnosed at a late stage (Kosary et al., 1995). Breast, colorectal, and cervical cancer in African American women are areas of particular concern.

BREAST CANCER

Cancer of the breast is the most common incident cancer among women in the United States (Parker et al., 1996). The average annual incidence for breast cancer among black women is less than that for white women, 95.8 versus 112.7 per

100,000 women, respectively (Miller et al., 1993), but the average annual mortality rates for the two groups of women are nearly identical (Wingo et al., 1996). In addition, 5-year survival rates for breast cancer are lower for black women compared to white women (Parker et al., 1996).

The use of clinical breast exam (CBE) and mammography has been demonstrated to reduce mortality from breast cancer by 30% in women 50 years old and older (Shapiro, Strax, & Venet, 1990). Although utilization rates of screening mammography have improved over the last several years, many women have not made mammography an annual examination. In a review of mammography utilization, White, Urban, and Taylor (1993) concluded that to achieve meaningful reductions in breast cancer mortality, more women over age 50 need to be screened regularly and receive follow-up for abnormal findings. Estimates indicate that only 41% of women age 50 and older receive annual mammography, about half the national goal of 80% (Horton, Romans, & Cruess, 1992). In addition, certain subgroups of women, namely minority women, older women, and women of low socioeconomic levels, have poorer utilization rates for mammography (Marchant & Sutton, 1990).

Several knowledge-, belief-, access-, and physician-related barriers to mammography have been reported. The most common reason given by women for not having a mammogram was that they had not thought about it, or had thought it was not necessary because they had no problems (National Cancer Institute [NCI] Breast Cancer Screening Consortium, 1990). Fear of radiation, fear of finding something, and embarrassment are reported by some women, especially African American and Hispanic women (Fox & Stein, 1991). Although concern about the pain or discomfort associated with a mammogram has been reported by some women, this does not seem to be a major barrier to mammography utilization (Stomper et al., 1988). Access barriers include family or work responsibilities, lack of time, inconvenience, and distance from a mammography facility (Fink, Shapiro, & Roester, 1982; French et al., 1982; Goodspeed, DeLucia, Parravano, & Goldfield, 1988; Maclean, Sinfeld, Klein, & Harndon, 1984; Richardson, 1990; Schechter, Vanchieri, & Crofton, 1990). Cost may pose a barrier to certain subgroups of women, for example, African American urban women; however, it is not one of the main barriers cited by most women (NCI Breast Cancer Screening Consortium, 1990). When the cost factor is removed, other psychosocial barriers remain (Rimer, Keintz, Kesslers, Engstrom, & Rosan, 1989). Many women underestimate the true lifetime risk of breast cancer, do not feel susceptible to breast cancer, fail to recognize that the risk of breast cancer increases with increasing age, and believe that they do not need mammograms in the absence of a family history of breast cancer (Burack & Liang, 1987, 1989; Marchant & Sutton, 1990; Rimer et al., 1989; Schechter et al., 1990). Women who receive regular checkups, desire peace of mind and reassurance, view themselves as vulnerable to breast cancer, believe in the benefits of mammography, and have health insurance coverage are more likely to get a mammogram (Calnan, 1984;

French et al., 1982; Maclean et al., 1984; NCI Breast Cancer Screening Consortium, 1990; NCI Cancer Screening Consortium for Underserved Women, 1995; Paskett et al., 1996; Slenker & Grant, 1989; Taylor, Taplin, Urban, White, & Peacock, 1995). These trends are also reported among African American women (Parker et al., 1996) who are less likely to receive mammograms than non-Hispanic white women, even after adjustment for primary care visits (Burns et al., 1996).

Utilization rates for CBE are higher than those for mammography; however, subgroups of women are still underserved by regular CBE (NCI Breast Cancer Screening Consortium, 1990; NCI Cancer Screening Consortium for Underserved Women, 1995). Factors associated with low likelihood of receiving CBE include older age, lower educational attainment, Caucasian race, lower income, currently working, less knowledge of breast cancer risk factors and screening guidelines, lack of regular contact with health providers, and no family history of breast cancer (Burg, Lane, & Polednak, 1990; Grady, Lemkay, McVay, & Reisine, 1991; Lerman, Rimer, Trock, Balshem, & Engstrom, 1990; Polednak, Lane, & Burg, 1991).

CERVICAL CANCER

Cancer of the cervix is an alarming cancer because the introduction of the Pap smear test for early detection should virtually eliminate mortality from this cancer (Guzick, 1978). According to data from the Surveillance and Epidemiology End Results Program, black women have an average annual incidence for cervical cancer twice that of white women and a mortality rate from cancer of the cervix of 2.6 times that of white women (Reis, Hankey, & Edwards, 1990).

The recommended method of early detection for cervical cancer is the Pap smear test (Guzick, 1978). On average, 72% of women report having had a Pap smear within the last 3 years (Anderson & May, 1995). African American women are screened at similar or higher rates than Caucasian women (Harlan, Bernstein, & Kessler, 1991; Wilcox & Mosher, 1993). Women of lower socioeconomic levels, regardless of race, underutilize Pap smear screening, as do women who never married, are widowed, or who failed to complete high school (Calle, Flanders, Thun, & Martin, 1993; Harlan et al., 1991; Moody-Thomas & Fick, 1994; Weinrich, Coker, Weinrich, Eleazer, & Greene, 1995).

The most frequently stated reasons for not having a Pap smear were that women believed it was unnecessary, had no problems, or just procrastinated. Reasons also vary by income, race, and age. Women in upper income groups cited lack of time as one of the prohibitive factors, women in middle-income groups mentioned the cost of the test as a barrier, and women in lower income groups reported cost as well as other responses such as "I don't want to go," "no appointment was made," or "I wasn't pregnant" (Moody-Thomas & Fick, 1994). White women tend to cite having had a hysterectomy as the reason for not having a Pap smear more often than African American or Hispanic women do, whereas non-white women state that the test was not recommended by their physician (Harlan et al., 1991). Another reason for the excess mortality among African American women is less successful follow-up and treatment of detected cervical abnormalities (Garfinkel, Poindexter, & Silverberg, 1980; Harlan et al., 1991; Moss & Wilder, 1977). The noncompliance rate for follow-up recommendations among white women with cervical abnormalities is 40% (Singer, 1986), whereas 57% of black women fail to comply (Michielutte, Dignan, Bahnson, & Wells, 1994).

COLORECTAL CANCER

Colorectal cancer, the third most common cancer among men and women, affects African American and white men equally (Parker et al., 1996); however, African American women have a 20% higher incidence than white women (Wingo et al., 1996). Mortality rates for colorectal cancer are 20% to 30% higher (Wingo et al., 1996), 5-year survival rates are poorer (Miller et al., 1993), and fewer colorectal cancers are detected at localized stages among African Americans as compared to whites (Wingo et al., 1996). Whereas colorectal cancer mortality rates have been decreasing for whites, these rates have been increasing for African Americans (Miller et al., 1993).

Recently, strong evidence has emerged showing that colorectal cancer screening with flexible sigmoidoscopy (FS; Newcomb, Norfleet, Storer, Surawicz, & Marcus, 1992; Selby, Friedman, Quesenberry, & Weiss, 1992) or fecal occult blood testing (FOBT) reduces mortality from colorectal cancer. In general, screening FS is underutilized, with estimates of use ranging from 1% to 15% of eligible patients in general medical clinics to 42% in family practice settings (McPhee, Richard, & Solkowitz, 1986; Rodney, Beaber, Johnson, & Wuan, 1985; Woo, Wood, Cook, Weisberg, & Goldman, 1985). Breen and Kessler (1996) reported that national estimates of the utilization of colorectal cancer screening tests indicate that, compared to whites, fewer African Americans have utilized colorectal cancer screening tests (46% vs. 41%, respectively, for men, and 44% vs. 39%, respectively, for women).

Reasons for low utilization include patient factors such as perceived discomfort and anxiety and physician reluctance to order the exam due to cost, inconvenience, and lack of agreement with the guidelines (American Cancer Society [ACS], 1990; McPhee et al., 1986). To date, one study has examined patient attitudes, compliance, and reactions to screening FS (McCarthy & Moskowitz, 1993). This study found that although patients reported a high level of anxiety about the test, 75% complied with the recommendation from their physician to have the test and thought the procedure was significantly less embarrassing and less painful than expected. Among those who reported embarrassment and discomfort with the procedure, only 1.4% of the patients said they would probably not have the test again. The majority of patients reported high levels of perceived importance and satisfaction with the physician's explanation of the test.

FOBT utilization rates are not well known and are thought to be low. The ACS initiated a large-scale public awareness campaign from 1983 to 1986, during which time the percentage of asymptomatic individuals who had ever had an FOBT rose from 28% to 39% (ACS, 1986). FOBT has reported compliance rates of 51% to 88% for patients asked to return cards (Thompson, Michnick, Gray, Friedlander, & Gilson, 1986). Compliance was found to be the highest in programs in which primary-care physicians recommended the test as part of a regular annual exam (Winawer et al., 1980) or among attendees at community education programs sponsored by the ASC (Elwood, Erickson, & Lieberman, 1978), whereas lowest rates were found in general practice settings.

As this review indicates, racial differences exist in the utilization of screening exams for these cancers. In addition, several studies have suggested that low socioeconomic status may explain the majority of the differential in screening-test utilization. This study focuses on the differences in screening behaviors among African American and white women who have a relatively similar low socioeconomic status.

METHODS

Setting

The Forsyth County Cancer Screening (FoCaS) Project, funded by the NCI as one of six "Public Health Approaches to Breast and Cervical Cancer Screening" grants, was designed to test the effectiveness of public health clinic inreach and community outreach interventions in improving screening utilization by low-income minority women (NCI Screening Consortium for Underserved Women, 1995). The FoCaS project population included women 40 years old and older who resided in subsidized housing communities in Forsyth and Guilford Counties in North Carolina. The majority of residents in these communities were African American women; however, a sizable group of white women over age 65 also lived in these communities. In the intervention community of Forsyth County, the population of the nine housing communities was 95% African American. In the comparison county, the population was 93% African American, distributed among 18 subsidized housing communities. A total of 1,929 women (908 in Winston-Salem and 1,021 in Greensboro) in these communities formed our population of interest.

Description of Intervention

The objectives of FoCaS were to reduce the morbidity and mortality associated with breast and cervical cancer by improving knowledge, attitudes, and participation in breast and cervical cancer screening, and to identify barriers to early cancer detection faced by the target population and health care providers. Secondary objectives were to assess and improve compliance with follow-up recommendations for abnormal findings from mammography, CBEs, and Pap smears through a local clinic. Two types of intervention strategies were used: a community outreach program and a community health clinic-based inreach program. The community program included educational sessions, literature distribution, community events, media, and church programs. The community health clinic inreach strategies included chart reminders, exam room prompts, in-service meetings, and patient-directed literature. The FoCaS Project also utilized a consortium of local community agencies led by the Bowman Gray School of Medicine and Reynolds Health Center, a large, publicly funded multispecialty clinic in Forsyth County dedicated to serving low-income residents of the target area and providing in-house mammography as well as other medical care on a sliding fee-scale basis.

Sample

A mixed cross-section and cohort design was used to evaluate the success of the project. Independent cross-sectional surveys, conducted before and after the intervention, were used to assess community trends over time. The cohort was formed by randomly selecting half of the women who participated in the baseline survey to be also interviewed at the conclusion of the project. During Year 4 of the project, a survey of women's knowledge, attitudes, and practices related to breast, cervical, and colorectal cancer screening was conducted. For this study, only the women in the cross-sectional sample in Year 4 were included.

For the cross-sectional group of women, a random sample of 424 women from the housing communities, stratified by city and age group (40–64 years, and 65 and older), was selected to participate in the survey by simple random selection. Women were interviewed face to face by interviewers of the same ethnic background. The interviews lasted approximately 45 min and were conducted mainly in the women's homes. A total of 320 women completed a survey (75% response rate, with 84% in Forsyth County and 68% in Guilford County). For this study, we limited our analyses to African American and Caucasian women who resided in the housing communities; thus, the 20 women (6% of total sample) who are of other racial groups were not included in these analyses.

Statistical Analyses

Descriptive statistics were calculated for demographic and health care characteristics by racial group and compared using unadjusted chi-square tests. Knowledge, attitudes, and belief scores were calculated based on the participants' responses to a series of questions, described in the Appendix, which addressed areas of knowledge, attitudes, and beliefs for each cancer and screening test. Perceived risk of cancer was assessed by asking women to rate their risk of developing each cancer (high, average, or low). Compliance with screening guidelines was defined as follows. For mammography, women between 40 and 49 years old were within guidelines if they had received a mammogram within the last 2 years, and women 50 and older were within guidelines if they had a mammogram within the last year. An annual CBE and a Pap smear within the last 3 years defined women in compliance with guidelines for these exams. Guidelines used for FOBT were testing within the last year, and for FS, testing within the last 5 years. Analyses included all participants for breast and cervical cancer screening questions, but were restricted to participants aged 50 and older for colorectal cancer screening questions.

Comparisons between racial groups were made using chi-square tests. Adjusted p values were obtained using analysis of covariance models or logistic models (dichotomous responses) that included the covariates age (as a continuous response), city, health insurance, marital status, and work status, in addition to the variable of interest, race. Interactions between race and covariates were also examined, and were kept in the model if $p \leq .05$.

Variables tested in the logistic models were chosen as the results of stepwise variable selection as follows. For each outcome, an initial model was fitted that included main effects, plus all two-way interactions between race and the main effects. Main effects considered were those terms shown in Table 1, along with the beliefs, barriers, knowledge, and risk scores associated with the outcome. A backward stepwise algorithm (PROC REG for continuous outcomes and PROC LOGISTIC for dichotomous outcomes, in Statistical Analysis Software) was used to remove any interaction terms with a $p > .05$. Once this model was obtained, a final model was obtained using backward stepwise regression by forcing race and any main effects involved in significant interactions into the model; next, interaction terms themselves, along with other main effects, were examined and allowed to be removed from the model if $p > .05$.

RESULTS

Characteristics of the Sample

Of the 300 women who participated in this cross-sectional survey, 79% ($n = 237$) were African American and 21% ($n = 63$) were white. Demographic and health care utilization characteristics of these women are shown in Table 1 by racial group. African American women in the sample were younger (average age 66 years) compared to white women (average age 73 years, $p < .001$). The low-income housing communities are designed to serve persons with low income, and have separate communities that cater to the needs of seniors. African American women tend to be eligible on income level at younger ages, whereas more white women

TABLE 1
Demographic and Health Care Characteristics of Sample by Racial Group

| | Racial Group | | | | |
| | African American[a] | | White[b] | | |
Variable	n	%	n	%	p value
Age (years)					
< 65	102	44	10	16	.001
≥ 65	132	56	53	84	
Marital status					
Currently married	39	17	4	6	
Previously married	157	67	56	89	.002
Never married	40	17	3	5	
Education					
< Eighth grade	70	30	28	44	
Some high school	88	38	15	24	.053
High school graduate	75	32	20	32	
Parity					
Parous	191	84	46	82	.77
Nulliparous	37	16	10	18	
Health insurance					
Yes	202	89	55	98	.04
No	24	11	1	2	
Regular annual checkups					
Yes	190	83	47	84	.91
No	38	17	9	16	
Working status					
Yes	36	16	0	0	.001
No	190	84	56	100	
Smoking status					
Never	109	48	25	44	
Former	56	25	17	30	.70
Current	61	27	14	25	
Medical condition					
Yes	78	34	16	29	.42
No	150	66	40	71	

[a]$n = 237.$ [b]$n = 63.$

enter the communities at older ages. This difference in age affects other demographic characteristics of the sample, as shown in Table 1.

White women were less likely then African American women to be currently married (6% vs. 17%, $p = .002$) and were less likely to have had at least some high school education (56% vs. 70%, $p = .05$). In addition, more white women reported having health insurance (98% vs. 89%, $p = .04$), including Medicare coverage, and not working (100% vs. 84%, $p = .001$) compared to African American women. The two groups were similar in terms of parity (84% parous), proportion that had a regular checkup within the last year (83%), smoking status (27% current smokers), and prevalence of a chronic medical condition (33%).

Screening Patterns

Breast cancer.   The unadjusted univariate analyses for knowledge, attitudes, perceived risk of cancer, and utilization of breast, cervical, and colorectal cancer screening exams are shown in Table 2, along with the analyses adjusted for the variables that were significantly different between races in Table 1 (i.e., age as a continuous variable, city of residence, health insurance coverage, marital status, and work status). Only one variable, barriers to mammography screening, was significantly different in the univariate analyses, and no statistically significant differences in knowledge, beliefs, perceived risk, barriers, or breast cancer screening practices were noted in the adjusted analyses. Interestingly, about one third to one half of the women in both racial groups had poor to fair knowledge of and negative beliefs about mammography. Only 40% of the women had some perceived risk of breast cancer. Younger women (less than 65 years old) were more likely to report barriers to screening compared to women older than 65 (61% vs. 47%). About half of the women had a mammogram within age-specific guidelines, and only about 60% had a CBE within the last year.

Cervical cancer.   A similar picture is seen for cervical cancer variables, with two exceptions. A significant interaction between city of residence and race was found for perceived risk of cervical cancer (Table 3). In Greensboro, white women were 3.2 times more likely to perceive themselves at risk for developing cervical cancer ($p = .014$), whereas in Winston-Salem no statistically significant differences by race were observed. Although not significantly different, fewer white women had a Pap smear within the last 3 years ($p = .34$, adjusted). The majority of women in both groups had poor to fair knowledge about Pap smears and cervical cancer. White women tended to have more negative beliefs about Pap smears than did African American women (71% vs. 49%, $p = .097$), although this difference was not statistically significant. Neither group had many barriers to Pap smear screening.

Colorectal cancer.   Both groups of women had good knowledge about colorectal cancer and screening for colorectal cancer. Positive beliefs about FS were found for 20% to 33% of the women. Significantly more white women perceived themselves at high risk for colorectal cancer than did African American women (14% vs. 4%, $p = .007$, adjusted). Overall, about 60% of the women had never had an FS exam (Table 2), and about 20% of the entire sample had an FOBT within the last year. Significant interactions between city of residence and race were noted for beliefs about FOBT and regular FS exams. As shown in Table 3, women in

TABLE 2
Knowledge, Attitudes, and Utilization of Breast, Cervical, and Colorectal Cancer Screening Exams by Racial Group

| | Racial Group | | | | Adjusted | |
| | African American[a] | | White[b] | | | |
Variable	n	%	n	%	Unadjusted p Value	Adjusted p Value[c]
Breast cancer						
Knowledge about mammography screening						
Poor	51	22	19	30	.075	.274
Fair	30	13	7	11		
Good	51	22	6	10		
Very good	58	24	12	19		
Excellent	47	20	19	30		
Beliefs about mammography						
Negative	35	15	18	29	.119	.157
Slightly negative	53	22	15	23		
Slightly positive	91	38	18	29		
Positive	58	24	12	19		
Perceived risk of breast cancer						
None	141	60	36	57	.736	.143
Some	96	40	27	43		
Barriers to mammography screening						
Few	73	31	7	11	.003	.278
Some	71	30	22	35		
Many	63	27	17	27		
A lot	30	13	17	27		
Had mammogram within guidelines[d]						
Yes	121	52	25	40	.090	.528
No	113	48	38	60		
Had CBE within last year						
Yes	156	60	35	56	.132	.828
No	81	40	28	44		
Cervical cancer						
Knowledge about Pap smears and cervical cancer						
Poor	73	31	25	40	.705	.824
Fair	56	24	15	24		
Good	44	19	9	14		
Very good	54	23	12	19		
Excellent	10	4	2	3		
Beliefs about Pap smear screening						
Negative	61	27	27	48	.005	.097
Slightly negative	49	22	13	23		
Slightly positive	11	5	0	0		
Positive	107	47	16	29		

(Continued)

TABLE 2 *(Continued)*

	Racial Group				Adjusted	
	African American[a]		White[b]			
Variable	n	%	n	%	Unadjusted p value	Adjusted p value[c]
Perceived risk of cervical cancer						
None	159	67	47	75	.253	[e]
Some	78	33	16	25		
Barriers to Pap smear screening						
Few	110	46	26	41	.548	.784
Some	99	42	27	43		
Many	21	9	9	14		
A lot	7	3	1	2		
Had Pap smear within last 3 years						
Yes	180	80	32	59	.002	.339
No	46	20	22	41		
Colorectal cancer						
Knowledge about colorectal cancer screening						
Poor	38	20	7	14	.14	.500
Fair	25	13	11	22		
Good	46	24	8	16		
Very good	64	33	15	29		
Excellent	20	10	10	20		
Beliefs about FOBT						
Negative	34	18	10	20	.167	[e]
Slightly positive	95	49	31	60		
Positive	64	33	10	20		
Beliefs about flexible sigmoidoscopy						
Negative	33	17	9	18	.996	.089
Slightly positive	88	47	24	47		
Positive	68	36	18	35		
Perceived risk of colorectal cancer						
Low	166	96	37	86	.014	.007
High	7	4	6	14		
Had FOBT within last year						
Yes	38	21	8	17	.46	.22
No	139	79	40	83		
Had flexible sigmoidoscopy						
≤ 5 years ago	42	24	15	31	.57	[e]
> 5 years ago	20	11	4	8		
Never	114	65	30	61		

Note. FOBT = Fecal Occult Blood Test.

[a] $n = 237$. [b] $n = 63$. [c] All models are adjusted for age (as a continuous variable), city of residence, health insurance coverage, marital status, and work status. [d] Guidelines are age 40–49 within last 2 years; 50 years and older within last year. [e] Significant interaction between race and city of residence. Results are reported in Table 3.

TABLE 3
Variables With Significant Interaction Between Race and City of Residence

| | Racial Group | | |
Variable	African American	White	Adjusted p Value[a]
Perceived risk of cervical cancer		Odds ratio	
(High)			
Greensboro	1.0	3.4	.014
Winston-Salem	1.0	0.6	.437
Beliefs about FOBT		M	
Greensboro	4.21	3.15	.067
Winston-Salem	1.42	1.68	.74
Had a flexible sigmoidoscopy (≤ 5		Odds ratio	
years ago)			
Greensboro	1.0	2.86	.030
Winston-Salem	1.0	0.28	.120

[a]Adjusted for age (as a continuous variable), city of residence, health insurance coverage, marital status, and work status.

Greensboro had more positive beliefs about FOBT than did women in Winston-Salem. White women in Greensboro were almost three times more likely to have had an FS exam within guidelines as compared to African American women in Greensboro ($p = .03$). Although not significantly different, fewer white women in Winston-Salem had an FS within the recommended guidelines when compared to African American women.

Predictors of Screening

The results of the multivariate analyses of predictors of regular screening adjusted for city of residence are shown in Table 4. In these analyses, age, beliefs, knowledge, and barrier scores were considered as continuous variables. For regular mammography screening, four variables were important predictors for African American women: having fewer barriers to obtaining the exam (odds ratio [OR] = 1.4, $p <$ .001), being an ex-smoker or never smoking (OR = 1.9, $p = .04$), having regular checkups (OR = 4.6, $p < .001$), and having more positive beliefs (OR = 1.3, $p =$ .001). The three variables that predicted regular mammography among white women were those previously mentioned, with the exception of the barriers scale: age, beliefs, and knowledge. Thus, among African American women, those with fewer barriers to obtaining a mammogram were more likely to obtain a mammogram, whereas barriers did not affect whether or not white women received a regular mammogram. For African American women, the receipt of a CBE within the last year was related to not having a chronic medical condition, (OR = 1.9, $p = .04$),

TABLE 4
Multivariate Models for Receipt of Breast, Cervical, and Colorectal Cancer Screening Tests

Variable	Odds Ratio	95% Confidence Interval	p Value
Recent mammogram[a]			
Barriers (1-unit decrease)			
AfricanAmerican	1.4	1.2, 1.6	.0001
White	0.87	0.72, 1.14	.3910
Smoker (ex- or never vs. current)	1.9	1.0, 3.6	.0435
Regular checkups (yes)	4.6	1.9, 11.0	.0006
Beliefs (1-unit increase in score)	1.3	1.1, 1.5	.0011
CBE in last year			
Medical condition (yes)			
African American	0.52	0.28, 0.98	.0440
White	2.7	0.69, 3.6	.1419
Age			
5 years younger	1.2	1.02, 1.29	.0180
Regular checkups (yes)	6.4	3.0, 13.6	.0001
Pap smear in last 3 years			
Regular checkups (yes)			
African American	13.9	5.6, 34.8	.0001
White	0.55	0.10, 3.03	.4953
Knowledge score (1-unit increase)	1.3	1.4, 4.0	.0001
FOBT in last year			
Beliefs (1-unit increase in score)	1.40	1.21, 1.61	.0001
Flexible sigmoidoscopy in last 5 years			
Beliefs (1-unit increase in score)			
African American	1.09	1.001, 1.21	.049
White	1.74	1.15, 4.598	.009
Perceived colorectal cancer risk (high)			
African American	1.21	0.22, 6.68	.82
White	47.9	2.37, 971.3	.012

Note. Breast and cervical cancer screening models are adjusted for city of residence. CBE = clinical breast exam; FOBT = Fecal Occult Blood Test.
[a]Recent defined as age 40–49 last 2 years; 50 and older last year.

being younger (OR = 1.2, p = .02), and having regular checkups (OR = 6.4, p = .0001). Among white women living in the intervention community, younger age and receiving regular checkups were related to receiving a CBE within the last year.

Among African American women, two variables were associated with receiving a recent Pap smear among African American women: obtaining a regular annual checkup (OR = 13.9, p < .001), and greater knowledge about Pap smears and cervical cancer (OR = 1.3, p = .001). For white women, having regular checkups was not a significant predictor of receiving Pap smears, and greater knowledge of Pap smears and cervical cancer was the only significant variable.

Factors associated with colorectal cancer screening appear to be somewhat different than those associated with breast and cervical cancer screening. For women in both racial groups, those with more positive beliefs about FOBT were more likely to have had an FOBT within the last year (OR = 1.40, p = .0001). For white women, increasingly positive attitudes about FS and colorectal cancer screening increased the odds of having had an FS within the last 5 years (OR = 1.74, p = .009). This relation was not as strong among African American women (OR = 1.09, p = .049). The most striking relation was seen in women with perceived risk of colon cancer. White women were more likely to have had an FS within the last 5 years if they had some perceived risk of colorectal cancer (OR = 47.9, p = .012), whereas this relation was not statistically significant among African American women (OR = 1.21, p = .82).

DISCUSSION

This study examined the use of breast, cervical, and colorectal cancer screening exams among low-income women. In general, these screening tests were underutilized by the women and racial differences in screening rates were observed. Only 52% of African American women and 40% of white women had a mammogram within guidelines. These figures are below the Year 2000 objective of 60% (U.S. Department of Health and Human Services [DHHS], 1990). About 60% had a CBE within the last year, although about 80% had visited a physician within the last year for a regular checkup. Fewer white women had a Pap smear within the last year, but African American women had achieved the 80% goal set by the year 2000 objectives (DHHS, 1990). Colorectal cancer screening test utilization rates were low among both groups of women and well below the Year 2000 objectives of 50% and 40% for FOBT and FS exams, respectively (DHHS, 1990).

Overall, factors related to screening were similar among African American and white women in that no statistically significant differences were observed. Significant racial differences were noted for four of the five screening tests examined in logistic regression analyses. African American women who received regular checkups were more likely to have received a Pap smear within the last 3 years (OR = 13.9, p = .0001), whereas having a regular checkup had no effect on white women getting regular Pap smears. Barriers had no effect on whether white women received a regular mammogram, but barriers were important for African American women (OR = 1.4, p = .0001). African American women with a medical condition were less likely to receive a CBE (OR = 0.52, p = .04), whereas this was not seen in white women. Beliefs about colorectal cancer screening were important predictors of the receipt of FOBT for women of both races (OR = 1.4, p = .0001). For the receipt of regular FS exams, beliefs in the test were significantly different for both racial groups ($p < .05$), and the effect was stronger among white women than among African American women (OR = 1.74 vs. 1.09 for African American and white women, respectively). Perceived risk of colorectal cancer had greater impact on receiving regular FS exams among white women (OR = 47.9, $p = .012$).

Limitations of this study include the fact that we relied on self-reports of screening behavior. Although these reports may overestimate the actual screening rates, previous work in this population has found that self-reports can be used to identify predictors of screening among low-income women fairly well for mammography (Paskett et al., 1996). Another limitation of the study is our low response rate among women in the comparison community (68% response rate). We attribute this to the fact that we were well known in the intervention community and thus were more successful in getting women to complete our survey (84% response rate). Nonresponders tended to be similar to those women who participated in the survey in terms of age and race, the only variables we have knowledge of for these women. A last limitation is the fact that women in the intervention community had been exposed to clinic-based and community interventions about breast and cervical cancer screening. As we hypothesized an effect from this intervention in terms of breast and cervical cancer knowledge, attitudes, and screening behaviors, we adjusted for city of residence in our multivariate model. Results of the intervention program in terms of improving knowledge, attitudes, and behaviors are still being analyzed and will be reported elsewhere. The strengths of this study include the relative homogeneity of the sample in terms of income, which allows for an examination of racial differences in knowledge, attitudes, and screening behavior related to breast, cervical, and colorectal cancer among low-income women. Relatively few studies have examined patterns and predictors of colorectal cancer screening in this population; however, the results of this study are limited to women who reside in similar types of subsidized housing communities.

The results of this study are similar to those reported from other studies that examined cancer screening behaviors of women. Data from the 1992 Cancer Control Supplement of the National Health Interview Survey (NHIS) indicated that 23% of African American women had a mammogram within the last year, compared to 30% of white women (Martin et al., 1996). Data from this study indicate that the screening rates were higher, 52% for African American women and 40% for white women. The NHIS data also indicated that mammography utilization declined as income and years of schooling decreased; however, from our data, no differences in mammography utilization were seen when adjustments were made for age, income, and education. Women without a usual source of health care underutilized mammography in the NHIS data; however, in this study, women who received regular checkups were regular mammography users.

Mickey, Durski, Worden, and Danigelis (1995) found that women who had never heard of mammography had poor knowledge about breast cancer screening, were less educated, and had lower incomes compared to women who had heard of mammography. Women who had not had a CBE exam within the last year were less likely to have a regular place to get medical care, and had poorer knowledge about breast cancer screening than did women who had a CBE within the last year. Price (1994) reported that urban African American women had misconceptions about breast cancer screening, such as not viewing themselves as at risk for the disease and that pain was a barrier to getting a mammogram. Previous studies have cited as barriers to regular screening among African American women more negative beliefs among African American women who do not get mammograms, failure of physicians to recommend mammograms, cost, and poorer knowledge about breast cancer risk (Ackermann, Brackbill, Bewerse, & Sanderson, 1992; Burack & Liang, 1989; Caplan, Wells, & Haynes, 1992; Kiefe, McKay, Halevy, & Brody, 1994; Vernon et al., 1992). Calle et al. (1993) found that income level, rather than race, was an important predictor of mammography utilization; and that African American women were significantly more likely to have had a Pap smear within the last year than white women. In contrast to previous studies where older age was related to underuse of both Pap smear and mammography exams (Calle et al., 1993; Rimer, 1994), this study found this underutilization pattern only in relation to CBE.

For Pap smear utilization, the NHIS found that older women, widows, women with higher income, and African American women were more likely to have had a Pap smear. Women with less than 12 years of education and those without a usual source of health care underutilized Pap smear exams. This study found that fewer white women than African American women had a Pap smear within guidelines (59% vs. 80% for white and African American women, respectively); however, having regular checkups, rather than having a usual source of health care, was a consistent significant predictor of receiving regular cervical cancer screening.

In terms of colorectal cancer screening exams, Breen and Kessler (1996) reported from the 1992 NHIS data that 12% of African American women and 16% of white women reported having an FOBT within the last year, whereas 8% of African American women and 6% of white women reported having had an FS within the last 3 years (21% of African American and 27% of white women had ever had the test). Compared to the NHIS data, data from this study indicate higher utilization rates for both tests among both racial groups. This study also adds important information about colorectal cancer screening among low-income populations, as few studies have been previously reported. Jepson, Kessler, Portnoy, and Gibbs (1991) found that black–white differences in utilization of FOBT were eliminated after knowledge, attitudes, and education variables were included in the multivariate model. We found similar results in this study. To add insight into this finding, Hoffman and Abcarian (1991) reported that a significant number of their low-income African American patients believed that surgery can expose cancer to air and cause the spread of cancer. This belief was greater among patients who did not participate in an FOBT program, and was a result of experiences in the community in which surgery was performed on patients with advanced cancer. Where barriers to colorectal cancer screening tests, including embarrassment, worry, discomfort, inconvenience, and dislike of the procedure have been associated with noncompliance (Macrae et al., 1984), our study found that beliefs were more important than perceived barriers to screening. Similar results were also reported by Silman and Mitchell (1984).

In summary, few differences in receiving screening exams were noted by race among this low-income population. Overall, few women were receiving FS exams and about half the women were receiving regular mammograms. Because they tended to be older, white women were less likely to receive regular Pap smears. Only 60% of the sample received an annual CBE, and 17% to 20% received an FOBT within the last year. After adjustment for significant factors, important issues related to obtaining regular screening exams included the receipt of regular checkups, and knowledge, beliefs, and barriers related to the specific screening test, regardless of race. These data suggest that efforts to improve mortality rates from these cancers among low-income women should include messages tailored to improve beliefs and convey understanding of risk. These efforts will assist in bringing us closer to the Year 2000 goals for all women and help to reduce the disproportionate cancer mortality rates among low-income populations.

ACKNOWLEDGMENT

This research was supported by Grant CA57016 from the National Cancer Institute, Public Health Service.

REFERENCES

Ackermann, S. P., Brackbill, R. M., Bewerse, B. A., & Sanderson, L. M. (1992). Cancer screening behaviors among U.S. women: Breast cancer, 1987–1989, and cervical cancer, 1988–1989. *Mortality and Morbidity Weekly Report Centers for Disease Control Surveillance Summary, 41*, 17–25.

American Cancer Society. (1986). Cancer of the colon and rectum. *Gallup Report, 38*, 1–38.

American Cancer Society. (1990). 1989 survey of physicians' attitudes and practices in early cancer detection. *CA: A Cancer Journal for Clinicians, 40*, 77–101.

Anderson, L. M., & May, D. S. (1995). Has the use of cervical, breast, and colorectal cancer screening increased in the United States? *American Journal of Public Health, 85*, 840–842.

Baquet, C. R., Clayton, L. A., & Robinson, R. G. (1986). *Cancer prevention and control: Minorities and cancer.* New York: Springer-Verlag.

Breen, N., & Kessler, L. (1996). Current trends in cancer screening: 1987 and 1992. *Morbidity and Mortality Weekly Reports, 26*, 57–61.

Burack, R. C., & Liang, J. (1987). The early detection of cancer in the primary-care setting: Factors associated with the acceptance and completion of recommended procedures. *Preventive Medicine, 16*, 739–751.

Burack, R. C., & Liang, J. (1989). The acceptance and completion of mammography by older black women. *American Journal of Public Health, 79*, 721–726.

Burg, M. A., Lane, D. S., & Polednak, A. P. (1990). Age group differences in the use of breast cancer screening tests. *Journal of Aging and Health, 2,* 514–530.

Burns R. B., McCarthy, E. P., Freund, K. M., Marwill, S. L., Shwartz, M., Ash, A., & Moskowitz, M. A. (1996). Black women receive less mammography even with similar use of primary care. *Annals of Internal Medicine, 125,* 173–182.

Calle, E. E., Flanders, D. W., Thun, M. J., & Martin, L. M. (1993). Demographic predictors of mammography and Pap smear screening in U.S. women. *American Journal of Public Health, 83,* 53–60.

Calnan, M. (1984). The health belief model and participation in programmes for the early detection of breast cancer: A comparative analysis. *Social Sciences in Medicine, 19,* 823–830.

Caplan, L. S., Wells, B. L., & Haynes S. (1992). Breast cancer screening among older racial/ethnic minorities and whites: Barriers to early detection. *Journal of Gerontology, 47,* 101–110.

Elwood, T. W., Erickson, A., & Lieberman, S. (1978). Comparative educational approaches to screening for colorectal cancer. *American Journal of Public Health, 68,* 135–138.

Fink, R., Shapiro, S., & Roester, R. (1982). Impact of efforts to increase participation in repetitive screenings for early breast cancer detection. *American Journal of Public Health, 62,* 328–336.

Fletcher, S. W., Harris, R. P., Gonzalez, J. J., Degnan, D., Lannin, D. R., Strecher, V. J., Pilgrim, C., Quade, D., Earp, J. A., & Clark, R. L. (1993). Increasing mammography utilization: A controlled study. *Journal of the National Cancer Institute, 85,* 112–120.

Fox, S. A., & Stein, J. A. (1991). The effect of physician–patient communication on mammography utilization by different ethnic groups. *Medical Care, 29,* 1065–1082.

Freeman, H. P. (1989). Cancer in the socioeconomically disadvantaged. *CA: A Cancer Journal for Clinicians, 39,* 266–288.

French, K., Porter, A. M. D., Robinson, S. E., McCallum, F. M., Howie, J., & Roberts, M. M. (1982). Attendance at a breast screening clinic: A problem of administration or attitudes. *British Medical Journal (Clinical Research Edition), 285,* 617–620.

Garfinkel, L., Poindexter, C. E., & Silverberg, E. (1980). Cancer in black Americans. *CA: A Cancer Journal for Clinicians, 30,* 39–44.

Goodspeed, R. B., DeLucia, A. G., Parravano, J., & Goldfield, N. (1988). Compliance with mammography recommendations at the worksite. *Journal of Occupational Medicine, 30,* 40–42.

Grady, K. E., Lemkay, J. P., McVay, J. M., & Reisine, S. T. (1991). The importance of physician encouragement in breast cancer screening in older women. *Archives of Internal Medicine, 151,* 50–56.

Guzick, D. S. (1978). Efficacy of screening for cervical cancer: A review. *American Journal of Public Health, 68,* 125.

Harlan, L. C., Bernstein, A. B., & Kessler, L. G. (1991). Cervical cancer screening: Who is not screened and why? *American Journal of Public Health, 81,* 885–890.

Hoffman, A., & Abcarian, H. (1991). Six years of occult blood screening in an urban public hospital: Concepts, methods, and reflections on approaches to reducing avoidable mortality among black Americans. *Journal of the National Medical Association, 83,* 994–999.

Horton, J. A., Romans, M. C., & Cruess, D. F. (1992). Mammography attitudes and usage study. *Women's Health Issues, 2,* 180–186.

Jepson, C., Kessler, G. L., Portnoy, B., & Gibbs, T. (1991). Black–White differences in cancer prevention knowledge and behavior. *American Journal of Public Health, 81,* 501–504.

Kiefe, C. I., McKay, S. V., Halevy, A., & Brody, B. A. (1994). Is cost a barrier to screening mammography for low-income women receiving Medicare benefits? A randomized trial. *Archives of Internal Medicine, 154,* 1217–1224.

Kosary, C. L., Reis, L. A. G., Miller, B. A., Hankey, B. F., Harras, A., Devesa, S. S., & Edwards, B. K. (1995). *SEER cancer statistics review, 1973–1992: Tables and graphs* (NIH Publication No. 95-2789). Bethesda, MD: National Cancer Institute.

Lerman, C., Rimer, B., Trock, B., Balshem, A., & Engstrom, P. F. (1990). Factors associated with repeat adherence to breast cancer screening. *Preventive Medicine, 2,* 514–530.

Maclean, U., Sinfeld, D., Klein, S., & Harnden, B. (1984). Women who decline breast screening. *Journal of Epidemiology and Community Health, 38,* 278–283.

Macrae, F. A., Hill, D. J., St. John, J. B., Ambikapapthy, A., & Garner, J. F. (1984). Predicting colon cancer screening behavior from health beliefs. *Preventive Medicine, 13,* 115–126.

Mandel, J. S., Bond, J. H., Church, T. R., Snover, D. C., Bradley, G. M., Shuman, L. M., & Ederer, F., for the Minnesota Colon Cancer Control Study. (1993). Reducing mortality from colorectal cancer by screening for fecal occult blood. *New England Journal of Medicine, 328,* 1365–1371.

Marchant, D. J., & Sutton, S. M. (1990). Use of mammography—United States, 1990. *Morbidity and Mortality Weekly Report, 39,* 621–630.

Martin, L. M., Calle, E. E., Wingo, P. A., & Heath, C. W., Jr. (1996). Comparison of mammography and Pap test use from the 1987 and 1992 national health interview surveys: Are we closing the gaps? *American Journal of Preventive Medicine, 12,* 82–90.

McCarthy, B. D., & Moskowitz, M. A. (1993). Screening flexible sigmoidoscopy: Patient attitudes and compliance. *Journal of General Internal Medicine, 8,* 120–125.

McPhee, S. J., Richard, R. J., & Solkowitz, S. N. (1986). Performance of cancer screening in a university general internal medicine practice: Comparison with the 1980 American Cancer Society Guidelines. *Journal of General Internal Medicine, 1,* 275–281.

Michielutte, R., Dignan, M., Bahnson, J., & Wells, H. B. (1994). The Forsyth County Cervical Cancer Prevention Project–II: Compliance with screening follow-up of abnormal cervical smears. *Health Education Research, 9,* 421–432.

Mickey, R. M., Durski, J., Worden, J. K., & Danigelis, N. L. (1995). Breast cancer screening and associated factors for low-income African-American women. *Preventive Medicine, 24,* 467–476.

Miller, B. A., Ries, L. A., Hankey, B. F., Kosary, C. L., Harras, A., Devesa, S. S., & Edwards, B. K. (1993). *Annual cancer statistics review. SEER Program* (NIH Publication No. 93–2789). Washington, DC: National Cancer Advisory Board.

Moody-Thomas, S., & Fick, A. C. (1994). Women's health: Early detection and screening practices for breast and cervical cancer. *Journal of Louisana State Medical Society, 146,* 152–158.

Moss, A. J., & Wilder, M. H. (1977). *Use of selected medical procedures associated with prevention care, United States: 1973* (DHEW Publication No. HRA 77–1538; Vital and health statistics, Series 10, No. 110). Rockville, MD: U.S. Department of Health, Education, and Welfare, Public Health Service.

National Cancer Institute Breast Cancer Screening Consortium. (1990). Screening mammography: A missed clinical opportunity? *Journal of the American Medical Association, 264,* 54–58.

National Cancer Institute Cancer Screening Consortium for Underserved Women. (1995). Breast and cervical cancer screening among underserved women. *Archives of Family Medicine, 4,* 617–624.

Newcomb, P. A., Norfleet, R. G., Storer, B. E., Surawicz, T. S., & Marcus, P. M. (1992). Screening sigmoidoscopy and colorectal cancer mortality. *Journal of the National Cancer Institute, 84,* 1572–1575.

Parker, S. L., Tong, T., Bolden, S., & Wingo, P. A. (1996). Cancer statistics, 1996. *CA: A Cancer Journal for Clinicians, 65,* 517.

Paskett, E. D., Tatum, C. M., Mack, D. W., Hoen, H., Case, L. D., & Velez, R. (1996). Validation of self-reported breast and cervical cancer screening tests among low-income minority women. *Cancer, Epidemiology, Biomarkers & Prevention, 5,* 721–726.

Polednak, A. P., Lane, D. S., & Burg, M. A. (1991). Risk perception, family history, and use of breast cancer screening tests. *Cancer Detection and Prevention, 15,* 257–263.

Price, J. H. (1994). Economically disadvantaged females' perceptions of breast cancer and breast cancer screening. *Journal of the National Medical Association, 86,* 899–906.

Reis, L. A. G., Hankey, B. F., & Edwards, B. K. (1990). *Cancer statistics review 1973–1987.* Bethesda, MD: National Cancer Institute.

Richardson, A. (1990). Factors likely to affect participation in mammographic screening. *North Carolina Medical Journal, 103,* 155–156.

Rimer, B. K. (1994). Lifespan and ethnicity issues. *Cancer, 74,* 323–328.

Rimer, B. K., Keintz, M. K., Kesslers, H. B., Engstrom, P. F., & Rosan, J. R. (1989). Why women resist screening mammography: Patient-related barriers. *Radiology, 172,* 243–246.

Rodney, W. M., Beaber, R. J., Johnson, R., & Wuan, M. (1985). Physician compliance with colorectal cancer screening (1978–1983): The impact of flexible sigmoidoscopy. *Journal of Family Practice, 20,* 265–269.

Schechter, C., Vanchieri, C. F., & Crofton, C. (1990). Evaluating women's attitudes and perceptions in developing mammography promotion messages. *Public Health Reports, 105,* 253–257.

Selby, J. V., Friedman, G. D., Quesenberry, C. P. J., & Weiss, N. S. (1992). A case-control study of screening sigmoidoscopy and mortality from colorectal cancer. *New England Journal of Medicine, 326,* 653–657.

Shapiro, S., Strax, P., & Venet, L. (1990). Evaluation of periodic breast cancer screening with mammography: Methodology and early observations. *CA: A Cancer Journal for Clinicians, 40,* 111–125.

Silman, A., & Mitchell, P. (1984). Attitudes of non-participants in an occupation based programme of screening for colorectal cancer. *Community Medicine, 6,* 8–11.

Singer, A. (1986). The abnormal cervical smear. *British Medical Journal, 293,* 1551.

Slenker, S. E., & Grant, M. C. (1989). Attitudes, beliefs, and knowledge about mammography among women over forty years of age. *Journal of Cancer Education, 4,* 61–65.

Stomper, P. C., Kopans, D. B., Sadowksy, N. L., Sonnenfeld, M. R., Swann, C. A., Gelman, R. S., Meyer, J. E., Jochelson, M. S., Hunt, M. S., & Allen, P. D. (1988). Is mammography painful? A multicenter patient survey. *Archives of Internal Medicine, 148,* 521–524.

Taylor, V. M., Taplin, S. H., Urban, N., White, E., & Peacock, S. (1995). Repeat mammography use among women ages 50–75. *Cancer, Epidemiology, Biomarkers & Prevention, 4,* 409–413.

Thompson, R. S., Michnick, M. E., Gray, J., Friedlander, L., & Gilson, B. (1986). Maximizing compliance with hemoccult screening for colon cancer in clinical practice. *Medical Care, 24,* 904–914.

U.S. Department of Health and Human Services. (1990). *Healthy people 2000: National health promotion and disease prevention objectives* (DHHS Publication No. 91-50212). Washington, DC: Author.

Vernon, S. W., Vogel, V. G., Halabi, S., Jackson, G. L., Lundy, R. O., & Peters, G. N. (1992). Breast cancer screening behaviors and attitudes in three racial/ethnic groups. *Cancer, 69,* 165–174.

Weinrich, S., Coker, A. L., Weinrich, M., Eleazer, P. G., & Greene, F. L. (1995). Predictors of Pap smear screening in socioeconomically disadvantaged elderly women. *Journal of American Geriatrics Society, 43,* 267–270.

White, E., Urban, N., & Taylor, V. (1993). Mammography utilization, public health impact, and cost-effectiveness in the United States. *Annual Review of Public Health, 14,* 605–614.

Wilcox, L. S., & Mosher, W. D. (1993). Factors associated with obtaining health screening among women of reproductive age. *Public Health Reports, 108,* 76–86.

Winawer, S. J., Andrews, M., Flehinger, B., Sherlock, P., Schottenfeld, D., & Miller, D. G. (1980). Progress report on controlled trial of fecal occult blood testing for the detection of colorectal neoplasia. *Cancer, 45,* 2952–2964.

Wingo, P. A., Bolden, S., Tong, T., Parker, S. L., Martin, L. M., & Heath, C. W., Jr. (1996). Cancer statistics for African Americans. *CA: A Cancer Journal for Clinicians, 46,* 113–125.

Woo, B., Wood, B., Cook, E. F., Weisberg, M., & Goldman, L. (1985). Screening procedures in the asymptomatic adult. Comparison of physicians' recommendations, patients' desires, published guidelines, and actual practice. *Journal of the American Medical Association, 254,* 1480–1484.

APPENDIX
Description of Items for Belief, Knowledge, and Barrier Scales for Breast, Cervical, and Colorectal Cancer Screening

	Code	
Mammography/Breast Cancer	*Agree*	*Disagree*
Belief Scale (Score groupings: negative = −4 to −1; slightly negative = 0–1; slightly positive = 2–3; positive = 4)		
It's embarrassing to get a mammogram.	−1	1
The radiation you get from a mammogram can give you cancer.	−1	1
A mammogram hurts.	−1	1
I feel okay so why bother getting a mammogram, it won't find anything.	−1	1
Knowledge Scale (Score groupings: poor = −13 to 0; fair = 1–2; good = 3–4; very good = 5–6; excellent = 7–13)		
Women over the age of 50 should have mammograms regularly.	1	−1
Knowledge of correct guidelines women should get screening mammograms.	1	−1
Knowledge of correct age women should begin regular screening mammograms.	1	−1
Women should never stop getting regular screening mammograms.	1	−1
Women over the age of 50 should have a breast exam by a physician every year.	1	1
Women who never have had any children are less likely to get breast cancer.	−1	1
After a couple of mammograms that show everything is okay, it is no longer necessary to have any mammograms.	−1	1
Breast cancer runs in families.	1	−1
Women can tell if they have breast cancer without going to the doctor for any tests.	−1	1
Black women are more likely to get breast cancer than white women.	−1	1
Older women are more likely to get breast cancer than younger women.	1	−1
The only good treatment for breast cancer is an operation to remove the breast.	−1	1
I feel okay so why bother getting a mammogram, it won't find anything.	−1	1
Barriers (Score Groupings: few = −13 to −9; some = −8 to −7; many = −6 to −3; a lot = −2 to 13)		
I have to sit and wait too long before the doctor sees me.	1	−1
It's too hard to get to the doctor's office.	1	−1
The doctor or nurses do not treat me with respect.	1	−1
I don't know where to get a mammogram.	1	−1
It's too hard to find time to get a mammogram.	1	−1
The technician at the mammogram place doesn't treat me with respect.	1	−1
I don't like having to go to a different place to get a mammogram.	1	−1
My doctor recommended a mammogram but I did not get it.	1	−1
Insurance/medicaid pays towards a screening mammogram.	−1	1
I believe my regular doctor wants me to get a mammogram.	−1	1
Someone encouraged me to have a mammogram.	−1	1
I never got a mammogram on my own.	−1	1
I asked a doctor to order a mammogram for me.	1	−1

(continued)

	Code	
Pap Smears/Cervical Cancer	*Agree*	*Disagree*
Belief Scale (Score Groupings: negative = –5 to –1; slightly negative = 0–1; slightly positive = 2; positive = 3–5)		
Getting a Pap smear is uncomfortable and can hurt.	–1	1
It's embarrassing to get a Pap smear.	–1	1
I have the responsibility to see that I get regular Pap smears.	1	–1
I feel ok so why bother getting a Pap smear, it won't find anything.	–1	1
I believe that my regular doctor wants me to get a Pap smear.	1	–1
Knowledge (Scale Score Groupings: poor = –14 to 2; fair = 3–4; good = 5–6; very good = 7–8; excellent = 9–14)		
I feel ok so why bother getting a Pap smear, it won't find anything.	–1	1
If the test found something, they might have to remove my womb.	–1	1
If you have cancer, it can't be cured anyway, so why bother getting a Pap smear.	–1	1
Women can tell if they have cervical cancer without going to a doctor for any tests.	–1	1
Women don't need a Pap smear if they aren't having sex.	–1	1
If a woman has stopped having her period, she doesn't need Pap smears anymore.	–1	1
After a couple of Pap smears that show everything is ok, it is no longer necessary to have any Pap smears.	–1	1
Cervical cancer runs in families.	–1	1
Young women are more likely to get cervical cancer than older women.	–1	1
Women who have had a hysterectomy (had their womb removed) no longer need to get Pap smears.	–1	1
Only women who have had many sex partners need Pap smears.	–1	1
Black women are more likely to get cervical cancer than white women.	–1	1
Women who smoke are more likely to get cervical cancer.	1	–1
Healthy adult women should have routine Pap smears according to guidelines (1–3 years).	1	–1
Barriers (Score Groupings: few = 5; some = –4 to –3; many = –2 to –1; a lot = 0–5)		
I have to sit and wait too long before the doctor sees me.	1	–1
It's too hard to get to the doctor's office.	1	–1
The doctor or nurses do not treat me with respect.	1	–1
I don't know where to get a Pap smear.	1	–1
Someone encouraged me to have a Pap smear.	1	–1

Colorectal Cancer

Belief Scale Fecal Occult Blood Test (negative = –7 to –1; slightly positive = 0–4; positive = 5–7)		
I feel ok so why bother getting a Fecal Occult Blood Test, it won't find anything.	–1	1
If the test found something, they might have to do more tests.	–1	1

(continued)

225

	Code	
	Agree	*Disagree*
Doing a Fecal Occult Blood Test is messy.	−1	1
If you have colon cancer, it can't be cured anyway, so why bother getting a Fecal Occult Blood Test.	−1	1
It takes too much time to do a Fecal Occult Blood Test.	−1	1
It's too hard to do a Fecal Occult Blood Test.	−1	1
I don't know where to get a Fecal Occult Blood Test.	−1	1
Knowledge Scale (poor = 0–1; fair = 2; good = 3; very good = 4; excellent = 5–6)		
After a couple of tests that show everything is ok in my colon, it is no longer necessary to have any more colon cancer tests.	0	1
Colon cancer runs in families.	1	0
Black people are more likely to get colon cancer than white people.	1	0
Young people are more likely to get colon cancer than older people.	0	1
Only people who eat poorly will get colon cancer.	0	1
Men are more likely to get colon cancer than women.	0	1
Beliefs Flexible Sigmoidoscopy (negative = −10 to −1; slightly positive = 0–4; positive = 5–10)		
I feel ok so why bother getting a flexible sigmoidoscopy exam, it won't find anything.	−1	1
If the test found something, they might have to remove part of my colon.	−1	1
Getting a flexible sigmoidoscopy exam is uncomfortable and can hurt.	−1	1
If you have colon cancer, it can't be cured anyway, so why bother getting a flexible sigmoidoscopy exam.	−1	1
It's embarrassing to get a rectal exam.	−1	1
It is too much bother to use the enemas to prepare for a flexible sigmoidoscopy exam.	−1	1
A person can tell if they have colon cancer without going to a doctor for any tests.	−1	1
I don't know where to get a flexible sigmoidoscopy exam.	−1	1
It costs too much to have a flexible sigmoidoscopy exam.	−1	1
It takes too much time to get a flexible sigmoidoscopy exam.	−1	1

WOMEN'S HEALTH: RESEARCH ON GENDER, BEHAVIOR, AND POLICY, 3(3&4), 227–242

Importance of Psychological Variables in Understanding Risk Perceptions and Breast Cancer Screening of African American Women

Deborah Bowen, Kari-Mae Hickman, and Diane Powers

*Division of Public Health Sciences, Fred Hutchinson Cancer Research Center
Seattle, WA*

African American women are less likely than white women to receive and perform adequate breast screening, and represent a group that has not been thoroughly researched in the area of breast cancer risk. In general, perceptions of risk and worry about cancer are both related to obtaining mammography and possibly other screening activities. We examine African American women's worry and beliefs about breast cancer, and their intentions to perform breast and genetic screening behaviors, using the self-regulatory model. Participants were recruited via media announcements; they completed questionnaires addressing several aspects of the self-regulatory model. Forty-one percent of participants were underestimators, 23% were overestimators, and 37% were extreme overestimators of their own personal risk for breast cancer. Several variables were significant predictors of willingness to undergo mammography and genetic screening, including ethnic identity, attitudes toward the physician, emotional distress, and risk overestimation. These data highlight the importance of psychological variables in understanding screening in African American women and hold promise for intervention design.

Key words: ethnicity, risk perceptions, cancer screening, transactional model

Breast cancer is a public health problem for African American women. The risk for breast cancer occurrence in black women 45 years old or younger is higher, 35.6

Correspondence concerning this article should be addressed to Deborah Bowen, Fred Hutchinson Cancer Research Center, 1124 Columbia Street, MP702, Seattle, WA 98104.

per 100,000 per year, than for white women of those ages, 31.9 per 100,000 per year (Ries et al., 1994). In the western Washington area, the incidence rate is even higher in these young black women: 69.6 per 100,000 per year compared with 51.8 per 100,000 per year in white women 45 years old or younger. Breast cancer presents at a later stage, higher grade, and greater tumor size at diagnosis in African American women (Ownby et al., 1985; Polednak, 1986) and results in greater mortality from the disease (Eley et al., 1994). Furthermore, black women are less likely than white women to receive and perform adequate breast screening (Burack & Liang, 1989), and represent a group that has not been extensively targeted for breast cancer risk research. These data point to a need to target African American women for breast health services. In particular, there are no published studies on the risk perceptions, cancer worries and anxieties, and related screening behaviors in African American women that can guide such services.

Perceived risk is a critical component of understanding why women obtain screening. Perceptions of risk and worry about cancer are both related to obtaining mammography and possibly other screening activities. Perception of risk, or perceived vulnerability, is a central component of most current models of health promotion and health-protective behaviors (Shumaker, Schron, & Ockene, 1990). Perceived risk has been linearly related to increased health behavior performance for behaviors such as seatbelt and condom use (Cochran & Peplau, 1991; Stasson & Fishbein, 1990); however, the case for breast cancer is not so clear. Studies linking perceived risk and performance of mammography have reported mixed results: Some have reported linear relations, whereas others have reported an inverted U-shaped relation with very low and very high levels of risk perception associated with lowered levels of screening (McCaul, Branstetter, Schroeder, & Glasgow, 1996; McCaul, Schroeder, & Reid, 1996). In general, women report overestimates of their own risk for breast cancer (Black, Nease, & Tosteson, 1995; Lerman et al., 1993) and report increased levels of worry and distress associated with breast cancer (Lerman, Kash, & Stefanek, 1994; Lerman & Schwartz, 1993), particularly if they have any family history of breast cancer. Taken together, the management of risk perception and worry and distress regarding cancer should be a priority to improve screening rates. This is particularly true when considering the impact of risk and worry on quality of life. Health-related quality of life should include a general assessment of functioning in health and other (psychological, cultural, etc.) domains (U.S. Department of Health & Human Services, 1990). Chronic worry and overestimation of one's risk for disease could impact quality of life on many fronts. Therefore, quality of life should be considered as an important area for assessment in research on breast cancer risk and worry.

Several studies can provide insight into the unique psychological issues facing African American women regarding their breast cancer risk. For example, in some studies African American and Caucasian women reported similar delays in care-seeking behavior, and levels of anxiety were important predictors for both groups of women (Lauver, 1994). In other studies, however, African American women delayed longer than did Caucasian women (Lauver & Ho, 1993) and race interacted with psychological variables to explain seeking medical care (Lauver, 1992). Race predicted compliance with hypertensive medications, independent of other demographic variables (Daniels, René, & Daniels, 1994), suggesting that race contributes something unique to a psychological profile. Perceptions of health were poorer among African Americans compared to Caucasians in large-scale surveys, again independent of income or education (Blendon et al., 1995). Finally, several studies have documented issues in Black and African American women's lives that could influence health, health care, and coping (e.g., Thomas & Quinn, 1993; Wyche, 1993).

Despite the breast cancer mortality differences and the potential psychological influences unique to African American women's health, few empirical studies have focused on psychological predictors of breast cancer screening for African American women (Powell, 1994). In these few studies, important factors included beliefs and knowledge, worry and anxiety, perceived risk, fear of finding cancer, and the consequences of cancer (Duke, Gordon-Sosby, Reynolds, & Gram 1994; Miller & Hailey, 1994; Royak-Schaler et al., 1995; Tessaro, Eng, & Smith, 1994). Clearly, both emotional and "rational" belief-type variables are important in predicting screening behaviors in African American and Black women.

Two issues potentially important to African American and Black women in the United States were measured in this study. One is the potential lack of trust in the medical establishment (Dula, 1994). Reports of the Tuskegee Experiment, in which Black men with syphilis were maintained in an untreated follow-up condition beyond ethical or medical standards for years, have been published in both the medical and lay press (Jones, 1993). Black and African American women have lack of trust, comfort, and faith in the medical establishment as a reason for not obtaining regular care (Dula, 1994). If present, this lack of trust could be due to publicly acknowledged failures, such as Tuskegee, or to the Caucasian dominance of the medical profession and the resulting racism (Carter, 1995). Whatever the potential cause, this phenomenon must be investigated empirically, and if a cause of lack of medical care, eliminated at all levels.

Therefore, this article identifies African American women's trust of their health care provider and examines its role in perceiving risk and seeking cancer screening. We do not know how trust in a physician relates to the other psychological variables; therefore, for this study we consider it a background variable capable of influencing the entire model. The second issue of interest in this population is the issue of self-definition of ethnic identity. Many labels have been used to describe African Americans, from both inside the community and from outsiders, including African American, Black, Afro-American, and Negro. Literature is not extensive on the meaning of these labels or the relation between use of a specific label and health variables. We included a measure of a woman's self-label to use as a predictor of our breast cancer risk outcomes of interest.

We use a model developed by Leventhal and colleagues (Leventhal & Cameron, 1987) to examine African American women's worry and beliefs about breast cancer and their intentions to perform breast and genetic screening behaviors. The transactional or self-regulation model of health behavior addresses health-risk communications and the use and effects of health screening. This model emphasizes the ways in which people actively cope with information about their health and make decisions regarding medical procedures, and the importance of understanding both a woman's understanding of her health risk and her emotional reaction to that risk. It has been used both to develop the intervention to be tested and to develop the evaluation plan. According to this model, a woman begins coping with her risk for breast cancer when she learns that she is at risk for the disease. This realization may occur to her on her own, when she learns of a friend or relative's illness, when she learns that breast cancer may be partially hereditary, or when she is invited to participate in a screening program. Regardless of the timing or nature of this realization, the woman reacts emotionally to the realization and develops an internal understanding or mental representation of what her elevated risk for breast cancer means to her. This mental representation will include her knowledge and beliefs about breast cancer, and more specifically, her beliefs about her own risk for breast cancer. The representations will then influence her emotional reactions, including her development and execution of plans for action regarding her risk and her emotional reactions to that risk. Emotional variables include the woman's specific reactions to breast cancer and cancer risk, as well as general levels of anxiety and depression. These emotional reactions will in turn influence both the mental representations and the action plan. The development of an action plan may include consideration of several approaches, including health behavior change, screening, denying the importance of the risk, avoiding thinking about her risk, or a combination of these approaches. Because a woman's risk for breast cancer continues throughout her life, her best strategy for coping with this risk may evolve over time as she participates in screening or learns more about her risk. This evolution occurs through a process of repeated evaluations of the representation or coping plan. These reevaluations may occur periodically throughout her life and be triggered by a variety of cues.

METHODS

Recruitment

Participants ($N = 129$) were recruited via notices in religious organizations and in two local African American newspapers asking for participants interested in a research project. We approached community representatives of several local churches and of the newspapers, asking for their help and support in disseminating invitations to participate. The invitations gave a two-sentence description of the research and the study line number. Potential participants called the study line and received a return call and a brief telephone survey screening for interest and eligibility. Eligibility criteria included age between 18 and 74 years old, interest in completing questionnaires and possibly receiving counseling about breast cancer risk, no personal history of breast or ovarian cancer, and a low-to-moderate familial risk for breast or ovarian cancer. Women were ineligible if they had more than two first-degree relatives with breast cancer. These high-risk women were referred to more appropriate counseling and genetic information.

Description of the Sample

Forty-nine percent of the recruited participants had at least one family member with breast or ovarian cancer. The average age was 44 (range = 20–72 years) and 40% of the participants were currently married or living with a partner, 30% were never married, and 23% were divorced or separated. Twenty-six percent had a combined annual household income of under $30,000, and 15% had an income of $70,000 or more, indicating a wide range of income levels. Eleven percent completed only high school, another 41% had post-high-school training, 23% held a college degree, and 23% had professional or graduate training. All women lived within a 60-mile radius of the research center, indicating either urban or suburban living.

To measure ethnic identity, participants completed a question asking about the best description of their ethnic identity. Participants described themselves as African American (64%), Black (30%), Afro-American (4%), or other (3%).

Measures

Demographic variables.   We measured important demographic variables using simple single-item measures. Educational level, income level, and marital status were measured by asking participants to choose from among categories of each variable. Age was measured in years.

Attitudes toward physicians.   Two questions were developed to measure attitudes toward physicians. The first statement was "I feel that I can trust my doctor's judgment," and the second was "I would like to discuss my anxiety about breast cancer with my health care provider." Both statements had response categories on a 4-point scale ranging from 1 (*strongly disagree*) to 4 (*strongly agree*).

Perceived risk. Breast cancer risk knowledge was measured using a single item measuring personal perceived breast cancer risk. This risk question, "On a scale of 0–100, what do you think your chances of getting breast cancer are, where 0 is no chance of getting breast cancer and 100 means you will definitely get it?", was modeled after questions discussed by Weinstein (1987). We found that the response to this single question correlated .8 to .9 with other types of perceived risk questions, including comparing personal risk to risk of other women in the same age group, and a categorical measure of perceived risk.

Mental representations. The second domain of breast cancer knowledge items measured the five categories of mental representations defined by Leventhal and Cameron (1987; causes of breast cancer risk, labels of breast cancer risk, symptoms of breast cancer risk, timeline, and consequences). Participants respond to each item using a 5-point Likert scale with anchors of 5 (*strongly agree*) to 1 (*strongly disagree*).

Actual breast cancer risk information. We collected information on demographic, reproductive, and hormonal risk factors for breast cancer using questions from our previous study of breast cancer risk counseling. These questions measured family history of breast cancer, age, age at menarche and at first birth, and other variables, all combined into a standard risk algorithm (Gail et al., 1989). The model used to calculate breast cancer risk (i.e., the Gail model) produced a risk estimate number in percent for lifetime risk of breast cancer. We produced a risk inaccuracy score by simply dividing the actual risk by the perceived risk reported by each participant. This gave us a method of assessing women's perceptions of their risk, relative to the actual medical risk as represented by the model.

Emotional reactions. We measured emotional reactions about breast cancer risk in two ways. We used the Brief Symptom Inventory to measure general anxiety and depression (Derogatis & Melisaratos, 1983). This instrument is a shortened version of the Hopkins Symptom Checklist and is a reliable, valid measure of emotional and psychiatric variables. The instrument consists of 49 items with 5-point Likert scales. Participants respond to the question, "How much have you been bothered by the following during the past 7 days, including today?" Participants answered each of the 49 items with anchors of 0 (*not at all*) to 4 (*extremely*). We used the Cancer Worry Scale (Lerman et al., 1991) to measure cancer-specific worry. This widely used and simple questionnaire is a four-item scale with 4-point response categories measuring the frequency of worry about breast cancer in different settings. The questions include, "During the past month, how often have thoughts about your chances of getting breast cancer affected your mood?" and "During the past month, how often have thoughts about your chances of getting breast cancer affected your ability to perform your daily activities?" The answers range from 1 (*not at all or rarely*) to 4 (*a lot*). The minimum score is a 4 and the maximum score possible is a 16. The a coefficient for this questionnaire was .76, and it is consistently used in studies measuring women's worries and concerns about breast cancer.

Coping.   We measured participants' methods of coping with stressful events or issues using the Lazarus Ways of Coping Inventory (Folkman & Lazarus, 1980a, 1980b). The instrument consists of 40 items with 5-point Likert scales ranging from 0 (*does not apply and/or not used*) to 4 (*used a great deal*). This widely used and well-validated measure provides a score for two broad categories of coping style: problem-focused coping and emotion-focused coping. Problem-focused coping involves some action that tries to directly change the issue or problem to reduce stress. Emotion-focused coping involves some action to reduce the impact of the problem on the individual without changing the problem items. Both methods of coping could be relevant to the strategies used by women at risk for breast cancer.

Screening behaviors.   For this study we defined behavioral action plans as actions women can take, including intentions to perform breast cancer screening behaviors and intentions to obtain breast cancer mutation screening. Breast cancer-related screening behaviors will be assessed using specific questions for each type of screening behavior. These questions are a modified version of those developed for the Community Mammography Consortium of the National Cancer Institute. Intentions to obtain screening are measured with a single question for each behavior (mammography, breast self-examination, and clinical breast examination) with a 5-point scale with endpoint anchors. Companion questions measure frequency of mammography, clinical breast exam, and breast self-exam, and allow for staging of mammography. We used intentions to obtain appropriate screening rather than actual screening behavior for our main outcome because of the broad age range of the participants. As asking about performance of actual mammography would have been inappropriate for a younger woman, we examined patterns of obtaining mammography in the older subsample of our study. Intentions to obtain genetic mutation screening for breast cancer were measured by a series of questions developed for our Cancer Genetics consortium on genetic screening. Two particular questions—intentions to seek screening, and belief that one is an appropriate candidate for genetic screening—were used here. These questions are each a single item.

Procedures

Women were screened for interest in the study and for eligibility by telephone. If eligible and interested, they received a copy of the baseline questionnaire in the U.S. mail to complete at home. They mailed the completed questionnaire to the research institute in a stamped, addressed envelope mailed with the questionnaire. If study staff did not receive an envelope within 2 weeks, the woman received a reminder call. An opportunity to complete a subsection of the baseline questionnaire was offered to women who did not respond to the reminder call. Seventy-three women completed the baseline questionnaire by mail, and 43 completed the questionnaire subsection by telephone.

Analyses

The analyses for this study were organized into three steps. First, descriptive statistics were calculated to understand participants' demographic patterns and responses to their personal risk. The second wave of analyses included bivariate groupings of all key variables selected from the theoretical model. Statistics for the bivariate analyses included chi-squares and t tests, as appropriate. Scheffé tests were performed to identify significant pairwise differences. Finally, multivariate regression models were used to predict screening intentions using hierarchical regressions (Cohen & Cohen, 1983). This method enters sets of variables into the regression equation based on a priori hypotheses about the relations among the predictor variables. This analytic method is appropriate for applications of the self-regulation model because this model has an underlying causal structure that should be tested in addition to the significance of individual variables.

RESULTS

Participants' perceptions of their own risk relative to their medical risk varied widely. The average Gail algorithm value was 8% ($SD = 3$), and the average perceived risk was 30% ($SD = 29$). For analysis purposes the values for the perceived-to-actual ratio were clustered into three groups for all participants: underestimators, or those participants whose ratio was between 0 and 1; overestimators, those participants with ratios between 1 and 5; and extreme overestimators, with ratios over 5. Forty-one percent of participants were underestimators, 23% were overestimators, and 36% were extreme overestimators. The mean ratio of the underestimators was .41 ($SD = 0.57$). The mean ratio of the overestimators was 3.4 ($SD = 0.72$). The mean ratio of the extreme overestimators was 8.9 ($SD = 4.0$).

Table 1 examines the groupings of risk categories by demographic variables. Given the sample size, many of the cells were represented by small numbers, and therefore the comparisons among the cells within each cross-tab are tentative. Nevertheless, there were no significant differences within each cross-tabulation of demographic group and estimation of personal risk relative to medical risk. When simple perceived risk was substituted for the ratio of perceived to actual risk, no differences were found as well.

The levels of psychological variables by risk categories are presented in Table 2. As clearly shown in this table, levels of several of the psychological variables differed by risk estimation category. Level of cancer worry was highest in the extreme overestimators, as were levels of general anxiety and general depression (all pairwise $ps < .05$). However, levels of general anxiety and depression were also high in the overestimator group (pairwise $ps < .05$), and were not for cancer worry. Emotion-focused coping strategies were reported more frequently by extreme

TABLE 1
Demographic Values for Women in Differing Risk Estimate Categories

Demographic Categories	Underestimators	Overestimators	Extreme Overestimators
Ethnic identity[a]			
Percent Black	32.3	37.5	22.2
Percent African American	64.5	50.0	70.4
Percent Afro-American	3.2	6.3	3.7
Percent other	—	6.3	3.7
Education[b]			
Percent high school degree	18.0	3.6	8.7
Percent post-high school	36.0	46.4	45.7
Percent college degree	22.0	28.6	19.6
Percent graduate or professional school	24.0	21.4	26.1
Marital status[c]			
Percent married or partnered	40.8	46.4	36.1
Percent single	28.6	28.6	36.2
Percent widowed	8.2	—	2.2
Percent divorced or separated	22.5	25.0	26.1
Age in years[d]			
M	45.0	41.0	45.0
SD	10.0	9.0	13.0
Annual income[e]			
Percent < $15,000	21.7	—	11.4
Percent $15,000–29,000	10.9	14.3	22.7
Percent $30,000–49,000	32.6	53.6	29.5
Percent $50,000–69,000	23.9	14.3	15.9
Percent > $70,000	10.9	17.9	20.5

[a]$n = 74$. [b]$n = 124$. [c]$n = 123$. [d]$n = 127$. [e]$n = 116$.

TABLE 2
Average Level of Psychological Variables for Women in Differing Risk Categories

Average Psychological Values	N	Underestimators		Overestimators		Extreme Overestimators	
		M	SD	M	SD	M	SD
Emotions							
Cancer Worry Scale	127	5.67	1.9	5.66	1.6	6.89[a]	2.5
General anxiety	123	.25	.43	.46	.46	.47	.54
General depression	123	.27	.34	.63	.88	.46[a]	.59
Coping							
Problem-focused coping	75	9.77	12.7	13.18	14.1	11.19[a]	11.3
Emotion-focused coping	75	11.16	13.9	15.41	14.9	16.22[a]	15.1
Mental representation symptoms							
Concerned about breast symptoms	73	2.31	1.0	3.00	1.1	2.89	1.3
Thought that symptoms were cancer	73	2.00	.93	2.47	.94	2.74	1.3
Label							
Having cancer is serious illness	75	3.13	.99	3.12	1.2	3.59	1.3
Cancer is upsetting	74	4.07	.78	4.65	.49	4.56	.58
Treatment is painful	73	3.31	.66	3.47	.72	3.67	.88
Causes							
Cancer explanation is family heredity	75	3.48	1.0	3.82	.95	3.78	.64
HRT causes cancer	74	3.27	.74	3.47	.72	3.15	1.0
Pollutants cause cancer	74	3.83	.79	4.12	.70	4.00	.68
Timeline							
Breast cancer cured if found early	74	4.20	.61	4.29	.69	4.04	.85
Aging increases risk	74	3.60	.72	3.71	.85	3.89	.97
Consequences							
Breast cancer causes family problems	73	2.86	.58	3.06	.56	2.96	.98
Breast cancer cured without breast loss	73	3.90	.77	4.00	.61	3.70	.82

[a]Significantly different among risk groups; $p < .05$.

overestimators, as compared with overestimators, and by overestimators as compared with underestimators (pairwise $ps < .05$). However, problem-focused coping was reported more frequently by the middle group of overestimators (pairwise $ps < .05$).

Several of the mental representations were differentially reported by the three risk-estimation groups. Labeling the cancer was endorsed more frequently by the highest estimation group, whereas beliefs about the timeline and about the consequences were more frequently endorsed by the lower risk-estimation groups (pairwise p's < .05).

Table 3 provides the results of regression analyses to predict intentions to perform mammography using clusters of variables from the self-regulation model, and Table 4 presents the same model predicting intentions to obtain genetic mutation testing for breast cancer. The first set entered was a group of background variables, including label of each woman's ethnic identity and her attitudes toward physicians. Second, the emotional variables were entered as predictor variables. The third set included the personal-to-actual risk ratio as a simple mental representation of one's beliefs about one's personal risk.

TABLE 3
Predicting Mammography Intentions Using the Self-Regulatory Model

Set	β	SE	t	p
1: Background variables[a]				
Ethnic identity	−.26	.14	−1.86	.05
I trust my doctor's judgment	.39	.28	1.38	ns
I want to talk to my doctor about my breast cancer anxiety	−.409	.25	−1.6	.09
2: Emotions[b]				
Cancer worry	.25	.07	3.30	.001
General anxiety	−1.05	.40	−2.62	.01
General depression	.008	.293	.29	.77
3: Mental representation[c]				
Perceived over actual risk	−.013	.034	−.386	.70

[a]Set 1: $p < .05$; $R^2 = 21\%$. [b]Set 2: $p < .003$; additional $R^2 = 23\%$. [c]Set 3: $p < .45$; additional $R^2 = 0$.

TABLE 4
Predicting Intentions to Obtain Mutation Testing Using the Self-Regulatory Model

Set	β	SE	t	p
1: Background variables[a]				
Ethnic identity	.24	.08	2.83	.005
Trust my doctor's judgment	−.0018	.17	−.10	.91
Talk to my doctor about my breast cancer anxiety	−.009	.16	−.58	.56
2: Emotions[b]				
Cancer worry	.004	.25	.91	.36
General anxiety	.004	.04	.17	.87
General depression	−.15	.18	−.79	.42
3: Mental representation				
Perceived over actual risk	.38	.07	3.26	.001

[a]Set 1: $p < .05$; $R^2 = 6\%$. [b]Set 2: $p < .15$; additional $R^2 = 7\%$. [c]Set 3: $p < .0001$; $R^2 = 71\%$.

The data from Table 3 indicate that several variables were significant predictors of mammography screening. In particular, the ethnic label of African American or Black significantly predicted intentions to get a mammogram, in that self-identified African American women were more likely than self-identified Black women to report intentions to obtain a mammogram. Both cancer worry and general anxiety in the second set entered into the equation-predicted intentions to obtain mammograms. Perceived risk relative to actual risk did not significantly predict intentions after the affect variables were entered. We reversed the order of entry for Sets 2 and 3 to see if emotional variables were still significant predictors of intentions after the risk variable was entered. The pattern of results did not change for this reversed analysis.

The data from Table 4 present differing patterns of predictors of intentions to obtain genetic mutation testing for breast cancer risk. The most powerful and the only predictors of intentions to obtain mutation testing were a woman's ethnic identity and her risk ratio. Women who labeled themselves as Black were more likely to have higher intentions to obtain genetic screening, as were women at higher overestimation of their breast cancer risk.

DISCUSSION

The data presented here provide us with a view of the perceptions and affect of African American women regarding their breast cancer risk and mammography screening. This sample may be different from others in this issue, in that it does not focus on low-income African American women or women with lower educational levels. The sample recruited here reported a range of demographic values for education and for income, indicating that the participants in this study were from diverse situations and backgrounds. These backgrounds surely influenced the psychological variables presented here, as well as the behavioral ones. But the psychological variables are more important for intervention design, because it is the psychological variables that an intervention will target for change, not the demographic ones such as race or income. Therefore, we chose to focus on the differences among women in psychological predictors as opposed to the demographic ones.

There were consistent psychological differences among women who estimated their risk more or less accurately. The effect of risk estimation on emotion was not in the form of a "dose-response" in that the extreme overestimators reported the highest levels of distress, compared with the other two lower risk-estimation groups. This is supported by the bivariate correlations among these variables, which were weak (rs between .1 and .23). Depression actually showed a more intriguing inverted U-shaped relation with risk ratio, as did problem-focused coping.

The levels of cancer worry in this study indicate that African American women do have concerns about breast cancer. The levels in this study are comparable to or higher than those found in other research with primarily Caucasian women (Lerman et al., 1991; Lerman & Schwartz, 1993). In the previous literature, levels of cancer worry from 5 to 8 have been labeled as high, and our values were between 5 and 7. This indicates that the issues that keep African American women from obtaining screening are not simply access issues. Access issues are critically important and the focus of other research, intervention, and outreach projects. These findings identify a different aspect of the functioning of African American and Black women: the psychological variables that interfere with screening and are present at all levels of demographic variables in this study. These, too, deserve research and intervention attention.

The multivariate analyses predicting mammography support the findings of the simple bivariate analyses. Ethnic identity, willingness to discuss anxiety with the doctor, and emotional variables were all predictors of intentions to obtain appropriate mammography screening. In particular, women who labeled themselves as African American reported higher intentions to obtain mammography, as did women who wanted to discuss their anxiety with their doctors. As with the demographic variables, women reported a range of levels of trust in their physician, in that the average responses to the two trust questions were 3.2 and 3.0, respectively, for the "trust my doctor" and "talk to my doctor about anxiety" questions. Fully 25% of participants reported low trust in their physician (response less than 2) for each item. Of course, the sample recruited here probably had a bias toward higher levels of trust than do African American and Black women in the general public, because of willingness to participate in a research program by coming to the research facility, providing data, and so forth. Therefore, it is difficult to generalize to nonparticipants on this issue.

The regression data predicting intentions to obtain genetic mutation testing for breast cancer risk showed a different profile of significant predictors. Ethnic identity again predicted intentions to obtain screening, but in the opposite direction: Black women were more likely to intend to obtain genetic screening. The differences between self-identified African American and self-identified Black women did not appear in the demographic data reported, nor in patterns of correlation with the psychological variables. Therefore, we do not have any information from this study on the differences among labeled groups that could explain these findings. This is an area of important study, because if personal identity is altering patterns of screening, then we should identify the reasons for this difference and consider altering information and presentation of appropriate screening programs to appeal to all identities of African American and Black women. Our hypothesis, which we plan to test in future research, is that the self-label of African American is more political and more conscious of ties to international heritage, and that these variables are related to the ways in which women perceive their connection to the mainstream culture. The self-label of Black could carry an identity of belonging in a multicultural framework, hypothetically, and these women would have perhaps a stronger connection with the dominant culture in the United States. These variables could alter health outcomes, and deserve research attention.

In our study we excluded all women at extremely high risk for breast cancer, focusing the exclusion on women whose family history showed a pattern consistent with autosomal dominant breast cancer inheritance. Therefore, none of these women would be likely candidates for breast cancer genetic mutation testing. It is interesting that over 70% of women in this sample indicated some intention to obtain testing, and that overestimation of personal breast cancer risk is an incredibly powerful predictor of the intention to obtain testing. This means that African American and Black women are not informed as to the realities and limitations of genetic testing. This is disturbing, particularly because there is likely to be a bias in this volunteer sample regarding higher levels of knowledge and information about medical issues. Obviously genetic screening is dissimilar from mammography screening in predictors. However, we have identified a potential for inappropriate use of testing and screening due to misinformation about the relation of risk to current tests available.

These data can be used to design interventions to promote the appropriate use of mammography and genetic screening. Ethnic identity, in the form of self-label, is important in predicting both types of intentions, but the reasons for this are not clear from the existing data. This is an area of critical psychological investigation. Emotional variables are critical in the intentions of these women to obtain mammography screening. Both specific and general distress interfere with their motivation for mammography. These psychological variables must be addressed in research on intervention to increase mammography use among African American and Black women. Second, emotional distress does not seem to be important in the intentions of these participants to obtain genetic mutation testing. The field should be very careful of potential misunderstandings in the public that can increase intentions to obtain this relatively new technology, because if women at only moderately increased risk intend to obtain genetic screening, then public pressure could convince physicians to apply this screening in inappropriate settings. The use of this model has helped to highlight differences among differing screening behaviors, and should be applied more frequently in future research.

ACKNOWLEDGMENTS

This research was supported by grant HG/CA 01190 from the National Institute for Human Genome Research, the National Cancer Institute, and the Office for Research on Women's Health.

REFERENCES

Black, W. C., Nease, R. F., Jr., & Tosteson, A. N. A. (1995). Perceptions of breast cancer risk and screening effectiveness in women younger than 50 years of age. *Journal of the National Cancer Institute, 87,* 720–731.

Blendon, R. J., Scheck, A. C., Donelan, K., Hill, C. A., Smith, M., Beatrice, D., & Altman, D. (1995). How White and African Americans view their health and social problems: Different experiences, different expectations. *Journal of the American Medical Association, 273,* 341–346.

Burack, R. C., & Liang, J. (1989). The acceptance and completion of mammography by older black women. *American Journal of Public Health, 79,* 721–726.

Carter, J. H. (1995). Psychosocial/cultural issues in medicine and psychiatry: Treating African-Americans. *Journal of the National Medical Association, 87,* 857–860.

Cochran, S. D., & Peplau, L. A. (1991). Sexual risk reduction behaviors among young heterosexual adults. *Social Science and Medicine, 33,* 25–36.

Cohen, J., & Cohen, P. (1983). *Applied multiple regression/correlation analysis for the behavioral sciences* (2nd ed.). Hillsdale, NJ: Lawrence Erlbaum Associates, Inc.

Daniels, D. E., René, A. A., & Daniels, V. R. (1994). Race: An explanation of patient compliance—Fact or fiction? *Journal of the National Medical Association, 86,* 20–25.

Derogatis, L. R., & Melisaratos, N. (1983). The Brief Symptom Inventory: An introductory report. *Psychological Medicine, 13,* 595–605.

Duke, S. S., Gordon-Sosby, K., Reynolds, K. D., & Gram, I. T. (1994). A study of breast cancer detection practices and beliefs in black women attending public health clinics. *Health Education Research, 9,* 331–342.

Dula, A. (1994). African American suspicion of the healthcare system is justified: What do we do about it? *Cambridge Quarterly of Healthcare Ethics, 3,* 347–357.

Eley, J. W., Hill, H. A., Chen, V. W., Austin, D. F., Wesley, M. N., Muss, H. B., Greenberg, R. S., Coates, R. J., Correa, P., Redmond, C. K., Hunter, C. P., Herman, A. A., Kurman, R., Blacklow, R., Shapiro, S., & Edwards, B. K. (1994). Racial differences in survival from breast cancer results of the National Cancer Institute Black/White Cancer Survival Study. *Journal of the American Medical Association, 272,* 947–954.

Folkman, S., & Lazarus, R. S. (1980a). An analysis of coping in a middle-aged community sample. *Journal of Health and Social Behavior, 21,* 219–239.

Folkman, S., & Lazarus, R. S. (1980b). If it changes it must be a process: A study of emotion and coping during three stages of a college examination. *Journal of Personality and Social Psychology, 48,* 150–170.

Gail, M., Brinton, L., Byar, D., Corle, D. K., Green, S. B., Schairer, C., & Mulvihill, J. J. (1989). Projecting individualized probabilities of developing breast cancer for white females who are being examined annually. *Journal of the National Cancer Institute, 81,* 1879.

Jones, J. H. (1993). *Bad blood: The Tuskegee syphilis experiment* (New expanded ed.). New York: Free Press.

Lauver, D. (1992). Psychosocial variables, race, and intention to seek care for breast cancer symptoms. *Nursing Research, 41,* 236–241.

Lauver, D. (1994). Care-seeking behavior with breast cancer symptoms in Caucasian and African-American women. *Research in Nursing & Health, 17,* 421–431.

Lauver, D., & Ho, C-H. (1993). Explaining delay in care seeking for breast cancer symptoms. *Journal of Applied Social Psychology, 23,* 1806–1825.

Lerman, C., Daly, M., Sands, C., Balshem, A., Lustbader, E., Heggan, T., Goldstein, L., James, J., & Engstrom, P. (1993). Mammography adherence and psychological distress among women at risk for breast cancer. *Journal of the National Cancer Institute, 85,* 1074–1080.

Lerman, C., Kash, K., & Stefanek, M. (1994). Younger women at increased risk for breast cancer: Perceived risk, psychological well-being, and surveillance behavior. *Monographs of the National Cancer Institute, 16,* 171–176.

Lerman, C., & Schwartz, M. (1993). Adherence and psychological adjustment among women at high risk for breast cancer. *Breast Cancer Research and Treatment, 28,* 145–155.

Lerman, C., Trock, B., Rimer, B., Boyce, A., Jepson, C., & Engstrom, P. F. (1991). Psychological side effects of breast cancer screening. *Health Psychology, 10,* 259.

Leventhal, H., & Cameron, L. (1987). Behavioral theories and the problem of compliance. *Patient Education and Counseling, 10,* 117–138.

McCaul, K. D., Branstetter, A. D., Schroeder, D. M., & Glasgow, R. E. (1996). What is the relationship between breast cancer risk and mammography screening? A meta-analytic review. *Health Psychology, 15,* 423–429.

McCaul, K. D., Schroeder, D. M., & Reid, P. A. (1996). Breast cancer worry and screening: Some prospective data. *Health Psychology, 15,* 430–433.

Miller, L. Y., & Hailey, B. J. (1994). Cancer anxiety and breast cancer screening in African-American women: A preliminary study. *Women's Health Issues, 4,* 170–174.

Ownby, H. E., Frederick, J., Russo, J., Brooks, S. C., Swanson, G. M., Heppner, G. H., & Brennan, M. J. (1985). Racial differences in breast cancer patients. *Journal of the National Cancer Institute, 75,* 55–60.

Polednak, A. P. (1986). Breast cancer in black and white women in New York State: Case distribution and incidence rates by clinical stage at diagnosis. *Cancer, 58,* 807–815.

Powell, D. R. (1994). Social and psychological aspects of breast cancer in African-American women. *Annals of the New York Academy of Sciences, 736,* 131–139.

Ries, L. A. G., Miller, B. A., Hankey, B. F., Kosary, C. L., Harras, A., & Edwards, K. (Eds.). (1994). *SEER Cancer Statistics Review 1973–1991: Tables and graphs* (NCI, NIH Publication No. 94–2789). Bethesda, MD: National Cancer Institute and National Institutes of Health.

Royak-Schaler, R., DeVellis, B. M., Sorenson, J. R., Wilson, K. R., Lannin, D. R., & Emerson, J. A. (1995). Breast cancer in African-American families. Risk perception, cancer worry, and screening practices of first-degree relatives. *Annals of the New York Academy of Sciences, 768,* 281–285.

Shumaker, S. A., Schron, E. B., & Ockene, J. K. (Eds.). (1990). *The handbook of health behavior change.* New York: Springer.

Stasson, M., & Fishbein, M. (1990). The relation between perceived risk and preventive action: A within-subject analysis of perceived driving risk and intentions to wear seatbelts. *Journal of Applied Social Psychology, 20,* 1541–1557.

Tessaro, I., Eng, E., & Smith, J. (1994). Breast cancer screening in older African-American women: Qualitative research findings. *American Journal of Health Promotion, 8,* 286–293.

Thomas, S. B., & Quinn, S. C. (1993). The burdens of race and history on Black Americans' attitudes toward needle exchange policy to prevent HIV disease. *Journal of Public Health Policy, 14,* 320–347.

U.S. Department of Health and Human Services. (1990). *Quality of life assessment: Practice, problems, and promise* (NIH Publication No. 93-3503). Bethesda, MD: National Institutes of Health.

Weinstein, N. D. (Ed.). (1987). *Taking care: Understanding and encouraging self-protective behavior.* New York: Cambridge University Press.

Wyche, K. F. (1993). Psychology and African-American women: Findings from applied research. *Applied & Preventive Psychology, 2,* 115–121.

WOMEN'S HEALTH: RESEARCH ON GENDER, BEHAVIOR, AND POLICY, 3(3&4), 243–274

Obesity Among African American Women: Prevalence, Consequences, Causes, and Developing Research

David B. Allison, Lynn Edlen-Nezin, and
Gaynelle Clay-Williams

Obesity Research Center, St. Luke's/Roosevelt Hospital Center
Columbia University College of Physicians and Surgeons

This article reviews data concerning the prevalence, causes, and consequences of obesity among African American women. It shows that approximately 50% of adult African American women are considered obese by prevailing standards. Moreover, this prevalence appears to be increasing. Obesity has an important influence on the development of a variety of morbidities among African American women. The effect of obesity on longevity among African American women is less clear. The reasons for the very high prevalence of obesity among African American women are unknown. Data supporting various putative genetic, physiological, and psychosocial influences are discussed.

Key words: obesity, overweight, blacks, African American, ideology, sequelae, cultural factors, dietary factors, exercise, metabolic rate

This article is divided into three major sections. In the first section, we review data on the prevalence of obesity among African American women. Using data from several nationally representative samples, it can be shown that (a) the prevalence of obesity among African American women is at near-epidemic proportions (i.e., within certain age groups more than 50% of African American women are obese), (b) the prevalence of obesity has been increasing among African American women, and (c) the prevalence of obesity among African American women is two to three times greater than among European American women. The second section dis-

Correspondence concerning this article should be addressed to David B. Allison, Obesity Research Center, St. Luke's/Roosevelt Hospital Center, 1090 Amsterdam Avenue, 14th Floor, New York, NY 10025. E-mail: dba8@columbia.edu.

cusses the physical and social consequences of obesity among African American women. Although data are somewhat limited, these data tentatively indicate that obesity may be less evocative of adverse consequences (both social–psychological and physical) among African American compared to European American women. The third section considers putative causes of the substantial prevalence of obesity among African American women. Although the data on this topic are limited, social–psychological, cultural, and genetic possibilities are discussed and the data in support of each of these possibilities are reviewed.

PREVALENCE OF OBESITY

Obesity Among African American Women Is at Near-Epidemic Proportions and Increasing

In epidemiological studies, adiposity (fatness) is typically assessed through the use of a weight-for-height index, the most popular being Quetelet's index or body mass index (BMI; weight in kilograms divided by the square of height in meters). The National Center for Health Statistics (NCHS) uses a BMI greater than or equal to 27.3 as a cutoff for defining moderate obesity in women; this is approximately equivalent to 120% of ideal weight according to the Metropolitan Life Insurance Company (1983). Severe obesity (approximately 140% of ideal weight) is defined as a BMI greater than or equal to 32.3 for women. According to these definitions, high prevalence rates of obesity in African American women have been consistently observed in national survey data (Gillum, 1987; Harlan, Landis, Flegal, Davis, & Miller, 1988; Kumanyika, 1987; Williamson, Serdula, Anda, Levy, & Byers, 1992). Table 1 summarizes data from four nationally representative surveys, spanning approximately 30 years. The most recent data are from the first phase of the National Health and Nutrition Examination Survey III (NHANES), conducted between 1988 and 1991 (Kuczmarski, Flegal, Campbell, & Johnson, 1994). NHANES consists of a series of national surveys designed to yield representative samples of the U.S. civilian noninstitutionalized population. The overall prevalence of overweight in non-Hispanic African American women is estimated as approximately 49.2%, with rates exceeding 60% for women 60 through 69 years old.

Obesity among African American women seems to be increasing (Kumanyika, 1994; see Pi-Sunyer, 1990; Table 1). The prevalence of obesity in African American women 20 to 74 years old increased approximately 6.5% in the 20-year period (1967–1987) between NHANES I and NHANES III (Russell, Williamson, & Byers, 1995). Recent dietary guidelines (U.S. Department of Agriculture, 1995) have suggested a more stringent BMI cutoff of 25 as the definition of overweight, which would increase the prevalence rates among African American women further (Flegal, Pamuk, Kuczmarski, & Johnson, 1996).

Although obesity is quite prevalent and increasing in all race, age, and sex groups in the United States (Kuczmarski et al., 1994), it is striking that the prevalence is

TABLE 1
Prevalence of Overweight in African American Women 20 to 74 Years Old in Four
Nationally Representative Studies

Survey	Mean BMI	Prevalence
NHES I (1960–1962)	26.8	41.6%
NHANES I (1971–1974)	27.3	43.1%
NHANES II (1976–1980)	27.5	44.5%
NHANES III (1988–1991)	28.3	49.2%

Note. BMI = body mass index.

much greater in African American than in European American women. Moreover, the differences observed in adults emerge at much younger ages, that is, by or before 9 to 10 years (Campaigne et al., 1994). An examination of prevalence rates of obesity by race and sex highlights the complexity of the epidemiology of obesity. Specifically, there is a strong, but unexplained, race by gender interaction. That is, although African American women are considerably fatter than European American women, on average, there is no clear and consistent difference in fatness between African American and European American men. This pattern is not consistent across all ethnic groups. For example, among Native Americans and Hispanic Americans, both men and women are far more obese than European American men and women (Broussard et al., 1995; Kumanyika, 1994; Ramirez, 1994; Valdez, González-Villalpando, Mitchell, Haffner, & Stern, 1995). The reasons for this race by sex interaction are unknown.

The disproportionate prevalence of obesity in African American women compared to European American women has been reported in several large-scale studies (Adams-Campbell et al., 1990; Bennett, 1991; Burke et al., 1992; Dawson, 1988; Lackland et al., 1992; Must, Gormaker, & Dietz, 1994; Rand & Kuldau, 1990; Stevens et al., 1992) summarized in Table 2.

Data from the NCHS calculate the overweight prevalence ratio of African American to European American women as approximately 2:1 (Kumanyika, 1994). This difference is observed in all age groups, at virtually every level of obesity considered (i.e., it is not dependent on the BMI cutpoint used) and regardless of what indicator of adiposity is used (Croft et al., 1996).

Are the Racial Differences Independent of Socioeconomic Status (SES)?

Relative to European Americans, African Americans continue to have lower SES (Cotton, 1989; Harrison & Gorham, 1992). Additionally, it is well documented that, among women in the United States, SES is inversely associated with relative weight

TABLE 2

African American and European American Differences in Female Obesity

Reference	Study	Sample	Study Design	Anthropometrics	African American	European American
Hypertension Detection, Follow-up Program Cooperative Group (1977)	Hypertension Detection and Follow-up Program	158,906 African American and European American persons, age 30–60 in 14 communities	Population-based samples assessed by interview	Self-reported height and weight	58.6% overweight	31.4% overweight
Dawson (1988)	1985 National Health Interview Survey	1,955 African American and 14,330 European American women aged 18 and older	Cross-sectional household interview survey	Self-reported height and weight BMI	25.1 (median)	22.9 (median)
Adams-Campbell et al. (1990)	Study of body-fat distribution patterns and blood pressure in African American and white women	Sample of female U.S. African American (93) and U.S. European American (88) and Nigerian(124) first-year U.S. college students	Cross-sectional	Measured height and weight	U.S.:29.6% overweight, 12.9% obese; Nigerian: 18.6% overweight, 1.6% obese	13.6% overweight, 2.3% obese
Rand & Kuldau (1990)	Health Survey	2,115 African American and European American adults age 18–96	Cross-sectional, interview	Self-reported height and weight	46% overweight	18% overweight

Reference	Study	Sample	Design	Measures		
Burke et al. (1992)	Coronary Artery Risk Development in Young Adults	5,115 young adults age 18–30, 2,801 African American and European American women	Cross-sectional examination	BMI Subscapular Skinfold Triceps skinfold	25.8–26.0 21.5	23.8–22.7 14.7
Lackland et al. (1992)	South Carolina Cardiovascular Disease Prevention Project	3,175 adult residents of South Carolina	Cross-sectional population-based sample of adults	BMI WHR	23.2 28.10 ± (7.43) .84 ± (0.11)	19.7 24.89 ± (5.74) .81 ± (0.09)
Stevens et al. (1992)	Charleston Heart Study	Probability sample of Charleston, South Carolina; 738 European American, 452 African American women	Longitudinal	Measured height and weight	46% overweight	25% overweight
Must et al. (1994)	National Longitudinal Study of Youth	11,591 Hispanic, African American, and European American youths	Longitudinal	Self-reported height and weight	14.2% overweight	7.3% overweight
Striegel-Moore, Wilfley, Caldwell, Needham, & Brown (1996)	Sample from *Consumer Reports* subscribers	162 African American and matched 162 European American women	Cross-sectional	Self-reported height and weight, BMI	BMI 30.16 ± (7.59)	BMI 27.9 ± (6.93)

(Sobal, 1991b; Sobal & Stunkard, 1989). This prompts the question of whether the observed difference in adiposity is independent of SES.

Several studies have examined this issue and all have found that even after controlling for SES indicators (most commonly income, education, or both) African American women have significantly higher relative weights than do European American women (Burke et al., 1992; Dawson, 1988; Deulberg, 1992; Rand & Kuldau, 1990; see Kumanyika 1987, 1994, for further references). SES has been shown to be inversely related to BMI levels in African American women (Croft et al., 1992; Sobal & Stunkard, 1989). However, high rates of obesity have been observed in African American women across all socioeconomic strata (Burke et al., 1992; Dawson, 1988; Domel, Alford, Cattlett, & Gench, 1992; Gillum, 1987). Therefore, the high prevalence of obesity among African American women cannot be solely attributable to low SES, as might be suspected. However, after reviewing the SES and obesity literature, Sobal and Stunkard (1989) stated:

> There is little consensus about conceptualizing and measuring SES, and different researchers choose different measures. Studies have assessed SES with a wide variety of indicators, most frequently income or education and less often occupation or other measures. Most studies used only one measure. (p. 260)

Thus, the measurement of SES is weak in many studies. Also, it is possible that the relation between SES and BMI is different among African American than among European American women, and some evidence for this has been found (Burke et al., 1992).

In sum, the overwhelming majority of the data suggest that African American women have higher relative weights than European American women do, even after controlling for SES. This finding does not seem to be an artifact of an inappropriate statistical model. However, some problematic issues remain with respect to concluding that observed differences are independent of SES. Specifically, one must wonder if the possibility of residual confounding (Becher, 1992) remains. More research is needed on this question.

CONSEQUENCES OF OBESITY

The high rate of obesity observed among African American women is troubling, given that obesity is associated with a broad array of adverse physical and so-cial–psychological consequences. These consequences are reviewed here.

Physical Consequences of Obesity

It has been established that African American women have unusually high prevalence rates of medical conditions, including non-insulin-dependent diabetes mellitus (NIDDM; Pi-Sunyer, 1990; Roseman, 1985), hyperinsulinemia (Nabulsi et al., 1995), hypertension (NCHS, 1981), and cardiovascular disease (Gillum, 1991), for which obesity, weight gain, and an upper body fat distribution are recognized as risk factors among people of European ancestry (Allison & Pi-Sunyer, 1995). Therefore, one might suppose a priori that obesity produces these conditions among African American women. However, before accepting this premise, it is essential to show that obesity is associated with these morbidities among African American women. It is possible that body weight and fatness may confer different degrees of risk in different groups through potentially different mechanisms (Kumanyika & Adams-Campbell, 1991).

Fat distribution. In trying to understand the health consequences of obesity among African American women, it is important to consider the anatomical distribution of body fat in addition to simply considering the total amount of body fat. Forty years ago, Vague (1956) pointed out the differential health consequences of upper versus lower body obesity. It has now been well established (at least in European Americans) that fat in the abdominal region, particularly intra-abdominal or visceral fat, represents a much greater health risk than fat in the periphery of the body. Only recently have investigators begun to examine fat distribution patterns in African American versus European American women (Croft et al., 1996). We provide a detailed tabulation (this tabulation can be considered an extension of that in Kumanyika & Adams-Campbell, 1991) of data from nine studies comprising a total of 14,194 participants in Table 3.

The overall message is clear. Regardless of which index is used to quantify centrality of fat distribution, African American women have a more central (or upper) distribution of adipose tissue for 10 of the 12 comparisons. Assuming a more central distribution of body fat has the same effect on African American and European American women, this places African American women at even greater risk for cardiovascular disease and diabetes mellitus. However, the assumption that visceral and abdominal fat has the same impact in African American and European American individuals may not be reasonable. Data relating to the validity of this assumption are discussed in a later section of this article.

Diabetes, impaired glucose tolerance, and hyperinsulinemia. Obesity is highly correlated with the development of NIDDM. African Americans have a two- to threefold excess risk of developing NIDDM compared to European Americans (Haffner et al., 1996). Impaired glucose tolerance and hyperinsulinemia, considered precursors to NIDDM, are also more frequent in African American women compared to European American women (Tinker, 1994). Gestational diabetes, for which obesity is a risk factor, is approximately 80% more frequent in African American women (American Diabetes Association, 1996).

TABLE 3
Data on the Comparative Fat Distribution of African American and
European American Women

		Blacks			Whites		
Source	Measure	N	M	SD	N	M	SD
Adams-Campbell et al. (1990)	WHR	93	.76	±N/A	88	.74	±N/A
Freedman et al. (1992)	STR	552	1.00	±.40	4,453	.80	±.40
Folsom et al. (1989)	WHR	1,447	.75	±.08	1,288	.73	±.07
Gillum (1987)	WHR	448	.93	±N/A	2,931	.87	±N/A
Lackland et al. (1992)	WHR	554	.84	±.11	1,425	.81	±.09
Stevens et al. (1991)	AMR	78	3.00	±.26	141	3.20	±.37
Summerson et al. (1992a)[a]	WHR	15	.84	±.20	15	.92	±.10
Summerson et al. (1992b)[b]	WHR	19	.90	±.10	22	.87	±.10
Wing et al. (1989)	STR	48	.95	±.34	490	.79	±.34
Zillikens & Conway (1990)	STR	45	.96	±N/A	42	.69	±N/A
	STR_2		.56	±N/A		.40	±N/A
	SSR		.99	±N/A		.63	±N/A

Note. WHR = waist-to-hip ratio; STR = subscapular-to-tricep skinfold ratio; STR_2 = subscapular-to-thigh skinfold ratio; SSR = subscapular-to-suprailliac skinfold ratio; AMR = abdominal-to-midarm circumference ratio.
[a]Premenopausal women. [b]Postmenopausal women.

According to data from the National Health Interview Survey, the prevalence of diabetes increased 33% between 1973 and 1983 for African American women of all ages (Harris, 1990). NIDDM in African American women is also accompanied by more severe diabetic complications, such as retinopathy and peripheral neuropathy, and end-stage renal disease (Anderson et al., 1991; Pi-Sunyer, 1990). Recent data show diabetes to be the fourth most frequently listed cause of death in African American women (American Diabetes Association, 1996). NHANES data (National Diabetes Data Group, 1995) describe a monotonic increase in the prevalence of NIDDM among African American women. Women with a BMI of 35 or greater have rates approximately 18 times higher than do women with a BMI less than 22.

NHANES II data have shown the risk of NIDDM associated with obesity to be greatest in African American women. Among African American women, there is a rapidly accelerating risk of NIDDM associated with comparatively small increments in BMI.

Hypertension.   African American women have a greater risk of developing high blood pressure than European American women do (Adams-Campbell et al., 1990; Lackland et al., 1992; Liu et al., 1989; Pollard, Brush, & Harrison, 1991; Sprafka, Folsom, Burke, & Edlavitch, 1988). Higher BMI and weight gain are both risk factors for the development of hypertension (Gillum, 1996). Approximately 3 million African American women have hypertension. Self-reported hypertension prevalence rates for African American women increase dramatically with age, ranging from 4.5% between ages 18 and 29 to 47.2% for women 65 years or older (Piani & Schoenborn, 1991).

Dustan (1990) suggested that the relation between obesity and hypertension may be quite different for African Americans than for European Americans: "The importance of obesity to the hypertension of African Americans is difficult to assess. Although there is considerable information available about obesity and hypertension in general, there is little about it in African Americans" (p. 395). Although the mechanisms of the ethnic disparity in hypertension prevalence rates are unknown, evidence is accumulating that hormonal and physiological differences may be partially responsible (Hildreth & Saunders, 1992).

Despite these caveats, the Pitt County Study of 25- to 50-year-old African American participants (Croft et al., 1993) found that among women, both higher BMI and waist-to-hip ratio (a measure of central fat deposition) were independently associated with higher systolic and diastolic blood pressure. These relations persisted after statistically controlling for age, smoking, physical activity, alcohol use, and SES. Thus, these (and other) data suggest that obesity is an important risk factor for hypertension among African American women.

Dyslipidemias.   Paradoxically, despite the elevated levels of adiposity, body fat distribution, blood pressure, and poorer glucose tolerance found among African American women, these women typically do not exhibit the more adverse serum lipid profiles seen in non-African American women with these elevations. We quantitatively synthesized (Hedges & Olkin, 1985) data on serum lipid levels among African American women from seven studies (Anderson, Burns, Wallace, Folsom, & Sprafka, 1992; Folsom et al., 1989; Freedman, Strogatz, Williamson, & Aubert, 1992; Sprafka, Norsted, Folsom, Burke, & Luepker, 1992; Srinivasan, Dahlen, Jarpa, Webber, & Berenson, 1991; Summerson, Konen, & Dignan, 1992b; Tyroler et al., 1975) in Table 4.

TABLE 4
Meta-Analytic Summary of Data From Seven Studies of Lipid Levels in U.S. Adult Women

	Black			White			
	N	M	SD	N	M	SD	p
Triglycerides	2,376	69.1	34.8	2,866	87.2	46.2	< .0001
HDL-cholesterol	3,604	56.6	17.2	2,866	53.4	23.6	< .0001
LDL-cholesterol	2,376	111.9	32.0	2,866	110.9	31.6	.26
VLDL-cholesterol	2,376	12.4	7.0	2,866	15.9	12.0	< .0001

Results indicated that across a variety of studies, African American women have lower levels of triglycerides and very low-density lipoprotein cholesterol, and higher levels of high-density lipoprotein cholesterol (no difference is apparent for low-density lipoprotein cholesterol), than non-African American women, suggesting a healthier lipid profile than is usually associated with obesity. Similarly, Conway, Yanovski, Avila, & Hubbard (1995) found African American women had significantly lower plasma triglyceride levels and significantly higher levels of high-density lipoproteins than the European American women in their study. This benign serum lipid profile in the presence of a high frequency of obesity, hypertension, and glucose intolerance is quite interesting and begs for explanation. One possibility is that African American women have a lifestyle (e.g., diet) that promotes obesity, NIDDM, hypertension, and dyslipidemias. However, they may have some strong genetic predisposition to a healthy serum lipid profile that serves to protect them in this one arena from the ill effects of their lifestyle. However, it must be emphasized that this possibility is solely speculative.

Mortality and obesity.   Although considerable data exist for European Americans (Van Itallie & Lew, 1995), fewer data are available on the effects of adiposity or relative weight on all-cause mortality among African Americans. The overall relation between obesity and mortality is not clear, despite the fact that obesity in African American women is associated with a number of cardiovascular and other risks (Gillum, 1991; Nabulsi et al., 1995; Pi-Sunyer, 1990). To our knowledge, there are eight studies assessing the association between obesity or adiposity and all-cause mortality among African Americans.

Comstock, Kendrick, and Livesay (1966) conducted a 14-year mortality study with X-ray-determined adiposity, and concluded that "excessive mortality among fat persons was generally more marked for European Americans than for Negroes" (p. 562). Analyses of 20-year cardiovascular disease mortality in the Evans County Study (Johnson, Heineman, Heiss, Hames, & Tyroler, 1986) found no effect of BMI on mortality among African American women. Wienpahl, Ragland, and Sidney (1990) followed 2,731 African American women members of the Kaiser Foundation Health Plan for 15 years and found that "over the entire range of BMI the adjusted BMI–mortality association was … essentially flat" (p. 949). These results were unchanged after controlling for smoking and excluding deaths during the first 5 years of follow-up. Similar results were found by Cornoni-Huntley et al. (1991). More recently, the Charleston Heart Study followed 452 African American women for 25 to 28 years (Stevens et al., 1992). The authors concluded that "The failure of BMI and fat patterning to predict mortality in African American women challenges previously held assumptions regarding the role of overweight in the higher mortality experienced by African American women" (p. 1257). Sorkin, Zonderman, Costa, and Andres (1996) analyzed mortality data from NHANES I, and found a U-shaped relation between BMI and mortality. The BMI levels associated with minimum mortality for African American women were found to be in the range of 29, compared to 26 for European American women. Durazo-Arivzu, Luke, McGee, and Cooper (1996) found similar results in the NHANES I Epidemiologic Follow-up Study. Analyses conducted by our research group using data from the Longitudinal Study of Aging also found a clear U-shaped relation between BMI and mortality with no statistically significant racial differences in the effects of BMI (Allison, Gallagher, Heo, Pi-Sunyer, & Heymsfield, 1997). However, it must be noted that the sample size was somewhat small for racial comparisons. Other data on BMI and mortality among African American women have been reported by Plankey et al. (1995), but insufficient information is available to evaluate this study at this time.

On balance, despite the high prevalence rates of obesity-related morbidities among African American women (Klesges, DeBon, & Meyers, 1996), the data previously mentioned are not clear and consistent enough to support strong conclusions regarding the relation between BMI and mortality in this ethnic group. This issue remains open to question.

Following three independent studies of the effects of obesity among black women in Africa (Walker, Walker, Manetsi, Tsotetsi, & Walker, 1990; Walker, Walker, Walker, & Vorster, 1989; Walker et al., 1991), Walker and colleagues (1991) stated that "obesity appeared less evocative of adverse sequelae than prevails in a white population" (p. 244). Moreover, as reviewed earlier, adiposity may not be as "life-threatening" among African Americans as it is among European American women. Part of this may have to do with the anatomical distribution of adipose tissue.

As stated earlier, adipose tissue in the viscera appears to be much more dangerous than subcutaneous adipose tissue. However, Dowling and Pi-Sunyer (1993) found that the waist-to-hip ratio, which was for a long time the most widely used surrogate for measured visceral adiposity, was not as strongly related to morbidities among African American women as among European American women. More recently, studies have suggested that even at equivalent waist-to-hip ratios, African American women may actually have less visceral adipose tissue than do European American women (Conway et al., 1995; Lovejoy, de la Bretonne, Klemperer, & Tulley, 1996). Thus, at least two factors may explain the seemingly less adverse consequences of obesity. First, visceral adipose tissue may be less harmful among African American women. Second, it may be that African American women may be less prone to deposit their adipose tissue viscerally. This remains to be fully sorted out.

Social Consequences

Obesity is associated with tremendous social stigma in contemporary American society (Allon, 1979, 1982; DeJong, 1980; Sobal, 1991a; Yuker & Allison, 1994). Obese individuals are frequently denigrated (Hiller, 1981; Homant & Kennedy,

1982) and discriminated against in a variety of contexts, including the search for housing (Karris, 1977), employment (Klesges et al., 1990; Matusewitch, 1983; Rothblum, Brand, Miller, & Oetjen, 1990), mates (Sonne-Holm & Sørensen, 1986), higher salaries (Frieze, Olson, & Good, 1990; Register & Williams, 1990), financial support for college (Crandall, 1991), academic grades (Ledoux, 1981/1982), social favors (Rodin & Slochower, 1974; Steinberg & Birk, 1983), and help from sales people (Pauley, 1989). Even in death, obese people often face derision and discrimination (Anonymous, 1987; Gruzen, 1996).

We are unaware of any literature that describes the discrimination-provoking effects of obesity as a function of race. However, some speculation can be offered. Both obese and African American persons are viewed by many people as lazy and lacking in self-control (Bess, 1982; Yuker & Allison, 1994). The literature of obese persons' experiences with obtaining housing and employment suggests that these individuals experience discrimination regularly in these and other areas of their daily life (Rothblum et al., 1990). The same negative and discriminatory attitudes exhibited toward the obese population, such as reduced job opportunities, decreased housing opportunities, limited social interactions, and lower educational attainments are similarly experienced by many African Americans because of their race (Kumanyika & Adams-Campbell, 1991; Outlaw, 1993).

Moreover, Crandall and Biernat (1990) showed that individuals with "antifat" attitudes share an ideologically conservative outlook on life and may endorse racist views as well. In their study, antifat attitudes and authoritarianism were closely correlated. Individuals exhibiting these two attitudes were more likely to have negative attitudes toward members of minority groups and people who are different. Thus, for many individuals with such attitude constellations, African American racial status and obesity status may act synergistically to elicit increased levels of discrimination. Future research should address this possibility.

PUTATIVE DETERMINANTS OF THE GREATER PREVALENCE OF OBESITY

It is clear from the information already presented that African American women are at substantially increased risk for obesity. However, what is not at all clear is why. There has been a great deal of speculation in this area. In the following subsections we address possible reasons for the increased risk of obesity among African American women. It should be pointed out from the outset, however, that much of this remains conjecture and far more research is needed in this area.

Possible Genetic Factors

That the mean level of adiposity (as indexed by relative weight or skinfold measurements) is greater among African American than among European American women is well known. What is less well known is that the variances of these measures are also quite a bit larger among African American than among European American women. To our knowledge, no published reviews or reports have focused on this issue. We tabulated relevant data from NHANES II for women 18 to 74 years old in data extracted from NCHS (1987). Table 5 shows the variances for BMI and skinfolds for both groups.

It can be seen that the variances for all these measures are significantly greater among African American than among European American women. Even if expressed as coefficients of variation to "control for" mean differences, the coefficients of variation for both BMI and triceps skinfold would still be significantly greater for African American than for European American women. We return to this point later as it relates to one hypothesis regarding possible causes of the between-race mean differences in adiposity.

Kumanyika (1987) pointed out that reasons for the between-race differences in female adiposity and adipose tissue distribution were unknown, and suggested that both environmental and genetic differences were possibilities. In a recent study of twins, Allison, Neale, Heshka, and Heymsfield (1994) found that among African American as compared to European American adolescents, there appeared to be both greater environmental and genetic variability for factors affecting BMI. One possible interpretation of the greater genetic variance among African Americans is that African Americans represent an admixed group with a gene pool contributed to by both Africans and Europeans. If Africans and Europeans have markedly different frequencies for alleles that influence adiposity, then a hybrid population is likely to have a greater variance than either of the parent populations (MacLean et al., 1974; MacLean & Workman, 1973a, 1973b). This is consistent with the data in Table 4. Future work should attempt to test this hypothesis using sophisticated measurements of body composition, genetic markers of admixture, and ethnic acculturation.

TABLE 5
Comparison of the Variance in Indicators of Fatness in African American Versus European American Women in NHANES-II

Measure	African American Women		European American Women		F Ratio	p Value
	N	S^2	N	S^2		
BMI	766	42.3	5,591	29.2	1.45	< .0001
Tricep	782	135.0	5,686	90.3	1.49	< .0001
Subscapular	782	177.0	5,686	137.0	1.29	< .0001

Note. S^2 = variance.

Resting Metabolic Rate

Resting metabolic rate (RMR), also called resting energy expenditure, is defined by the amount of energy an individual expends to maintain bodily integrity while at rest. It includes the energy cost of such activity as pumping blood, maintaining homeothermy, and so forth. Variations in RMR, which constitutes approximately 65% of total daily energy expenditure in sedentary persons (Ravussin, Lillioja, Andersen, Christin, & Bogardus, 1986), have been shown to longitudinally predict weight gain (Ravussin et al., 1988) as well as weight loss on a fixed intake (Garrow, Durant, & Mann, 1981). Until quite recently, there were no data available on the comparative metabolic rates of European Americans and African Americans (Kumanyika, 1987). However, a few studies have recently addressed this issue (Albu et al., 1996; Foster, Wadden, & Vogt, 1997; Jakicic & Wing, 1996; Yanovski et al., 1996). These studies are remarkable in their consistency. Each one found that, after controlling for body composition, African Americans had a lower RMR than European Americans. The results of these studies have been summarized meta-analytically (Hedges & Olkin, 1985) in Table 6.

We have summarized these data in meta-analytic fashion by calculating a mean effect size (d; Cohen, 1988) for each study. The weighted average effect size was $-.48$ and was highly statistically significant ($p = .00006$). Moreover, the results gave no significant indication of heterogeneity ($\chi^2 = 8.50$, $p = .075$), suggesting that the studies are providing a consistent answer.

Thus, on balance, this recent body of literature clearly and consistently shows that African American women have lower RMRs than do European American women. Although this may explain some of the increased obesity among African American women, it is unlikely to account for the degree of obesity seen among many African American women. Weinsier, Braco, and Schutz (1993) pointed out that even a difference as great as 200 kcal per day could result in an eventual weight gain of only about 15 kg (33 lb) if there were no increase in energy intake.

Parity

Segal and McAnarney (1994) found rapid weight gain in pregnant adolescents was associated with greater postpartum weight retention, resulting in obesity. Recently, Cameron, Graybill, Hobfoll, Crowther, and Ritter (1996) showed that inner-city African American women had different patterns of weight gain during pregnancy than did European American women. Weight gain occurred earlier in the pregnancy, which resulted in the average African American woman in their sample considered to be obese at the second trimester. This increased duration of overweight during pregnancy may be related to the retention of postpartum weight. Several studies have documented greater postpartum weight gain among African

TABLE 6

Quantitative Summary of Five Studies of Metabolic Rate in African American Versus European American Women

Reference	Age		BMI		African Americans			European Americans			
	M	SD	M	SD	N	M_{REE}	SD_{REE}	N	M_{REE}	SD_{REE}	d
Foster & Lukaski (1996)	40.6	±8.3	38.0	±5.7	44	1,637.6	236.9	122	1,731.4	262.0	-.377
Yanovski et al. (1996)	9.3	±0.5	17.3	±1.7	20	1,060.0	94.0	24	1,146.0	94.0	-.915
Jakicic et al. (1996)	37.2	±6.2	31.5	±3.1	15	1,790.0	141.0	13	1,949.0	142.0	-1.124
Albu et al. (1996)	36.9	±1.0	35.0	±1.0	22	1,454.0	178.2	20	1,574.0	245.9	-.573
Kushner, Racette, Neil, & Schoeller (1995)[a]	26–47		29.2–39.2		14	1,479.0	145.7	15	1,520.0	145.7	-.281

[a] Age and BMI given as range, not M and SD.

American as compared to European American women (Boardley, Sargent, Cojker, Mussey, & Sharpe, 1995; Keppel & Taffel, 1993; Parker & Abrams, 1993; Smith et al., 1994). Boardley et al. (1995) and Keppel and Taffel (1993), respectively, found that African American women retained 2.9 kg (6.4 lb) and 2.5 kg (5.5 lb) more of their pregnancy weight gain, as compared to European American women. A difference of this magnitude could account for a between-race difference of approximately one BMI unit for each pregnancy a woman brings to term. It appears that this is due primarily to differences in postpartum weight retention as opposed to differences in the amount of weight gained during pregnancy. Parker and Abrams (1993) found African American mothers were twice as likely to retain at least 20 lb postpartum as were European American mothers. Moreover, African American women tend to have more children and at younger ages than do European American women (Franklin, 1988), which may exacerbate this effect.

Physical Activity

Another putative factor contributing to obesity among African American women involves low levels of physical activity. Contemporary life in the United States tends to be quite sedentary. However, a number of studies have shown that African American women are particularly inactive (Ainsworth, Berry, Schnyder, & Vickers, 1992; Andersen et al., 1996; Crespo, Keteyian, Heath, & Sempos, 1996; Kelley, 1995; Lewis, Raczynski, Heath, Levinson, & Cutter, 1993; Macera, Croft, Brown, Ferguson, & Lane, 1995). It has been estimated that as many as 40% of African American women (compared to 27% of U.S. women overall) engage in no leisure-time physical activity (Crespo et al., 1996) and many also engage in very low levels of volitional nonleisure physical activity (Tuten, Petosa, Sarent, & Weson, 1995). Moreover, African American women tend to be more inactive than European American women. This has been shown in studies using both self-reported activity (Andersen et al., 1996; Crespo et al., 1996; Tuten et al., 1995; Washburn, Kline, Lackland, & Wheeler, 1992) and activity quantified through the use of doubly labeled water (Schoeller et al., 1986). Doubly labeled water is a biochemical technique for determining energy expenditure that does not depend on self-report.

Interestingly, African American men are considerably more active than African American women (Ainsworth et al., 1992; Andersen et al., 1996; Kelley, 1995; Kelly & Kelley, 1994; Lewis et al., 1993; Macera et al., 1995; Washburn et al., 1992) and no less active than European American men (Andersen et al., 1996; Macera et al., 1995). This suggests that activity patterns, like parity effects, may explain the fact that African American women are at greater risk of obesity than European American women, but that African American men are not at greater risk of obesity than European American men.

Psychosocial Factors

A variety of psychosocial factors have been studied as possible causes of the common obesity among African American women. Methodology has varied widely and methodological quality has generally been poor, although there are exceptions. Strong social psychological theorizing has generally not underpinned this research, standardized measurements of known reliability and validity have generally not been employed, and samples have often been small or convenience samples, or both. All of these factors combine to make it very difficult to review the psychosocial influences on obesity among African American women. The literature, although a morass, clearly supports the conclusion that, with respect to body shape, weight, and size, there are detectable differences about how African American women think or feel, compared to, for example, European American women. Beyond this incredibly imprecise general statement, it is difficult to know what to conclude from this literature. Nevertheless, there are a few subareas characterized by a degree of clarity and consistency. We review those here.

Body image.   The term *body image* is typically used to encompass a number of interrelated phenomena. Body image can be described as having behavioral, perceptual, and attitudinal components (Thompson, 1992). By the attitudinal component of body image, we mean an individual's subjective evaluation of the body. Most often this is conceived in terms of physical attractiveness. The overwhelming majority of the work relating to body image among African American women has dealt with the attitudinal component. Moreover, conjectures about reasons for the high prevalence of obesity among African American women have centered largely around the attitudinal component. Thus, when we refer to body image in the remainder of these sections, we are referring to the attitudinal component. However, there are a number of other components to this that include perception of one's body as powerful, healthy, respectable, and so forth (Nelson, 1996). Nevertheless, the majority of research has either dealt explicitly with attractiveness, seems to deal implicitly with attractiveness, or does not clearly specify the dimension that is assessed.

One of the most common assessment methods in body image research involves the use of silhouettes. In this technique, participants are shown silhouettes representing a range of weights from extremely underweight to extremely overweight. Participants are shown an array of figures and asked to select the silhouette that best represents their current body shape, their ideal body shape, the first body shape they think is too fat, the first body shape they think is too thin, the body shape they think will be most attractive to the opposite sex, and so forth. A number of such studies are summarized in Table 7. These studies suggest that across age ranges,

TABLE 7

Studies Comparing Figures Selected as Ideal, Desirable, or Attractive by African American and European American U.S. Females

Study	African American N	European American N	Ages	African American M	European American M	d	Significance	Silhouettes	Adjective
Allan et al. (1993)	31	36	18–55	2.2	2.2	.04	ns	Massara & Stunkard (1979)	Ideal
Allan et al. (1993)	≈84	≈75	11–14	2.2	1.9	.47	ns		Attractive
Cohn et al. (1991)	548 combined	combined		3.4	3.6	.32	+	Stunkard et al. (1983)	Ideal
Collins (1991)			preadolescent	3.52 combined		NA	+	Adapted from Stunkard et al. (1983)	Ideal
Kemper, Sargent, Drane, Valois, & Hussey (1994)	190	247	13–19	3.5	3.0	NA	+	Stunkard et al. (1983)	Ideal
Powell & Kahn (1995)	38	59	18–26	4.7	3.6	.84	+	Williamson et al. (1989)	Ideal
Rand (1995)	25	25	15–45	NA	NA	NA	ns	Stunkard et al. (1983)	Acceptable
Rucker & Cash (1992)	59	61	college students	4.1	3.3	.56	.002	Williamson et al. (1989)	Ideal or desired
Stevens, Kumanyika, & Keil (1994)	126	278	66–105	3.6	3.5	.11	ns	Stunkard et al. (1983)	Ideal
Wilson, Sargent, & Dias (1994)	80		14–17	NA	NA	.11	+	Massara & Stunkard (1979)	Ideal

Note. *d* is an effect size measure and is equivalent to the mean silhouette selected as ideal by the African American women minus the mean ideal for the European American women divided by the pooled within-group standard deviation. For significance, + indicates African American women gave responses indicating a preference for fatter figures than did European American women. *ns* = no significant difference; NA = information not available or not applicable.

African American women select heavier figures as ideal or attractive than do European American women.

However, a number of caveats apply. First, although African American women may rate "larger" figures as ideal, this should not be misconstrued to imply that African American women rate "large" figures as desirable. Rather, a more accurate description seems to be that, on average, both African American and European American women pick rather thin figures as ideal, but European American women select even thinner figures. Second, concerns have been raised about the validity of these assessment instruments. Silhouette series differ in degree of realism, as well as perceptual vantage point; that is, whether the figures are profile or full face. More important, there are questions as to whether or not participants adequately understand the instructions for the selection task. For example, Clay-Williams, Allison, Gallagher, Liu, and Heymsfield (1996) assessed perception of current body size versus desired body size among 600 African American women voluntarily participating in a weight-loss program. Nearly 5% of the participants chose desirable figures that were larger than their current figures. This finding suggests that the instructions were misinterpreted by many participants. Finally, it seems clear that the phrasing of the question has a substantial impact on the outcome. For example, Allan, Mayo, and Michel (1993) obtained different results depending on whether the word "ideal" or "attractive" was used.

Desired Weights

It has been suggested that African American women may prefer higher body weights than do European American women (Kumanyika, 1994). That is to say, the body weight that African American women label as ideal or desirable for themselves is higher than the corresponding weight chosen by European American women. We have found three published studies addressing this issue. Two additional studies of Africans residing on the continent of Africa were located but are not reviewed as African Americans were not directly assessed. The studies are summarized in Table 8. As can be seen, on average, it appears that African American women want to weigh between approximately 57 kg (approximately 125 lb) and 65 kg (143 lb). Expressed as a BMI, it appears that southern African American women desire a BMI on average of 26. This is in contrast to corresponding figures from European American women, who want to weigh on average approximately 60 kg (132 lb) and have a BMI of approximately 24. This suggests that African American women find weights desirable or acceptable at a level that is about 5 kg (11 lb) higher than that of European American women. Collectively, these data suggest that African American women do tolerate or desire greater body weights than do European American women. However, the difference is not overwhelming. Moreover, the direction of causation must be questioned. In our experience, it seems

TABLE 8
Comparison of Actual and Goal Weights

Reference	European Americans			African Americans		
	N	Actual Weight	Goal Weight	N	Actual Weight	Goal Weight
Thomas (1987)[a, b]				104	64.9	57.5
Williamson et al. (1992)[a]	9,836	73.6	59.7	1,182	82.3	64.8
Stevens et al. (1994)[c]	278	26.9	24.1	126	27.0	26.0

[a]Weight reported in kilograms. [b]No data for European Americans. [c]Body mass index used as a measure of weight.

to be assumed that these differences in attitudes about desirable body weights cause racial differences in actual body weights. However, it seems equally plausible that differences in actual body weights determine differences in desired body weights. That is, it seems as likely that African American women may tolerate or desire higher body weights than European American women do because they are used to experiencing such higher body weights in themselves and their peers.

Just as it is possible that women's own perceptions of what is a desirable body shape influence behavior, it is also possible that these perceptions are influenced by what men of their culture think is desirable. That is, African American women may be more tolerant of higher weights because African American men may be more tolerant (Collins, 1991; Harris, Walters, & Waschull, 1990; Powell & Kahn, 1995), or perhaps even desirous, of higher weights in African American women, relative to the attitudes held by European American men about the desirability of European American women. This hypothesis is bolstered by anecdotal evidence that African American men find women with larger body sizes attractive; however, the quantitative data on this issue are largely not supportive. Studies have generally found either no differences in attitudes about body shape desirability between African American and European American men (Allison, Hoy, Fournier, & Heymsfield, 1993; Allison, Hoy, & Heymsfield, 1994; Singh, 1994) or very small differences (Greenberg & LaPorte, 1996).

Self-esteem and obesity.   A characteristic may be described as central for an individual to the extent that his or her evaluation of that characteristic is highly correlated with, or predictive of, his or her evaluation of the total self (Boldrich, 1983). Thus, if relative weight is central to self-esteem, then self-esteem should be lower among obese persons. Furthermore, if weight were more central to self-esteem among European American women than among African American women, this might result in European American women being more motivated to maintain lower weights. This putative ethnic difference in the psychological centrality of obesity should also be manifested as a stronger association between relative body weight and self-esteem among European American as compared to African American women.

Several researchers have documented lower self-esteem among obese compared to nonobese persons (e.g., Davis, Wheeler, & Willy, 1987; Hoover, 1984; Martin et al., 1988; Stein, 1987). A meta-analytic review by Friedman and Brownell (1995) summarized nine studies exploring the association between self-concept and obesity, and reported a mean effect size (d) of .41. The association seems to be greatest among women (Rodin, Silberstein, & Striegel-Moore, 1985). However, a literature search revealed only five published studies that assessed the association between relative weight and self-esteem among African Americans in samples with 100 or more participants (Fisher, Pastore, Schneider, Pegler, & Napolitano, 1994; Gortmaker, Must, Perrin, Sobol, & Dietz, 1993; Kaplan & Wadden, 1986; Martin et al., 1988; O'Brien, Smith, Bush, & Peleg, 1990). Of these, only Gortmaker et al. (1993) used a nationally representative sample. Unfortunately, results were not reported separately for African American and European American individuals.

At this time, there appear to be no published studies assessing the association between self-esteem and obesity among African Americans in large nationally representative samples. We (Manibay, Faith, Griffith, & Allison, 1996) are currently conducting research using four national data sets. Manibay et al. (1996) analyzed data from the National Longitudinal Study of Youth ($N = 3,094$) and the Adolescent Health Care Evaluation Study ($N = 1,745$) and found no significant associations between self-esteem and relative body weight among African American males or females. Thus, the available data suggest that among European American women there is a weak inverse relation between BMI and self-esteem. In contrast, among African American women there appears to be no such association. This supports the hypothesis that African American women are relatively psychologically unaffected by their body weights as opposed to highly motivated to attain or maintain a particular (high) weight.

The Possible Protective Role of African American Ethnicity

One creative line of speculation involves the possible protective role of African American ethnicity. The line of argument is as follows: All individuals are exposed to social stimuli on a regular basis, social stimuli are often ambiguous, and how these stimuli are interpreted can have profound effects on an individual's state of mind. This is the essence of much cognitive theory and therapy (Beck, 1976; Ellis, 1995; Kelly, 1955). It is possible that membership in an oppressed minority group affects one's perceptions of ambiguous social stimuli in a way that, in some contexts, is protective of self-esteem.

Specifically, African Americans may interpret negative social feedback of an ambiguous origin as due to racial discrimination rather than weight-oriented discrimination. The attribution that one is receiving negative feedback because one is obese may lead to self-recrimination, because many people, including obese people, believe that obesity, as opposed to race, is controllable (Allison, Basile, & Yuker, 1991; Crandall & Biernat, 1990; Crocker & Major, 1989; Crocker, Voelkl, Testa, & Major, 1991; Yuker & Allison, 1994). Furthermore, contemporary society does not openly endorse or justify recriminations based on ethnicity. Therefore, if in fact African American women do have a predisposition to interpret ambiguous negative feedback as stemming from racial discrimination rather than their obesity status, this may serve to protect their self-esteem when confronted with the negative social feedback that obese people are likely to encounter throughout their lives. This is an exciting hypothesis. To our knowledge, it is as yet untested and a promising area for future research.

On balance, it appears that the data on putative psychosocial influences suggest that African American women are relatively unaffected psychologically by their body weight. However, the data do not seem to support the idea that women want to be overweight. Moreover, the reasons African American women seem relatively tolerant of overweight are unknown at this time and warrant further research.

SUMMARY

In conclusion, obesity among African American women is well documented by numerous studies consistently showing that the prevalence of obesity is extremely high and is steadily increasing. It is also clear that obesity is closely related to a variety of morbidities among African American women. But the mechanisms underlying these relations are less clear. More research is warranted regarding the relation between visceral fat and morbidity among African American women. Finally, the finding that African American women have a benign serum lipid profile despite high rates of obesity, NIDDM, and hypertension remains paradoxical and calls for further inquiry. Unlike the morbidity issue, the relation between obesity (or BMI) and mortality among African American women is not clear. Prospective cohort studies with large samples of African American women are necessary to clarify this relation.

The causes of obesity in general, and among African American women in particular, are not well understood. There is burgeoning research suggesting that low levels of both resting and nonresting energy expenditure may contribute to obesity among African American women. Some of this effect may be genetic in origin. Studies of genetic admixture (Chakraborty, 1986; Chakraborty, Kamboh, Nwankwo, & Ferrell, 1992; Chakraborty & Weiss, 1986) and related methods might be useful to test such hypotheses. Regarding psychosocial causes, the quality of the literature is poor, making firm conclusions difficult to draw. Associations observed in studies have generally been small and equivocal. Moreover, it has been impossible to determine direction of causation when associations have been observed. If progress is to be made in understanding the psychosocial influences on obesity among African American women, the development of strong psychological theories, reliable and valid measurement instruments, and sound study designs is essential.

Continued scientific inquiry will be required to effectively address these issues. It is hoped such research will eventually lead to effective means of both preventing and treating obesity and its pathological sequelae among African American women. This segment of our population has traditionally been underserved by the health care system. Future research will need to generate improved surveillance and clinical intervention strategies to enhance and protect the health of these women.

ACKNOWLEDGMENT

This research was supported in part by National Institutes of Health Grants DK26687, DK51716, and DK47256.

Lynn Edlen-Nezin is now at the American Health Foundation, New York.

REFERENCES

Adams-Campbell, L. L., Nwankwo, M., Ukoli, F., Omene, J., Haile, G. T., & Kuller, L. H. (1990). Body fat distribution patterns and blood pressure in African-American and White women. *Journal of the National Medical Association, 82,* 573–576.

Ainsworth, B. E., Berry, C. B., Schnyder, V. N., & Vickers, S. R. (1992). Leisure-time physical activity and aerobic fitness in African-American young adults. *Journal of Adolescent Health, 13,* 606–611.

Airhihenbuwa, C. O. (1992). Health promotion and disease prevention strategies for African-Americans: A conceptual model. In R. L. Braithwaite & S. E. Taylor (Eds.), *Health issues in the black community* (pp. 267–280). San Francisco: Jossey-Bass.

Albu, J., Shur, M., Curi, M., Murphy, L., Heymsfield, S., & Pi-Sunyer, F. X. (1996). Resting metabolic rate in African-American women. *FASEB Journal, 10,* A727.

Allan, J. D., Mayo, K., & Michel, Y. (1993). Body size values of white and black women. *Research in Nursing & Health, 16,* 323–333.

Allison, D. B., Basile, V. C., & Yuker, H. E. (1991). The measurement of attitudes toward and beliefs about obese persons. *International Journal of Eating Disorders, 10,* 599–607.

Allison, D. B., Gallagher, D., Heo, M., Pi-Sunyer, F. X., & Heymsfield, S. B. (1997). Body mass index and mortality among persons over age 70: Analysis of the Longitudinal Study of Aging. *International Journal of Obesity, 21,* 424–431.

Allison, D. B., Hoy, K., Fournier, A., & Heymsfield, S. B. (1993). Can ethnic differences in men's preferences for women's body shapes contribute to ethnic differences in female obesity? *Obesity Research, 1,* 425–432.

Allison, D. B., Hoy, M. K., & Heymsfield, S. B. (1994). Response to Must and Goldberg. *Obesity Research, 2,* 294–295.

Allison, D. B., Neale, M. C., Heshka, S., & Heymsfield, S. B. (1994). Race effects in the genetics of adolescents' body mass index. *International Journal of Obesity, 18,* 363–368.

Allison, D. B., & Pi-Sunyer, F. X. (1995). Obesity treatment: Examining the premises. *Endocrine Practice, 1,* 353–364.

Allon, N. (1979). Self-perceptions of the stigma of overweight in relationship to weight-losing patients. *American Journal of Nutrition, 32,* 470–480.

Allon, N. (1982). The stigma of overweight in everyday life. In B. B. Wolman (Ed.), *Psychological aspects of obesity: A handbook* (pp. 130–174). New York: Van Nostrand Reinhold.

American Diabetes Association. (1996). *Diabetes: 1996 vital statistics.* Alexandria, VA: Author.

Andersen, N., Jacobs, D. R., Jr., Sidney, S., Bild, D. E., Sternfeld, B., Slattery, M. L., & Hannan, P. (1996). Change and secular trends in physical activity patterns in young adults: A seven-year longitudinal follow-up in the Coronary Artery Risk Development in Young Adults Study (CARDIA). *American Journal of Epidemiology, 143,* 351–362.

Anderson, R. A., Burns, T. L., Wallace, R. B., Folsom, A. R., & Sprafka, J. M. (1992). Genetic markers associated with high density lipoprotein cholesterol levels in a biracial population sample. *Genetic Epidemiology, 9,* 109–121.

Anderson, R. M., Herman, W. H., Davis, J. M., Freedman, R. P., Funnell, M. M., & Neighbors, H. W. (1991). Barriers to improving diabetes care for blacks. *Diabetes Care, 14,* 605–609.

Anonymous. (1987, May 18). A British town's cemeteries begin charging extra for oversize clients, and the plot thickens. *People Weekly, 27,* 129.

Becher, H. (1992). The concept of residual confounding in regression models and some applications. *Statistics in Medicine, 11,* 1747–1758.

Beck, A. T. (1976). *Cognitive therapy and the emotional disorders.* New York: International Universities Press.

Bennett, E. M. (1991). Weight loss practices of overweight adults. *American Journal of Clinical Nutrition, 53,* S1519–S1521.

Bess, B. E. (1982). New perspectives that shed light on physicians' misconceptions. *Consultant, 22,* 220–223.

Boardley, D. J., Sargent, R. G., Cojker, A. L., Mussey, J. R., & Sharpe, P. A. (1995). The relationship between diet, activity, and other factors, and postpartum weight change by race. *Obstetrics & Gynecology, 86,* 834–838.

Boldrich, L. M. (1983). Psychological centrality of physical attributes: A reexamination of the relationship between subjective importance and self-esteem. *Journal of Psychology, 115,* 97–102.

Broussard, B. A., Sugarman, J. R., Bachman-Carter, K., Booth, K., Stephenson, L., Strauss, K., & Gohdes, D. (1995). Toward comprehensive obesity prevention programs in Native American communities. *Obesity Research, 3*(Suppl. 2), S289–S297.

Burke, G. L., Savage, P. J., Manolio, T. A., Sprafka, J. M., Wagenknecht, L. E., Sidney, S., Perkins, L. L., Liu, K., & Jacobs, D. R., Jr. (1992). Correlates of obesity in young Black and White women: The CARDIA Study. *American Journal of Public Health, 82,* 1621–1625.

Cameron, R. P., Grabill, C. M., Hobfoll, S. E., Crowther, J. H., & Ritter, C. (1996). Weight, self-esteem, ethnicity, and depressive symptomatology during pregnancy among inner-city women. *Health Psychology, 15,* 293–297.

Campaigne, B. N., Morrison, J. A., Schumann, B. C., Falkner, F., Lakatos, E., Sprecher, D., & Schreiber, G. B. (1994). Indexes of obesity and comparisons with previous national survey data in 9- and 10-year-old black and white girls: The National Heart, Lung, and Blood Institute Growth and Health Study. *Journal of Pediatrics 124*(5, Pt. 1), 675–680.

Chakraborty, R. (1986). Gene admixture in human populations: Models and predictions. *Yearbook of Physical Anthropology, 29,* 1–43.

Chakraborty, R., Kamboh, M. I., Nwankwo, M., & Ferrell, R. E. (1992). Caucasian genes in American Blacks: New data. *American Journal of Human Genetics, 50,* 145–155.

Chakraborty, R., & Weiss, K. M. (1986). Frequencies of complex diseases in hybrid populations. *American Journal of Physical Anthropology, 70,* 489–503.

Clay-Williams, G., Allison, D. B., Gallagher, D., Liu, W. Q., & Heymsfield, S. B. (1996). Body size preference, sexual interest in African-American women seeking weight loss. *FASEB Journal, 10,* A503.

Cohen, J. (1988). *Statistical power analysis for the behavioral sciences.* Hillsdale, NJ: Lawrence Erlbaum Associates, Inc.

Cohn, L. D., Adler, N. E., Irwin, C. E., Millstein, S. G., Kegeles, S. M., & Stone, G. (1987). Body-figure preferences in male and female adolescents. *Journal of Abnormal Psychology, 96,* 276–279.

Collins, M. E. (1991). Body figure perceptions and preferences among preadolescent children. *International Journal of Eating Disorders, 10,* 199–208.

Comstock, G. W., Kendrick, M. A., & Livesay, V. T. (1966). Subcutaneous fatness and mortality. *American Journal of Epidemiology, 83,* 548–563.

Conway, J. M., Yanovski, S. Z., Avila, N. A., & Hubbard, V. S. (1995). Visceral adipose tissue differences in black and white women. *American Journal of Clinical Nutrition, 61,* 765–771.

Cornoni-Huntley, J. C., Harris, T. B., Everett, D. F., Albanes, D., Micozzi, M. S., Miles, T. P., & Feldman, J. J. (1991). An overview of body weight of older persons, including the impact on mortality. *Journal of Clinical Epidemiology, 44,* 743–753.

Cotton, J. (1989). Opening the gap: The decline in Black economic indicators in the 1980's. *Social Science Quarterly, 70,* 803–819.

Crandall, C. S. (1991). Do heavy weight students have more difficulty paying for college? *Personality and Social Psychology Bulletin, 17,* 606–611.

Crandall, C. S., & Biernat, M. (1990). The ideology of anti-fat attitudes. *Journal of Applied Social Psychology, 20,* 227–243.

Crespo, C. J., Keteyian, S. J., Heath, G. W., & Sempos, C. T. (1996). Leisure-time physical activity among U.S. adults. Results from the Third National Health and Nutrition Examination Survey. *Archives of Internal Medicine, 156,* 93–98.

Crocker, J., & Major, B. (1989). Social stigma and self-esteem: The self-protective properties of stigma. *Psychological Review, 96,* 608–630.

Crocker, J., Voelkl, K., Testa, M., & Major, B. (1991). Social stigma: The affective consequences of attributional ambiguity. *Journal of Personality and Social Psychology, 60,* 218–228.

Croft, J. B., Strogatz, D. S., James, S. A., Keenan, N. L., Ammerman, A. S., Malarcher, A. M., & Haines, P. S. (1992). Socioeconomic and behavioral correlates of body mass index in Black adults: The Pitt County Study. *American Journal of Public Health, 82,* 821–826.

Croft, J. B., Strogatz, D. S., Keenan, N. L., James, S. A., Malarcher, A. M., & Garrett, J. M. (1993). The independent effects of obesity and body fat distribution on blood pressure in black adults: The Pitt County study. *International Journal of Obesity and Related Metabolic Disorders, 17,* 391–397.

Croft, J. B., Freedman, D. S., Keenan, N. L., Sheridan, D. P., Macera, C. A., & Wheeler, F. C. (1996). Education, health behaviors, and the black–white difference in waist-to-hip ratio. *Obesity Research, 4,* 505–512.

Davis, J. M., Wheeler, R. W., & Willy, E. (1987). Cognitive correlates of obesity in a nonclinical population. *Psychological Reports, 67,* 879–884.

Dawson, D. A. (1988). Ethnic differences in female overweight. Data from the 1985 National Health Interview Survey. *American Journal of Public Health, 78,* 1326–1329.

DeJong, W. (1980). The stigma of obesity: The consequences of naive assumptions concerning the causes of physical deviance. *Journal of Health Social Behavior, 21,* 75–87.

Deulberg, S. J. (1992). Preventive health behavior among Black and White women in urban and rural areas. *Social Science and Medicine, 34,* 191–198.

Domel, S. B., Alford, B. B., Cattlett, H. N., & Gench, B. E. (1992). Weight control for black women. *Journal of the American Dietetic Association, 92,* 346–348.

Dowling, H. J., & Pi-Sunyer, F. X. (1993). Race-dependent health risks of upper body obesity. *Diabetes, 42,* 537–543.

Durazo-Arivzu, R., Luke, A., McGee, D., & Cooper, R. (1996). Statistical issues in the analysis of the body mass index–mortality relationship. *Obesity Research, 4,* 12S.

Dustan, H. P. (1990). Obesity and hypertension in Blacks. *Cardiovascular Drugs and Therapy, 4*(Suppl. 2), 395–402.

Ellis, A. (1995). Rational emotive behavior therapy. In R. J. Corsini & D. Wedding (Eds.), *Current psychotherapies* (5th ed., pp. 197–238). Itasca, IL: Peacock.

Fisher, M., Pastore, D., Schneider, M., Pegler, C., & Napolitano, B. (1994). Eating attitudes in urban and suburban adolescents. *International Journal of Eating Disorders, 16,* 67–74.

Flegal, K. M., Pamuk, R. J., Kuczmarski, C. L., & Johnson, C. L. (1996). The association of cigarette smoking with body mass index and waist-hip ratio in the U.S. population. *Obesity Research, 1,* 23S.

Folsom, A. R., Burke, G. L., Ballew, C., Jacobs, D. R., Haskel, W. L., Donahue, R. P., Liu, K., & Hilner, J. E. (1989). Relation of body fatness and its distribution to cardiovascular risk factors in young Blacks and Whites. *American Journal of Epidemiology, 130,* 911–924.

Folsom, A. R., Cook, T. C., Sprafka, J. M., Burke, G. L., Norsted, S. W., & Jacobs, D. R., Jr. (1991). Differences in leisure-time physical activity levels between blacks and whites in population-based samples: The Minnesota Heart Study. *Journal of Behavioral Medicine, 14,* 1–9.

Foster, G. D., Wadden, T. A., & Vogt, R. A. (1997). Resting energy expenditure in obese African-American and Caucasian women. *Obesity Research, 5,* 1–8.

Foster, K. R., & Lukaski, H. C. (1996). Whole-body impedance—What does it measure? *American Journal of Clinical Nutrition, 64*(Suppl. 3), S388–S396.

Franklin, D. L. (1988). Race, class, and adolescent pregnancy: An ecological analysis. *American Journal of Orthopsychiatry, 58,* 339–354.

Freedman, D. S., Strogatz, D. S., Williamson, D. F., & Aubert, R. E. (1992). Education, race, and high-density lipoprotein cholesterol among U.S. adults. *American Journal of Public Health, 82,* 999–1006.

Friedman, M. A., & Brownell, K. D. (1995). Psychological correlates of obesity: Moving to the next research generation. *Psychological Bulletin, 117,* 3–20.

Frieze, I. H., Olson, J. E., & Good, D. C. (1990). Perceived and actual discrimination in the salaries of male and female managers. *Journal of Applied Social Psychology, 20,* 46–67.

Garrow, J. S., Durrant, M. L., & Mann, S. (1981). Factors determining weight loss in obese patients in a metabolic ward. *International Journal of Obesity, 2,* 441–447.

Gillum, R. F. (1987). The association of body fat distribution with hypertension, hypertensive heart disease, coronary heart disease, diabetes and cardiovascular risk factors in men and women aged 18–79 years. *Journal of Chronic Disease, 40,* 421–428.

Gillum, R. F. (1991). Cardiovascular disease in the United States: An epidemiological overview. In E. Saunders (Ed.), *Cardiovascular disease in Blacks* (pp. 3–16). Philadelphia: Davis.

Gillum, R. F. (1996) Epidemiology of hypertension in African-American women. *American Heart Journal, 131,* 385–395.

Gortmaker, S. L., Must, A., Perrin, J. M., Sobol, A. M., & Dietz, W. H. (1993). Social and economic consequences of overweight in adolescence and young adulthood. *New England Journal of Medicine, 32,* 1008–1012.

Greenberg D. R., & LaPorte, D. J. (1996). Racial differences in body type preferences of men for women. *International Journal of Eating Disorders, 19,* 275–278.

Gruzen, T. (1996, May 12). Treatment of obese woman's corpse blasted. *Chicago Tribune,* p. 27.

Haffner, S. M., D'Agostino, R., Saad, M. F., Rewers, M., Mykkanen, L., Selby, J., Savage, P. J., Hamman, R. F., & Wagenknecht, L. E. (1996). Increased insulin resistance and insulin secretion in nondiabetic African-American and Hispanics compared with non-Hispanic whites. The Insulin Resistance Atherosclerosis Study. *Diabetes, 45,* 742–748.

Harlan, W. R., Landis, J. R., Flegal, K. M., Davis, C. S., & Miller, M. E. (1988). Secular trends in body mass in the United States, 1960–1980. *American Journal of Epidemiology, 128,* 1065–1074.

Harris, M. B., Walters, L. C., & Waschull, S. (1990). Gender and ethnic differences in obesity-related behaviors and attitudes in a college sample. *Journal of Applied Social Psychology, 21,* 1545–1577.

Harris, M. I. (1990). Noninsulin-dependent diabetes mellitus in Black and White Americans. *Diabetes/Metabolism Reviews, 6,* 71–90.

Harrison, B., & Gorham, L. (1992). Growing inequality in Black wages in the 1980's and the emergence of an African American middle class. *Journal of Policy Analysis and Management, 11,* 235–253.

Hedges, L. V., & Olkin, I. (1985). *Statistical methods for meta-analysis.* Orlando, FL: Academic.

Hildreth, C. J., & Saunders, E. (1992). Heart disease, stroke, and hypertension in Blacks. In R. L. Braithwaite & S. E. Taylor (Eds.), *Health issues in the black community* (pp. 90–105). San Francisco: Jossey-Bass.

Hiller, D. V. (1981). The salience of overweight in personality characterization. *Journal of Psychology, 108,* 233–240.

Homant, R. J., & Kennedy, D. B. (1982). Attitudes toward ex-offenders: A comparison of social stigmas. *Journal of Criminal Justice, 10,* 383–391.

Hoover, M. L. (1984). The self-image of overweight adolescent females: A review of the literature. *Maternal-Child Nursing Journal, 13,* 125–137.

Hypertension Detection and Follow-Up Program Cooperative Group. (1977). Race, education and prevalence of hypertension. *American Journal of Epidemiology, 106,* 351–361.

Jakicic, J. M., & Wing, R. R. (1996). Metabolic differences between obese Caucasian and African-American females. *Obesity Research, 4,* S18.

Johnson, J. L., Heineman, E. F., Heiss, G., Hames, C. G., & Tyroler, H. A. (1986). Cardiovascular disease risk factors and mortality among Black women and White women aged 40–64 years in Evans County, Georgia. *American Journal of Epidemiology, 123,* 209–220.

Kaplan, K. M., & Wadden, T. A. (1986). Childhood obesity and self-esteem. *Journal of Pediatrics, 109,* 367–370.

Karris, L. (1977). Prejudice against obese renters. *Journal of Social Psychology, 101,* 159–160.

Kelley, G. A. (1995). Gender differences in the physical activity levels of young African-American adults. *Journal of the National Medical Association, 87,* 545–548.

Kelley, G. A., & Kelley, K. S. (1994). Physical activity habits of African-American college students. *Research Quarterly for Exercise & Sport, 65,* 207–212.

Kelly, G. (1955). *The psychology of personal constructs* (2 vols.). New York: Norton.

Kemper, K. A., Sargent, R. G., Drane, J. W., Valois, R. F., & Hussey, J. R. (1994). Black and white females' perceptions of ideal body size and social norms. *Obesity Research, 2,* 117–126.

Keppel, K. G., & Taffel, S. M. (1993). Pregnancy-related weight gain and retention: Implications of the 1990 Institute of Medicine guidelines. *American Journal of Public Health, 83,* 1082–1084.

Klesges, R. C., DeBon, M., & Meyers, A. (1996). Obesity in African-American women: Epidemiology, determinants, and treatment issues. In J. K. Thompson (Ed.), *Body image, eating disorders, and obesity: An integrative guide for assessment and treatment* (pp. 461–477). Washington, DC: American Psychological Association.

Klesges, R. C., Klem, M. L., Hanson, C. L., Eck, L. H., Ernst, J., O'Laughlin, D., Garrott, A., & Rife, R. (1990). The effects of applicant's health status and qualifications on simulated hiring decisions. *International Journal of Obesity, 14,* 525–535.

Kuczmarski, R. J., Flegal, K. M., Campbell, S. M., & Johnson, C. L. (1994). Increasing prevalence of overweight among U.S. adults. *Journal of the American Medical Association, 272,* 205–211.

Kumanyika, S. (1987). Obesity in Black women. *Epidemiologic Reviews, 9,* 31–50.

Kumanyika, S. K. (1994). Obesity in minority populations: An epidemiologic assessment. *Obesity Research, 2*(2), 166–182.

Kumanyika, S., & Adams-Campbell, L. L. (1991). Obesity, diet, and psychosocial factors contributing to cardiovascular disease in Blacks. *Cardiovascular Clinics, 21,* 47–73.

Kushner, R. F., Racette, S. B., Neil, K., & Schoeller, D. A. (1995). Measurement of physical activity among black and white obese women. *Obesity Research, 3*(Suppl. 2), 261S–265S.

Lackland, D. T., Orchard, T. J., Keil, J. E., Saunders, D. E., Wheeler, F. C., Adams-Campbell, L. L., McDonald, R. H., & Knapp, R. G. (1992). Are race differences in the prevalence of hypertension explained by body mass and fat distribution? A survey in a biracial population. *International Journal of Epidemiology, 21,* 236–245.

Ledoux, N. D. (1982). Weight as a factor in the evaluation of college freshman essays (Doctoral dissertation, Marquette University, 1981). *Dissertation Abstracts International, 42,* 3873–3874.

Lewis, C. E., Raczynski, J. M., Heath, G. W., Levinson, R., & Cutter, G. R. (1993). Physical activity of public housing residents in Birmingham, Alabama. *American Journal of Public Health, 83,* 1016–1020.

Liu, K., Ballew, C., Jacobs, D. R., Jr., Sidney, S., Savage, P. J., Dyer, A., Hughes, G., & Blanton, M. M. (1989). Ethnic differences in blood pressure, pulse rate, and related characteristics in young adults. The CARDIA study. *Hypertension, 14,* 218–226.

Lovejoy, J. C., de la Bretonne, J. A., Klemperer, M., & Tulley R. (1996). Abdominal fat distribution and metabolic risk factors: Effects of race. *Metabolism: Clinical & Experimental, 45,* 1119–1124.

Macera, C. A., Croft, J. B., Brown, D. R., Ferguson, J. E., & Lane, M. J. (1995). Predictors of adopting leisure-time physical activity among a biracial community cohort. *American Journal of Epidemiology, 142,* 629–635.

MacLean, C. J., Adams, M. S., Leyshon, W. C., Workman, P. L., Reed, T. E., Gershowitz, H., & Weitkamp, L. R. (1974). Genetic studies on hybrid populations. III. Blood pressure in an American Black community. *American Journal of Human Genetics, 26,* 614–626.

MacLean, C. J., & Workman, P. L. (1973a). Genetic studies on hybrid populations. I. Individual estimates of ancestry and their relation to quantitative traits. *Annals of Human Genetics, 36,* 341–351.

MacLean, C. J., & Workman, P. L. (1973b). Genetic studies on hybrid populations. II. Estimation of the distribution of ancestry. *Annals of Human Genetics, 36,* 459–465.

Manibay, E. P., Faith, M. S., Griffin, J. L., & Allison, D. B. (1996). Obesity & self-esteem in African-American Adolescents. *Obesity Research, 4,* S60.

Martin, S., Housley, K., McCoy, H., Greenhouse, P., Stigger, F., Kenney, M. A., Shoffner, S., Fu, V., Korslund, M., Ercanli-Huffman, F. G., et al. (1988). Self-esteem of adolescent girls as related to weight. *Perceptual and Motor Skills, 67,* 879–884.

Matusewitch, E. (1983). Employment discrimination against the obese. *Personnel Journal, 62,* 446–450.

Metropolitan Life Insurance Company. (1983). Metropolitan height and weight tables. *Statistical Bulletin of the Metropolitan Life Insurance Company, 64,* 2–9.

Must, A., Gortmaker, S. L., & Dietz, W. H. (1994). Risk factors for obesity in young adults: Hispanics, African-Americans and whites in the transition years, age 16–28 years. *Biomedicine and Pharmacotherapy, 48,* 143–156.

Nabulsi, A. A., Folsom, A. R., Heiss, G., Weir, S. S., Chambless, L. E., Watson, R. L., & Eckfeldt, H. H. (1995). Fasting hyperinsulinemia and cardiovascular disease risk factors in nondiabetic adults: Stronger associations in lean versus obese subjects. *Metabolism, 44,* 914–922.

National Center for Health Statistics. (1981). *Hypertension in adults 25–74 years of age: United States, 1971–75* (U.S. Vital and Health Statistics Series 11, No. 221). Washington, DC: U.S. Government Printing Office.

National Center for Health Statistics. (1987). *Anthropometric reference data and prevalence of overweight, United States, 1976–1980* (U.S. Vital and Health Statistics Series 11, No. 238). Washington, DC: U.S. Government Printing Office.

National Diabetes Data Group. (1995). *Diabetes in America* (2nd ed., NIH Publication No. 95–1468, p. 220). Bethesda, MD: National Institutes of Health, National Institute of Diabetes and Digestive and Kidney Diseases.

Nelson, S. (1996). *Relative body weight among Black American women: Relationships to acculturation, social class, attitudes, and perceived power.* Unpublished doctoral dissertation, Hofstra University, Hempstead, NY.

O'Brien, R. W., Smith, S. A., Bush, P. J., & Peleg, E. (1990). Obesity, self-esteem, and health locus of control in Black youths during transition to adolescence. *American Journal of Health Promotion, 5,* 133–139.

Outlaw, F. H. (1993). Stress and coping: The influence of racism on the cognitive appraisal processing of African-Americans. *Issues in Mental Health Nursing, 14,* 399–409.

Parker, J. D., & Abrams, B. (1993). Differences in postpartum weight retention between black and white mothers. *Obstetrics & Gynecology, 5,* 768–774.

Pauley, L. L. (1989). Customer weight as a variable in salespersons' response time. *Journal of Special Psychology, 129,* 713–714.

Piani, A., & Schoenborn, C. (1991). Health promotion and disease prevention: United States 1990. *Vital Health Statistics, 10*(185), 1–88.

Pi-Sunyer, F. X. (1990). Obesity and diabetes in Blacks. *Diabetes Care, 13,* 1144–1149.

Plankey, M. W., Stevens, J., Palesch, Y. Y., Rust, P. F., O'Neil, P. M., & Williamson, D. F. (1995). The impact of education and smoking on the BMI–mortality relationship in white and African American women. *Obesity Research, 3*(Suppl. 3), 386S.

Pollard, T. M., Brush, G., & Harrison, G. A. (1991). Geographic distributions of within-population variability in blood pressure. *Human Biology, 63,* 643–661.

Powell, A. D., & Kahn, A. S. (1995). Racial differences in women's desires to be thin. *International Journal of Eating Disorders, 17,* 191–195.

Ramirez, E. A. (1994). Cardiovascular health in Puerto Ricans compared to other population groups in the United States. *Boletin-Asociacion Medica de Puerto Rico, 86*(4–6), 28–36.

Rand, C. J. (1995). *Body size and the eyes of the beholder: The role of body fatness in romance, friendship and employment.* Unpublished doctoral dissertation, Columbia University, Teachers College, New York.

Rand, C. S. W., & Kuldau, J. M. (1990). The epidemiology of obesity and self-defined weight problem in the general population: Gender, race, age, and social class. *International Journal of Eating Disorders, 9,* 329–343.

Ravussin, E., Lillioja, S., Andersen, T. E., Christin, L., & Bogardus, C. (1986). Determinants of 24-hour energy expenditure in man. *Journal of Clinical Investigation, 78,* 1568–1578.

Ravussin, E., Lillioja, S., Knowler, W. C., Christin, L., Freymond, D., Abbott, W. G., Boyce, V., Howard, B. V., & Bogardus, C. (1988). Reduced rate of energy expenditure as a risk factor for body weight gain. *New England Journal of Medicine, 318,* 462–468.

Register, C. A., & Williams, D. R. (1990). Wage effects of obesity among young workers. *Social Science Quarterly, 71,* 130–141.

Rodin, J., Silberstein, L. R., & Striegel-Moore, R. H. (1985). Women and weight: A normative discontent. In T. B. Sonderegger (Ed.), *Psychology and gender. Nebraska symposium on gender, 1984* (pp. 267–307). Lincoln: University of Nebraska Press.

Rodin, J., & Slochower, J. (1974). Fat chance for a favor: Obese–normal differences in compliance and incidental learning. *Journal of Personality & Social Psychology, 29,* 557–565.

Roseman, J. M. (1985). Diabetes in Black Americans. In M. I. Harris & R. F. Hamman (Eds.), *Diabetes in America: Diabetes data compiled 1984* (pp. 1–24). Washington, DC: U.S. Government Printing Office.

Rothblum, E. D., Brand, P. A., Miller, C. T., & Oetjen, H. A. (1990). The relationship between obesity, employment discrimination, and employment-related victimization. *Journal of Vocational Behavior, 37,* 251–266.

Rucker, C. E., III, & Cash, T. F. (1992). Body images, body-size perceptions, and eating behavior among African-Americans and white college women. *International Journal of Eating Disorders, 12,* 291–299.

Russell, C. M., Williamson, D. F., & Byers, T. (1995). Can the Year 2000 objective for reducing overweight in the United States be reached?: A simulation study of the required changes in body weight. *International Journal of Obesity, 19,* 149–153.

Schoeller, D. A., Ravussin, E., Schutz, Y., Acheson, J., Baertschi, P., & Jequier, E. (1986). Energy expenditure by doubly labeled water: Validation in humans and proposed calculation. *American Journal of Physiology, 250,* R823–R830.

Segal, J. S., & McAnarney, E. R. (1994). Adolescent pregnancy and subsequent obesity in African-American girls. *Journal of Adolescent Health, 15,* 491–494.

Singh, D. (1994). Body fat distribution and perception of desirable female body shape by young black men and women. *International Journal of Eating Disorders, 16,* 289–294.

Smith, D. E., Lewis, C. E., Caveny, J. L., Perkins, L. L., Burke, G. L., & Bild, D. E. (1994). Longitudinal changes in adiposity associated with pregnancy and persistent changes in young black and white women. *Journal of the American Medical Association, 271,* 1788–1790.

Sobal, J. (1991a). Obesity and nutritional sociology: A model for coping with the stigma of obesity. *Clinical Sociology Review, 9,* 125–141.

Sobal, J. (1991b). Obesity and socioeconomic status: A framework for examining relationships between physical and social variables. *Medical Anthropology, 13,* 231–247.

Sobal, J., & Stunkard, A. J. (1989). Socioeconomic status and obesity: A review of the literature. *Psychological Bulletin, 105,* 260–275.

Sonne-Holm, S., & Sørensen, T. I. A. (1986). Prospective study of attainment of social class of severely obese subjects in relation to parental social class, intelligence, and education. *British Medical Journal, 292,* 586–589.

Sorkin, J. D., Zonderman, A. B., Costa, P. T., Jr., & Andres, A. (1996). Twenty-year follow-up of the NAHANES I cohort: Test of methodological hypotheses. *Obesity Research, 4,* S12.

Sprafka, J. M., Folsom, A. R., Burke, G. L., & Edlavitch, S. A. (1988). Prevalence of cardiovascular disease risk factors in Blacks and Whites: The Minnesota Heart Study. *American Journal of Public Health, 78,* 1546–1549.

Sprafka, J. M., Norsted, S. W., Folsom, A. R., Burke, G. L., & Luepker, R. V. (1992). Life-style factors do not explain racial differences in high-density lipoprotein cholesterol: The Minnesota Heart Study. *Epidemiology, 3,* 156–163.

Srinivasan, S. R., Dahlen, G. H., Jarpa, R. A., Webber, L. S., & Berenson, G. S. (1991). Race and gender differences in serum lipoproteins of children, adolescents, and young adults—Emergence of an adverse lipoprotein pattern in White males: The Bogalusa Heart Study. *Preventive Medicine, 20,* 671–684.

Stein, R. F. (1987). Comparison of self-concept of nonobese and obese university junior female nursing students. *Adolescence, 22,* 77–90.

Steinberg, C. L., & Birk, J. M. (1983). Weight and compliance: Male–female differences. *Journal of General Psychology, 109,* 95–102.

Stevens, J., Keil, J. E., Rust, P. F., Tyroler, H. A., Davis, C. E., & Gazes, P. C. (1992). Body mass index and body girths as predictors of mortality in Black and White women. *Archives of Internal Medicine, 152,* 1257–1262.

Stevens, J., Kumanyika, S. K., & Keil, J. E. (1994). Attitudes toward body size and dieting: Differences between elderly black and white women. *American Journal of Public Health, 84,* 1322–1325.

Striegel-Moore, R. H., Wilfley, D. E., Caldwell, M. B., Needham, M. L., & Brownell, K. D. (1996). Weight-related attitudes and behaviors of women who diet to lose weight: A comparison of Black dieters and white dieters. *Obesity Research, 4,* 109–115.

Summerson, J. H., Konen, J. C., & Dignan, M. B. (1992a). Race-related differences in metabolic control among adults with diabetes. *Southern Medical Journal, 85,* 953–956.

Summerson, J. H., Konen J. C., & Dignan, M. B. (1992b). Racial differences in lipid and lipoprotein levels in diabetes. *Metabolism, 41,* 851–855.

Thomas, V. G. (1987). Body-image satisfaction among black women. *The Journal of Social Psychology, 129,* 107–112.

Thompson, J. K. (1992). Body image: Extent of disturbance, associated features, theoretical models, assessment methodologies, intervention strategies, and a proposal for a new DSM IV diagnostic category—Body Image Disorder. In M. Hersa, R. M. Eisler, & P. M. Miller (Eds.), *Progress in behavior modification* (Vol. 28, pp. 3–54). Sycamore, IL: Sycamore.

Tinker, L. F. (1994). Diabetes mellitus—A priority health care issue for women. *Journal of the American Dietetic Association, 94,* 976–985.

Tuten, C., Petosa, R., Sargent, R., & Weson, A. (1995). Biracial differences in physical activity and body composition among women. *Obesity Research, 3,* 313–318.

Tyroler, H. A., Hames, C. G., Krishan, I., Heyden, S., Cooper, G., & Cassel, J. C. (1975). Black–White differences in serum lipids and lipoproteins in Evans County. *Preventive Medicine, 4,* 541–549.

U.S. Department of Agriculture. (1995). *Report of the Dietary Guidelines Advisory Committee on the dietary guidelines for Americans, 1995, to the Secretary of Health and Human Services and the Secretary of Agriculture.* Beltsville, MD: Author.

Vague, J. (1956). The degree of masculine differentiation of obesities: A factor determining predisposition to diabetes, atherosclerosis, gout, and uric calculous disease. *American Journal of Clinical Nutrition, 4,* 20–34.

Valdez, R., González-Villalpando, C., Mitchell, B. D., Haffner, S. M., & Stern, M. P. (1995). Differential impact of obesity in related population. *Obesity Research, 3*(Suppl. 2), S223–S232.

Van Itallie, T. B., & Lew, E. A. (1995). In search of optimal weights for U.S. men and women. In F. X. Pi-Sunyer & D. B. Allison (Eds.), *Obesity treatment: Establishing goals, improving outcomes, and reviewing the research agenda* (pp. 1–20). New York: Plenum.

Walker, A. R. P., Walker, B. F., Manetsi, B., Molefe, O., Walker, A. J., Vorster, H. H. (1991). Obesity in indigent elderly rural African women: Effects on hypertension, hyperlipidaemia and hyperglycaemia. *International Journal of Vitamin and Nutrition Research, 61,* 244–250.

Walker, A. R. P., Walker, B. F., Manetsi, B., Tsotetsi, N. G., & Walker, A. J. (1990). Obesity in Black women in Soweto, South Africa: Minimal effects on hypertension, hyperlipidaemia and hyperglycaemia. *Journal of the Royal Society of Health, 110,* 101–103.

Walker, A. R. P., Walker, B. F., Walker, A. J., & Vorster, H. H. (1989). Low frequency of adverse sequelae of obesity in South African rural Black women. *International Journal of Vitaminology and Nutrition Research, 59,* 224–228.

Washburn, R. A., Kline, G., Lackland, D. T., & Wheeler, F. C. (1992). Leisure time physical activity: Are there black/white differences? *Preventive Medicine, 21,* 127–135.

Weinpahl, J., Ragland, D. R., & Sidney, S. (1990). Body mass index and 15-year mortality in a cohort of Black men and women. *Journal of Clinical Epidemiology, 43,* 949–960.

Weinsier, R. L., Bracco, D., & Schutz, Y. (1993). Predicted effects of small decreases in energy expenditure on weight gain in adult women. *International Journal of Obesity, 17,* 693–700.

Williamson, D. F., Serdula, M. K., Anda, R. F., Levy, A., & Byers, T. (1992). Weight loss attempts in adults: Goals, duration, and rate of weight loss. *American Journal of Public Health, 82,* 1251–1257.

Wilson, D. B., Sargent, R., & Dias, J. (1994). Racial differences in selection of ideal body size by female adolescents. *Obesity Research, 2,* 38–43.

Wing, R. R., Kuller, L. H., Bunker, C., Matthews, K., Caggiula, A., Meihlan, E., & Kelsey, S. (1989). Obesity, obesity-related behaviors and coronary heart disease risk factors in Black and White women. *International Journal of Obesity, 13,* 511–519.

Yanovski, S. Z., Yanovski, J. A., Filmer, K., Flood, M., Hubbard, V. S., & Reynolds, J. (1996). Resting metabolic rate in African American and Caucasian girls. *Obesity Research, 4,* S18.

Yuker, H. E., & Allison, D. B. (1994). Obesity: Sociocultural perspectives. In L. Alexander-Mott & D. B. Lumsden (Eds.), *Understanding eating disorders* (pp. 243–270). London: Taylor & Francis.

Zillikens, M. C., & Conway, J. M. (1990). Anthropometry in blacks: Applicability of generalized skinfold equations and differences in fat patterning between blacks and whites. *American Journal of Clinical Nutrition, 52,* 45–51.

WOMEN'S HEALTH: RESEARCH ON GENDER, BEHAVIOR, AND POLICY, *3*(3&4), 275–300

Diabetes in African American Women: The Silent Epidemic

Wylie McNabb, Michael Quinn, and Janet Tobian

Chicago Diabetes Research and Training Center
University of Chicago

Non-insulin-dependent diabetes mellitus is a serious metabolic disorder that affects an estimated 16 million Americans. Among African American women, diabetes has reached epidemic proportions, with 1 in 4 black women 55 years and older having diabetes. It is only within the last decade that diabetes research has begun to examine racial differences in the etiology, treatment, and long-term complications of diabetes. This review brings together the research that focuses on African American women within the context of diabetes research in the general population. Particular emphasis is placed on diabetes risk factors, complications of diabetes, and pharmacologic and nonpharmacologic treatment approaches. Diabetes prevention and public health issues related to diabetes and the African American woman are discussed. The literature reviewed points to the importance of screening and early detection of diabetes among high-risk African American women, as well as the need for improved quality of care and patient educational services and programs in diabetes appropriate to the needs of African American women.

Key words: African American women, diabetes, NIDDM

Non-insulin-dependent diabetes mellitus (NIDDM) is a serious metabolic disorder that affects an estimated 16 million Americans (Harris, 1993, 1995b). Almost 60% of individuals with NIDDM are women (Cowie & Eberhardt, 1995). Unlike insulin-dependent diabetes mellitus (IDDM), which affects both blacks and whites at about the same rate, the NIDDM rate among African Americans is twice that of whites (Brancati, Whelton, Kuller, & Klag, 1996). Among African American

---

Correspondence concerning this article should be addressed to Wylie McNabb, Associate Director, Chicago Diabetes Research and Training Center, University of Chicago, 5841 South Maryland Avenue, Chicago, IL 60637.

women, diabetes has reached epidemic proportion, with one in four black women 55 years and older having diabetes (Murphy & Elders, 1992; Tull & Roseman, 1995).

Because of the high prevalence of diabetes among African American women, it seems reasonable that a great deal of research would have been done in this area. However, beyond prevalence data, very little is known about diabetes in African American women. It is only within the last decade that diabetes research has begun to examine racial differences in the etiology, treatment, and long-term complications of diabetes. Very little diabetes research has focused on women (Tinker, 1994). This review will bring together the research that focuses on African American women within the context of diabetes research in the general population.

DEFINITIONS AND DIAGNOSIS OF DIABETES

Diabetes mellitus is a disorder characterized by fasting hyperglycemia (significantly elevated levels of glucose in the blood while in a fasting state) or levels of plasma glucose elevated above defined limits during glucose tolerance testing. The World Health Organization (WHO, 1980, 1985) and the National Diabetes Data Group (1979) have recognized four major types of diabetes: IDDM, NIDDM, gestational diabetes mellitus (GDM), and diabetes secondary to other conditions (such as pancreatic disease, hormonal disease, or certain genetic syndromes). IDDM affects only 5% to 10% of individuals with diabetes (Harris, 1995b) and it is characterized by the failure of the pancreas to produce insulin. Individuals with IDDM usually acquire the disorder in childhood and require exogenous insulin to control the disorder throughout their lives. The prevalence of IDDM in blacks is similar to (if not less than) that in whites. NIDDM is by far the most common form of diabetes, affecting 90% to 95% of the individuals with diabetes (Harris, 1995b). Proportionately affecting blacks more than whites, NIDDM is particularly prevalent among black women (Harris, 1990). Generally occurring later in life, NIDDM is characterized by the body's inability to produce or utilize, or both produce and utilize, insulin effectively. GDM is a form of impaired glucose tolerance that occurs during pregnancy (Coustan, 1995). Women with GDM may develop NIDDM within 5 to 15 years after parturition. All types of diabetes mellitus share the common feature of elevated blood glucose levels, or hyperglycemia, although they are actually a heterogeneous group of disorders with various etiologies. Of these four types of diabetes, African American women are most affected by NIDDM and GDM (Tull & Roseman, 1995). Both NIDDM and IDDM typically present with characteristic symptoms of excessive urination, excessive thirst, and weight loss in the setting of marked hyperglycemia (blood glucose levels > 200 mg/dl). Typically, the diagnosis is made by documenting the presence of hyperglycemia (blood glucose levels >140 mg/dl) in the fasting state or by using an oral glucose tolerance test. The measurement of plasma glucose using blood from a "finger stick" and a portable glucometer may indicate the need for further testing, but is not an accepted method of definitive diagnosis.

The WHO system of classification also recognizes impaired glucose tolerance (IGT), which occurs in individuals whose glucose tolerance is higher than the normal range but lower than the levels that are diagnostic of diabetes (National Diabetes Data Group, 1979). In most patients, IGT represents a transient stage during the development of NIDDM and is associated with all of the NIDDM risk factors but not with the chronic microvascular complications. However, IGT poses an increased risk for cardiovascular disease (CVD; Haffner et al., 1992). Among individuals with IGT, 30% to 40% eventually develop NIDDM, and the rate of progression from IGT to NIDDM is approximately 1% to 5% per year (National Diabetes Data Group, 1979). Risk factors associated with increased rate of progression to NIDDM include having a family history of NIDDM, being obese, and being African American (Harris, Hadden, & Bennett, 1987).

INCIDENCE AND PREVALENCE OF DIABETES

The prevalence and incidence of diabetes have been estimated largely from two major national surveys. The National Health Interview Survey (NHIS) has been conducted continuously in the United States since 1958. Conducted in selected U.S. households by personnel of the U.S. Bureau of the Census, the NHIS estimates the prevalence of diabetes by asking a subsample of survey participants questions about diabetes. Participants are asked whether they have ever been told that they have diabetes and, if so, the date of the diagnosis (see Adams & Benson, 1991, for details on sampling). The second major survey, the Second National Health and Nutrition Examination Survey (NHANES II), which was conducted from 1976 to 1980, contained a similar household interview for diabetes, along with a physical examination for a subsample of adults without a medical history of diabetes (National Center for Health Statistics, 1981). Data on diabetes obtained from these two surveys have been the subject of a number of epidemiological studies (e.g., Cowie, Harris, Silverman, Johnson, & Rust, 1993; Fain, 1993; Lipton, Liao, Cao, Cooper, & McGee, 1993; Tull & Roseman, 1995). These studies suggest that only one half of the estimated 16 million people with diabetes in the United States have been diagnosed (Harris, 1995b). Among African Americans, the prevalence of diabetes increased four times from an estimated 228,000 in 1963 to approximately 1 million in 1985; in contrast, the number of whites with diabetes increased two and one-half times (Fain, 1993). Although some of this increase may be due in part to a shift in the age of the U.S. population (diabetes increases with age) as well as more accurate diagnosis of the disorder, the WHO has nonetheless concluded that an apparent epidemic of diabetes has occurred—or is occurring—in adults throughout the world, citing lifestyle and economic change as the most likely causes (King & Rewers, 1994). With respect to data on gender and race, all epidemiological studies have reported similar conclusions, namely that diabetes is more prevalent in African American women than in African American men, or in white Americans of either gender. The prevalence of diabetes increases with age in both blacks and whites; however, for black women, the rate is strikingly higher after 45 years of age, as shown in Figure 1. Because diabetes affects so many older African American women, diabetes and its related morbidity are particular threats to the physical functioning of the black aged (Bernard, 1993).

RISK FACTORS FOR DIABETES

Risk factors for diabetes can be discussed best when they are conceptualized as being modifiable, nonmodifiable, or situational. Modifiable risk factors are those largely under the control of the individual, generally involving lifestyle. Nonmodifiable risk factors are those over which the individual has no control, such as age, gender, and genetics (ethnic identity and family history). Another category of risk factors includes those of a situational nature over which an individual has only

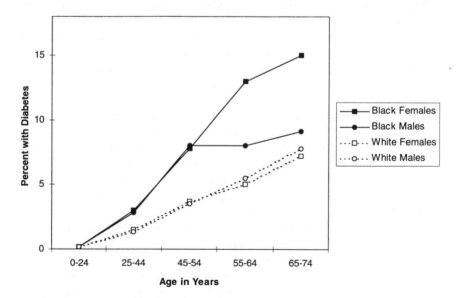

FIGURE 1 Prevalence of age-related diabetes in black and white Americans by gender, 1979–1981. From "Noninsulin-dependent diabetes mellitus in black and white Americans," by M. I. Harris, 1990, *Diabetes/Metabolism Reviews, 6,* p. 73. Copyright 1990 by John Wiley & Sons Limited. Adapted with permission.

partial or marginal control, such as socioeconomic status, geographic location (including urban or rural living), and access to health care.

Modifiable Risk Factors

Although there are a number of modifiable factors that put African American women at higher risk for diabetes, one of the most important is obesity. In the National Center for Health Statistics data for 1970 through 1980, 48% of African American women between the ages of 25 and 74 years were found to be overweight, compared with 26% of white women of the same age group (Kumanyika, 1987). More recently, in the 1991–1992 self-report protocol of the Centers for Disease Control Behavioral Risk Factor Survey, 38% of African American women over the age of 18 were overweight, compared with 22% of white women (*Morbidity and Mortality Weekly Report,* 1994). Obesity and NIDDM are highly correlated, especially among women. Diabetic women of both races (black and white) are more obese then their male counterparts, and 62% of white women and 83% of black women with diagnosed diabetes are overweight (Harris, 1990). This association of obesity as a risk factor for developing NIDDM has been reported by several investigators (Colditz et al., 1990; Cowie et al., 1993; Knowler, Pettitt, Savage, & Bennett, 1981; Lipton et al., 1993; West & Kalbfleisch, 1971). The distribution of body fat also plays a role in the way risk of diabetes is calculated. Women with central adiposity—who have most of their body fat deposited in the central abdominal region (waist area)—are at higher risk for diabetes than women of the same weight whose fat is deposited in their lower body, that is, hips and legs (Carey, Jenkins, Campbell, Freund, & Chisholm, 1996; Kaye, Folsom, Sprafka, Prineas, & Wallace, 1991). This association between diabetes and central adiposity was particularly noted in African American women (Svec, Rivera, & Huth, 1990). Research on Native American women and men has shown that duration of obesity—independent of degree of obesity—is a significant risk factor for the onset of NIDDM (Everhart, Pettitt, Bennett, & Knowler, 1992). If these data are applicable to other populations, it would suggest that young obese African American women who remain obese may be at a particularly high risk for acquiring diabetes by middle age. A second major risk factor for diabetes is physical inactivity, and African American women have been shown to be significantly less active than white women (Lipton et al., 1993; Myers, Kagawa-Singer, Kumanyika, Lex, & Markides, 1995; Washburn, Kline, Lackland, & Wheeler, 1992). As a sedentary lifestyle is a risk factor for diabetes, increased physical activity may be effective in preventing NIDDM, with the protective benefit being especially pronounced in individuals at the highest risk (Helmrich, Ragland, Leung, & Paffenbarger, 1991; Ruderman, Apelian, & Schneider, 1990).

Nonmodifiable Risk Factors

As has been reported earlier, several nonmodifiable risk factors appear to be operating in African American women with diabetes. Although gender per se may not be a risk factor for diabetes, there is clear evidence that African American women are more likely to have diabetes than African American men or white Americans of either gender. Although there are some inconsistencies across studies, U.S. data indicate that the prevalence of NIDDM is about 40% higher in women than men among both whites and African Americans (American Diabetes Association [ADA], 1996a). Age is a risk factor for diabetes in African Americans, with one in four black women having diabetes by the age of 55 years (Tull & Roseman, 1995). Genetics has also been identified as a probable risk factor for diabetes (Brancati et al., 1996; Cowie et al., 1993; Rewers & Hamman, 1995; Sacks & McDonald, 1996). Serving as a surrogate for genetics, family history of diabetes is an established risk factor for diabetes. Individuals having a family member with diabetes have a strikingly increased risk for NIDDM than do people without a family history of diabetes (ADA, 1996a; Harris, 1990). Hypertension is both a risk factor for NIDDM and a major risk for complications related to diabetes (Brancati et al., 1996; Carter, Pugh, & Monterrosa, 1996; Harris, 1990).

Situational Risk Factors

Other risk factors, only indirectly under the control of the individual, have been linked to NIDDM. One of these is socioeconomic status; in the United States, individuals in the lowest income brackets have a higher risk of diabetes (Brancati et al., 1996). There is evidence that obesity and low socioeconomic status are correlated—that is, low socioeconomic status may lead to obesity or both conditions may share the same unknown causes (Sørensen, 1995; Stunkard & Sørensen, 1993). Clearly, the reason for this is not known. The same is true for urbanization. Urban residents have higher rates of NIDDM than do rural residents, which may be a result of lifestyle factors, such as sedentary lifestyles, obesity, and levels of stress (Rewers & Hamman, 1995). Although it is very likely that African American women are especially affected by these situational risk factors (e.g., Anderson, McNeilly, & Myers, 1992), there is insufficient evidence in the literature to validate this assumption.

Delay of diagnosis is an additional risk factor that is associated with complications of diabetes. One of the most alarming findings related to the diagnosis of NIDDM is that the onset of the disease can predate the clinical diagnosis for up to 10 to 12 years (Harris 1995b; Harris, Klein, Welborn, & Knuiman, 1992). Often, individuals with NIDDM experience no symptoms and the disease can remain undiagnosed for many years. In fact, almost one half (49.9%) of people with

NIDDM reported that they had no symptoms of diabetes at the time of diagnosis (Harris, 1995a). In African Americans, cultural and socioeconomic factors often contribute to the lack of early diagnosis of NIDDM. First, there appears to be significant underuse of medical care by African Americans. Specifically, African Americans have been found to be significantly less likely than white Americans to have seen a doctor within the previous year; moreover, blacks have had, on average, fewer physician visits, even when controlling for income, age, and health status (Blendon, Aiken, Freeman, & Corey, 1989). In the context of a system that historically denied access to adequate health care services, many blacks may have negative attitudes toward the health care system and delay seeking care until their condition is quite serious (Neighbors, 1986). A study conducted by Bailey (1987) suggested that a culturally specific, sequenced pattern characterizes the health care seeking behavior of many African Americans. This pattern involves first perceiving symptoms, then delaying for a period of time to allow the body to heal itself, reducing daily activities, seeking the advice of family or friends, and finally seeking medical care. This pattern may lead to a delay in seeking care and may lead to a delay in the diagnosis for diabetes.

TREATMENT OF DIABETES

Treatment for NIDDM is best approached as an effort tailored to the needs of individual patients. General guidelines for therapy have been outlined in the medical literature and in standards established by the ADA (1996c). To be effective, diabetes management requires considerable coordinated effort on the part of the health provider and the patient. It is the provider who develops and presents the details of the management plan to the patient, but it is the patient who ultimately decides whether or not to expend the effort necessary to accept and follow the plan. Management of NIDDM generally consists of two components: pharmacologic (oral agents or insulin therapy, if warranted) and nonpharmacologic (nutrition and weight management, along with regular physical activity and exercise; Fertig, Simmons, & Martin, 1995). Each of these is discussed here in detail.

Pharmacologic Management of Diabetes

Pharmacologic treatment in NIDDM is aimed at ameliorating the underlying defects that are responsible for hyperglycemia. The goals of treatment are to alleviate symptoms, minimize acute complications, improve overall quality of life, and minimize the chronic complications associated with diabetes. These chronic complications include microvascular disease in the eyes, kidneys, and extremities, and macrovascular disease in the heart (Harris, 1995b). Unlike IDDM, in which the pancreas fails to produce insulin due to destruction of the insulin-producing cells, patients with NIDDM usually have elevated levels of insulin but are resistant to the effects of insulin in the body, especially in the liver, fat, and muscle. There are also abnormalities of insulin secretion, and overt diabetes ensues when the pancreas fails to keep up with the high demands for insulin. The magnitude of insulin resistance and of abnormalities in insulin secretion vary widely among patients, making it possible that some treatments are more efficacious in certain populations. Thus, although diet and exercise are the initial therapy in most patients with NIDDM, if progress toward glycemic control is not satisfactory within about 3 months, then the use of pharmacologic therapy is appropriate.

Pharmacologic therapies include oral antidiabetic agents and exogenous insulin. There are four classes of oral antidiabetic agents. Although the mechanisms of action differ, all work to restore metabolic normality by improving insulin resistance or improving insulin secretion, or both (Gerich, 1989). The available oral antidiabetic agents include sulfonylureas, biguanides (metformin), and alpha-glucosidase inhibitors. The thiazolidinediones are currently in clinical trials and will soon be available in the United States (Nolan, Ludvik, Beerdsen, Joyce, & Olefsky, 1994). In the United States, approximately 40% of persons with NIDDM are treated with oral agents and, of these, about 75% are treated with sulfonylureas (Gerich, 1989). The use of insulin in the treatment of NIDDM is appropriate when diet, exercise, and maximal doses of oral agents fail to provide adequate control. Insulin may be instituted without a trial of diet and oral agents in those patients that present initially with severe symptoms and metabolic disturbances. Approximately one third of all patients with diagnosed diabetes in the United States are treated with insulin (Fertig et al., 1995).

Nonpharmacologic Management of Diabetes

Nonpharmacologic management of diabetes has been shown to be effective in improving metabolic control in African Americans with NIDDM (Ziemer et al., 1996). Nonpharmacologic treatment generally involves nutrition and weight management, exercise, and patient education, each of which is discussed here.

Nutrition and weight management.   Lifestyle modification, in terms of proper nutrition and weight loss, is the cornerstone of diabetes management for individuals with NIDDM. Weight loss among obese individuals with NIDDM can lead to significant improvement in metabolic control (Henry, Wallace, & Olefsky, 1986). In obese NIDDM patients, the goal of nutrition therapy is for the patient to reach and maintain a realistic body weight (ADA, 1994). For example, even moderate weight loss of 5% to 10% of body weight has been shown to have positive effects on metabolic control (Henry et al., 1986; McNabb, Quinn, & Rosing, 1993). The difficulty, of course, lies in helping individuals achieve and maintain weight loss. This is particularly true of African American women who, as a group, appear less likely to benefit from weight-loss programs than their white counterparts (Kumanyika, Obarzanek, Stevens, Hebert, & Whelton, 1991). To be successful, weight-loss programs for black women must address a broad range of attitudes, beliefs, and sociocultural factors that facilitate or inhibit weight loss in minority women (Kumanyika & Charleston, 1992; McNabb, 1994). Inner-city minority women may have different educational needs (Gylys & Gylys, 1974), and their interactions with the health care system may limit the effectiveness of typical health education programs (Bailey, 1987). Economic deprivation may contribute to high rates of obesity among women in lower income groups (Jeffrey & French, 1996). In African American women, certain lifestyle practices are linked to the increased prevalence of obesity (Lipson, Kato-Palmer, Boggs, Moore, & Pope, 1988) and to the high prevalence of diabetes. Lifestyle practices related to nutrition were aptly reviewed by Veal (1996), the president of the National Medical Association:

> African Americans have eaten foods prepared with lard and other heavy oils because that is what they had available. The foods African Americans consumed were filling and presumably a fitting meal for a family. Traditionally, cooking methods such as frying were passed on from generation to generation as mothers taught their daughters how to cook and nourish their families. Economically, it was cheaper to cook beans in fatback than to purchase an array of meats and vegetables. African Americans did not have then, and still many today, do not have the financial means to buy the array of foods needed to provide a balanced diet. All of these factors have collectively been ingrained into African American culture and to a large extent make up the traditional foods that we consume. (p. 203)

Both cultural and economic variables create a unique African American lifestyle into which traditional weight-loss programs cannot be readily integrated. As such, it is understandable why so many traditional weight-loss programs are not successful with African American women. As noted earlier, African American women are less likely to benefit from weight-loss programs than white women. In a recent study comparing the response of blacks and whites to 52-week very low- and low-calorie diets, Wing and Anglin (1996) reported that blacks lost less weight than whites during the first 6 months of the program and were more likely than whites to regain weight after the intervention concluded.

To be effective, weight-loss programs for African American women must consider the numerous cultural, economic, and behavioral factors that mediate obesity among black women (Wilson, Nicholson, & Krishnamoorthy, 1997). Despite the importance of weight loss in the management of NIDDM, few studies have examined the effectiveness of weight-loss programs among African American women with NIDDM. In the literature, only one study has been reported that was specifically designed to address the cultural and behavioral needs of African American women with NIDDM: the PATHWAYS program developed by the

University of Chicago Diabetes Research and Training Center (McNabb et al., 1993). In this study, after 1 year, inner-city African American women with diabetes achieved and maintained an average weight loss of 9.8 lb, whereas participants in a comparison group gained 3.0 lb (McNabb et al., 1993). The success of the PATHWAYS program can be attributed to a number of features of the program that were intended to increase its relevance to African American women. First, the program used health benefits as the motivation for weight loss, not slenderness, as a large body size may be more acceptable in the African American culture. The program included extensive references to ethnic foods and inner-city sociocultural lifestyle situations. Finally, the program actively involved participants in setting their own weight loss and behavior change goals—goals that were relevant to their own culture and lifestyle.

Exercise in the treatment of NIDDM.   Like weight loss, exercise is a major nonpharmacological treatment for diabetes. Often, exercise is included as a component of a weight-loss program. However, exercise can and should be considered as an independent therapy. The benefits of exercise as related to diabetes are threefold: Exercise may reduce insulin resistance, allowing the body to operate with lower insulin levels (Flatt, 1995; Ruderman et al., 1990); exercise acts as an adjunct to diet in reducing obesity or assisting in maintaining weight loss (Maynard, 1991; Saris, 1995; Tremblay & Buemann, 1995; Tremblay et al., 1991; Wing et al., 1991); and exercise may reduce cardiovascular risk factors in patients with NIDDM (Gautier, Scheen, & Lefebvre, 1995; Hong et al., 1994; Maynard, 1991; Ruderman et al., 1990). The benefits of exercise for individuals with NIDDM have been amply supported by a number of experts (Garrow, 1995; Heath, Wilson, Smith, & Leonard, 1991; Helmrich et al., 1991; Jakicic & Leermakers, 1996; Kaplan, Hartwell, Wilson, & Wallace, 1987; King & Kriska, 1992; Soukup, Maynard, & Kovaleski, 1994). Although there remain some questions about the actual effects of exercise among individuals with NIDDM, regular physical activity, especially coupled with nutrition management, is strongly recommended (ADA, 1996b; Barnard, Jung, & Inkeles, 1994). For individuals with NIDDM, exercise can take any of several forms, with walking being the most popular form (Siegel, Brackbill, & Heath, 1995).

However, designing an exercise program that is appropriate to the needs of African American women with NIDDM and that assists them in overcoming many of the obstacles they face will be a difficult, challenging undertaking. In addition to lack of motivation to exercise, these obstacles include lack of access to exercise facilities, dangerous and unsuitable environments for walking, lack of time for exercise, and physical limitations due to injury or illness (Maillet, Melkus, & Spollet, 1996; Melnyk & Weinstein, 1994). Because there are certain risks involved in vigorous physical activity, even brisk walking, all experts recommend a physician's approval prior to beginning an exercise program. This is especially true for high-risk individuals with NIDDM who have a relatively sedentary lifestyle. It is noteworthy that, despite the evidence that increased physical activity will prevent NIDDM and improve glycemic control (Ruderman et al., 1990), no studies of exercise in black women with diabetes have been reported in the literature to date. Recently, Taylor, Beech, and Cummings (1997) reviewed exercise programs for African American youth and reported variable levels of success, with some programs being only slightly successful and others being quite successful. However, none of these programs dealt specifically with black women with diabetes.

Patient self-management education in diabetes.   Patient education in diabetes, more accurately termed self-management education, is intended to provide patients with the knowledge, attitudes, and skills required to manage their diabetes on a daily basis. In addition to making lifestyle changes, patients with diabetes may be expected to take medications (insulin or an oral hypoglycemic agent, as described earlier), monitor their blood glucose levels, respond to and self-treat diabetes-related symptoms, follow foot-care guidelines, and seek routine medical care for diabetes (McNabb, 1997). These requirements are further complicated by the need to integrate and sequence all of these behaviors into one's daily routine.

The demands on the part of the patient in terms of self-care make it mandatory that they be provided with enough patient education to empower them to assume their responsibilities. The importance of educating patients to care for their diabetes has been stressed by the ADA (1996b), Healthy People 2000 (U.S. Department of Health and Human Services, 1991), as well as findings from the Diabetes Control and Complications Trial (1993). Recently, Clement (1995) reviewed the effectiveness of diabetes self-management education and found that self-management education is associated with reduced hospitalizations for diabetes-related health problems and reduced diabetes-related health care costs. However, the level of patient education provided to patients with NIDDM is often inadequate. According to data from the NHIS, only 23.7% of patients with NIDDM who were not on insulin had received some form of patient education (Coonrod, Betschart, & Harris, 1994). Further, when patient education is received, it may be inadequate or culturally inappropriate (Hiss, 1996; Stolar, 1995). Often, patient education in diabetes consists of providing factual information about diabetes. This is far less successful than self-management education, which has a strong behavioral component and emphasizes the acquisition and practice of self-management behaviors (Mazzuca et al., 1986; McNabb, 1997).

DIABETES AND PREGNANCY

Pregnancy may be complicated by preexisting IDDM or NIDDM, or by the development of GDM in the course of the pregnancy. The goal of diabetes management during pregnancy is to maintain strict glycemic control. The primary therapeutic modality in the management of GDM is dietary therapy. Exogenous insulin administration may be required in some cases where tight blood glucose control can not be maintained by diet alone, and approximately 25% of women with GDM require insulin. Among women with preexisting diabetes, pregnancy poses particular problems. Because the hormonal changes occurring during pregnancy lead to higher and more variable insulin requirements, diabetes is more difficult to manage during pregnancy. Also, very strict glycemic control is required to avoid the risk for fetal malformations, macrosomia, and infant mortality associated with poor metabolic control. To maintain strict control, insulin must be administered in multiple daily injections and blood glucose must be monitored several times each day (Jovanovic-Peterson & Peterson, 1992). Oral antidiabetic agents are contraindicated during pregnancy (Metzger, 1991).

Among women with preexisting diabetes, it is important to provide preconception counseling to inform women about diabetes-specific risks to both mother and child. For example, in women with diabetes, pregnancy accelerates the development and progression of retinopathy (Jovanovic-Peterson & Peterson, 1992; Phelps, Sakol, Metzger, Jampol, & Freinkel, 1986; Rosenn et al., 1992). Active proliferative retinopathy, if untreated, is considered a contraindication to pregnancy. Moreover, pregnancy is known to increase the development and progression of nephropathy among women with diabetes; in most cases, kidney function returns to prepregnancy levels. However, in patients with chronic renal failure, pregnancy is contraindicated.

In addition to risks to the mother, diabetes poses specific risks for perinatal morbidity and mortality, including major congenital malformations, neonatal hypoglycemia, respiratory distress syndrome, hyperbilirubinemia, and increased incidence of spontaneous abortion and stillbirth. One relatively common morbidity, fetal macrosomia, can lead to traumatic delivery. However, when the mother maintains strict glycemic control, the risk to the baby is near that of children born to mothers without diabetes (Jovanovic-Peterson & Peterson, 1992).

Contraceptive counseling is important to avoid the risks associated with unplanned pregnancy among women with diabetes. Contraception planning should seek to balance the effectiveness of selected methods with their effect on diabetes control and complications. For example, although barrier methods interfere the least with glucose control, they have a high failure rate. On the other hand, although highly effective, oral contraceptives are associated with risk for thromboembolism, stroke, and myocardial infarction in nondiabetic women. Among women with diabetes who take oral contraceptives, these risks are increased. When used in women with diabetes, oral contraceptives with low-dose estrogen and progestin should be selected. Progestin-only pills are problematic with patients with diabetes, as they tend to be associated with elevated lipid levels. The use of intrauterine devices is controversial. Although they are highly effective, some studies show an increased risk of infection when used by women with diabetes. Once childbearing is completed, permanent sterilization as a contraceptive method ought to be considered (Jovanovic-Peterson & Peterson, 1992).

DIABETES COMPLICATIONS AND OTHER MEDICAL CONDITIONS

Diabetes is associated with microvascular complications, including eye disease (retinopathy), kidney disease (nephropathy), and nerve damage, especially in the extremities (neuropathy); and with macrovascular complications in the heart (coronary artery disease; Nathan, 1993). Because of the frequent delay in diagnosis, a significant percentage of patients will have already developed diabetic complications before the initiation of treatment. According to data from NHANES II, Harris and Modan (1994) reported that individuals with newly detected diabetes had abnormal heart findings (22%), angina (10%), peripheral vascular disease (8%), and stroke (6%). In other studies, retinopathy, a microvascular disorder of the eye that is a common complication of diabetes, was present in as many as 29% of patients at the time of diagnosis (Harris et al., 1992). Little is known about the prevalence of these complications specifically in African American women. For the African American population as a whole, the incidence and prevalence of vascular complications from diabetes appears to be higher than in whites, and the diabetic mortality rate of African Americans is almost twice that of white Americans (Harris, 1990).

Kidney Disease

The spectrum of diabetic kidney disease is wide ranging, from asymptomatic disturbances in filtration of proteins into the urine (albuminuria) to complete kidney failure (end-stage renal disease; ESRD) that requires dialysis. The presence of albuminuria has been shown to be higher in African Americans in general than in white Americans: 42% to 50% versus 19% to 42%, respectively (Dasmahapatra et al., 1994; Goldschmid, Domin, Ziemer, Gallina, & Phillips, 1995; Klein, Klein, & Moss, 1993; Neil et al., 1993). It is also known that the incidence of diabetic ESRD is 4.8 to 9.3 times higher in African Americans than in non-Hispanic whites (Brancati, Whittle, Whelton, Seidler, & Klag, 1992; Cowie et al., 1989; Pugh, Medina, Cornell, & Basu, 1995). The gender composition of black patients with ESRD has been stable over time, with about 48% of patients treated for ESRD being women (Feldman, Klag, Chiapella, & Whelton, 1992). Diabetes is second to hypertension as the leading cause of ESRD in the black population (Tull & Roseman, 1995).

Eye Disease

Diabetic retinopathy, the leading cause of new cases of blindness in the United States in the 20- to 74-year-old age group, has been reported to be twice as prevalent in African Americans as compared to whites (Kahn & Hiller, 1974). There are no data concerning the prevalence of diabetic retinopathy in African American women. The increased severity of diabetic retinopathy in African Americans may be due to the higher prevalence of hypertension (Rabb, Gagliano, & Sweeny, 1990).

Lower Extremity Vascular Disease

Diabetes increases the risk for lower extremity vascular disease resulting in non-healing ulcers, infection, and gangrene, and accounts for more than 50% of all nontraumatic amputations in the United States annually (Most & Sinnock, 1983). Rates of nontraumatic lower extremity amputation among persons with diabetes tend to be higher among blacks than whites (Geiss et al., 1993). However, one study reported that when blood pressure and blood glucose levels were controlled, race did not seem to confer additional risk (Selby & Zhang, 1995). Additional studies are needed to clarify the impact of race on lower extremity vascular disease.

CVD

CVD is more common among and is the major cause of mortality in patients with NIDDM. Among nondiabetic populations, men are by far at the highest risk for CVD; in contrast, women with diabetes have approximately equivalent risk for heart disease as do men (Raman & Nesto, 1996). Diabetes appears to be the only disease that causes women to have rates of heart disease similar to that of men (Wingard & Barrett-Connor, 1995). Women with diabetes appear to lose the protective effects of gender with respect to CVD, with diabetes conferring a 16-fold relative risk of mortality due to heart disease as compared to women without diabetes (DeStefano et al., 1993).

Hypertension

Hypertension, although not considered a complication of diabetes, affects similar populations as diabetes and has a significant negative impact on the microvascular and macrovascular complications associated with diabetes. In the diabetic population, blood pressure is higher in African Americans than in white Americans (Harris, 1990). Among women over 65 years of age, the risk for hypertension is much greater in blacks than in whites (National Center for Health Statistics, 1985).

Associated Complications of Diabetes Common in Women

Among women, diabetes is associated with a number of other complications. Women with IDDM are at risk for developing eating disorders, menstrual cycle irregularities, and endometrial cancer (Brinton et al., 1992; Wing, Norwalk, Marcus, Koeske, & Finegold, 1986). In addition, women with either IDDM or NIDDM appear to be more susceptible to certain infections, and report frequent and recurrent urinary tract infections and vaginitis (ADA, 1994).

CLINICAL STUDIES IN DIABETES PREVENTION

There is a growing body of clinical literature to suggest that diabetes may be prevented or its onset delayed through modification in lifestyle among high-risk individuals. In individuals with impaired glucose tolerance, one study suggested that diet and exercise interventions may reduce the incidence of diabetes (Pan, Li, & Hu, 1995). In severely obese individuals, weight loss was shown to significantly prevent the progression of IGT to diabetes (Long et al., 1994). Despite the findings of these studies, data are currently insufficient to allow us to prove conclusively that lifestyle modification can and will prevent NIDDM (Manson & Spelsberg, 1994). However, the findings of these and similar studies have been sufficient to warrant the undertaking of a large, multicenter clinical trial on the prevention of NIDDM. The Diabetes Prevention Program, currently being funded by the National Institutes of Diabetes and Digestive and Kidney Diseases of the National Institutes of Health, is being conducted to assess whether it is possible to prevent the development of NIDDM (Bloomgarden, 1996). One of the major interventions being studied in the Diabetes Prevention Program is an intensive lifestyle intervention involving weight loss and regular exercise. It is planned that a substantial number of African American women will be included as participants in this program.

Several weight-loss studies have been carried out with African American women at risk for diabetes. Modest weight loss has been reported among participants in these clinic-based programs (Holm, Taussig, & Carlton, 1983; Kanders et al., 1994; Stevens et al., 1993; Wassertheil-Smoller et al., 1985). Unfortunately, none of these studies was designed to provide data that would test the hypothesis that weight loss does, in fact, prevent or delay the onset of diabetes in African American women. However, this area of research is one of the most promising because of its clinical and public health implications.

DIABETES AS A PUBLIC HEALTH ISSUE

One of the primary goals in efforts to improve health care should be to prevent and control those factors that are responsible for the greatest costs (Wynder, 1996). Certainly, the costs of diabetes both to society and its citizens are substantial. In their review of the costs of diabetes, Javitt and Chiang (1995) concluded that the costs attributable to diabetes may amount to about 13% of U.S. health care expenditures. Much of the high cost is likely related to the treatment of diabetes complications. Then, any effort we can make to minimize the occurrence of diabetes complications would, in effect, lessen much of the cost associated with the disease. In diabetes, public health issues revolve around early detection (community screening for diabetes) and risk prevention (community-based lifestyle modification programs).

Community Screening for Diabetes

Because there is strong evidence of the prevalence of undiagnosed diabetes, and sufficient reason to believe that early detection and treatment can prevent or minimize the complications associated with diabetes, it would appear that widespread community screening is warranted. However, as discussed by Harris (1995a), there is controversy about screening for diabetes. First, the most easily utilized screening tool, fasting blood glucose, has a low sensitivity in detecting NIDDM. Second, conducting an oral glucose tolerance test is difficult and time consuming. However, if restricted to carefully selected high-risk populations, public screening for diabetes may be effective in detecting undiagnosed diabetes. Certainly, high-risk populations have been identified. Investigators at the Chicago Diabetes Research and Training Center, for example, conducted surveys in 18 African American churches in the Chicago metropolitan area to identify the prevalence of risk factors for diabetes among church members. When sedentary lifestyle was added as a risk factor, more than 80% of the nearly 2,500 African American women who completed the survey reported three or more risk factors for diabetes (McNabb, Cook, & Quinn, 1996). Although this was not a representative sample, it nevertheless provides an indication of the proportion of African American women who are at high risk for diabetes and who might benefit from community-based public health screening. To identify high-risk individuals, data on only a few factors are needed to yield a high level of sensitivity: age, gender, a history of delivering a high-birthweight child, obesity, sedentary lifestyle, and a family history of diabetes (Herman, Smith, Thompson, Engelgau, & Aubert, 1995).

Community-Based Programs in Diabetes

There are a number of programs throughout the country that provide education, services, and support to African Americans with diabetes. Although these programs are much needed and very important, their effectiveness in reducing the burden of diabetes on African Americans is not known. Few programs have been evaluated. With the goal of preventing diabetes or delaying its onset through lifestyle modification (diet, exercise, or a combination of the two), a number of weight-loss studies have been carried out in community-based settings such as churches, schools, and YMCAs (e.g., Domel, Alford, Cattlett, & Gench, 1992; Kumanyika & Charleston, 1992; Lasco et al., 1989; Pleas, 1988). Although some weight loss was reported, it is difficult to fully assess the effectiveness of these programs because of limited data. Many of the studies lacked control groups and reported no follow-up data. However, those programs that appear to offer the greatest promise incorporated culturally relevant activities, role modeling, social support from among intact groups, and sensitivity to unique local obstacles.

Exercise as a public health strategy was the focus of a major study in low-income African American communities (Lewis et al., 1993). Researchers developed carefully designed community-based exercise programs that involved substantial community participation. However, they were unable to demonstrate any increased physical activity in community residents, citing lack of resources and variable levels of commitment to the project by communities and exercise leaders as the reasons for lack of demonstrated success. Difficulty in achieving success in exercise programs is often attributed to the program's inability to overcome the many obstacles that prevent black women from engaging in regular physical activity. Effective programs need to specifically target obstacles commonly reported by African American women, such as lack of family and social support, an environment perceived as unsuitable or dangerous for exercise, and lack of transportation and child care (Maillet et al., 1996; Melnyk & Weinstein, 1994).

For the most part, these public health programs are few, are widely scattered throughout the country, and are not collecting data that will help demonstrate their effectiveness in increasing diabetes awareness, promoting early diagnosis, and minimizing complications.

SUMMARY, CONCLUSIONS, AND RECOMMENDATIONS

NIDDM is a major health problem affecting a disproportionate number of African American women. NIDDM is often dismissed as harmless: "I just have a little sugar." Quite the contrary. It is a very serious disease. Consider the following statistics: In women younger than 45 years old, the risk of death due to heart disease in the women with diabetes is 16 times greater than in women without diabetes (DeStefano et al., 1993). Although data on diabetic complications among African Americans are limited, existing evidence suggests that African Americans suffer considerably more morbidity due to diabetes and a higher frequency of diabetic complications than the U.S. white population (Tull & Roseman, 1995). For example, the rate of visual impairment due to diabetes is 40% higher in African Americans and, in African American women, blindness is three times higher than in whites (Harris, 1990).

Diabetes has clearly reached epidemic proportions among African American women, yet intervention studies of diabetes prevention and control among African American women are almost nonexistent. Although there is some evidence to suggest that weight loss might lessen a black woman's chances of acquiring NIDDM, there are no definitive studies to prove this hypothesis. Despite the fact that exercise might protect individuals against NIDDM, there is no published research regarding the effects of exercise in African American women with diabetes or those at risk for it (Ruderman et al., 1990).

The recommendations that follow are not new; they have been proposed in the literature for several years. When appropriate, citations from other sources are provided not only to support our recommendations, but also to show that many of these recommendations have remained unmet for almost a decade.

1.   The early detection of diabetes, particularly among African American women, should be emphasized. Individuals can have diabetes for years before it is diagnosed. During the time prior to diagnosis, serious complications can develop. African American women who are overweight, sedentary, and have a family history of diabetes are particularly at risk and should be tested for diabetes (Carter et al., 1996; Harris & Modan, 1994). A national screening program should be instituted that specifically addresses high-risk populations. With data to suggest that only half of individuals with diabetes are diagnosed and of those, half are diagnosed by chance (Harris, 1995a), there is an obvious need for health care providers to put in place a plan for the early identification and treatment of diabetes, especially in African American women who are at a particularly high risk. As a routine part of medical care, testing for diabetes should be considered in African American women who:

- Have first-degree relatives with diabetes.
- Are obese (> 120% of ideal body weight).
- Are over 40 years of age with any of the previously listed factors.
- Are hypertensive or have hyperlipidemia.
- Have been previously identified as having IGT.
- Are pregnant (at 24–28 weeks of pregnancy).
- Have a history of gestational diabetes or a history of delivering a high-birth-weight (> 9 lb) baby (ADA, 1994).

In private physician offices and other health care settings, screening for diabetes can be undertaken when testing for other medical conditions, such as hypertension, hyperlipidemia, and hypercholesterolemia (Harris, 1995a).

2.   The quality of care for African American women with diabetes should be improved. It is essential that we identify and overcome community and cultural barriers that prevent African American women with diabetes from receiving optimal care (Jewler, 1991). We must work to ensure that low-cost models of care, such as those being proposed in the managed care system, do not lead to a reduction in the already substandard quality of care for African American women with diabetes. We must especially provide early treatment for black women with diabetes to lessen the complications associated with it (Lipson, Kato-Palmer, Boggs, Moore, & Pope, 1988). Not only are African American women disproportionately affected

by diabetes, the disease is especially prevalent among elderly black women who suffer the most from complications.

3. Improved educational services and programs in diabetes are needed. A national diabetes education program should be initiated under a single organizing body that will promote the sharing of diabetes education programs and encourage the communication of crucial messages about diabetes, its prevention, and its control (Fisher et al., 1994). As part of the initiative, special programs should be developed and tested that focus on lifestyle modification for African American women with diabetes. We should also carry out studies to assess the effects of regular exercise in African American women with NIDDM. In this regard, we should make a concentrated effort to ensure that materials are culturally appropriate (Kumanyika et al., 1991).

It is our hope, with the research that is now being done in the area of prevention and control, that advances can be made before the year 2000 to overcome many of the hardships that diabetes imposes on African American women. This can only be accomplished through the initiation of more research and more services directed toward this much underserved population. However, if this diabetes-related research is to be successful, it is of utmost importance that more African American women become partners in the effort as both investigators and participants.

ACKNOWLEDGMENTS

This article was supported in part by Grant P60 DK20595–19 from the National Institutes of Diabetes and Digestive and Kidney Diseases to the University of Chicago.

We acknowledge the contributions of Carolyn Barrow, Sandy Cook, and Daniel Dücker in the preparation of this article.

REFERENCES

Adams, P., & Benson, V. (1991). Current estimates from the National Health Interview Survey. National Center for Health Statistics. *Vital and Health Statistics, 10*(181), 1–212.

American Diabetes Association. (1994). *Medical management of non-insulin-dependent (type II) diabetes.* Alexandria, VA: Author.

American Diabetes Association. (1996a). *Diabetes 1996: Vital statistics.* Alexandria, VA: Author.

American Diabetes Association. (1996b). National standards for diabetes self-management education programs and American Diabetes Association Review criteria. *Diabetes Care, 19*(Suppl. 1), S114–S118.

American Diabetes Association. (1996c). Standards of medical care for patients with diabetes mellitus. *Diabetes Care, 19*(Suppl. 1), S8–S15.

Anderson, N. B., McNeilly, M., & Myers, H. (1992). Toward understanding race differences in autonomic reactivity: A proposed contextual model. In J. R. Turner, A. Sherwood, & K. C. Light

(Eds.), *Individual differences in cardiovascular response to stress: Applications to models of cardiovascular disease* (pp. 125–146). New York: Plenum.

Bailey, E. J. (1987). Sociocultural factors and health care-seeking behavior among black Americans. *Journal of the National Medical Association, 79,* 389–392.

Barnard, R. J., Jung, T., & Inkeles, S. B. (1994). Diet and exercise in the treatment of NIDDM. *Diabetes Care, 17,* 1469–1472.

Bernard, M. A. (1993). The health status of African-American elderly. *Journal of the National Medical Association, 85,* 521–527.

Blendon, R. J., Aiken, L. H., Freeman, H. E., & Corey, C. R. (1989). Access to medical care for black and white Americans. *Journal of American Medical Association, 261,* 278–281.

Bloomgarden, Z. T. (1996). American Diabetes Association postgraduate course, 1996: Treatment and prevention of diabetes. *Diabetes Care, 19,* 784–786.

Brancati, F. L., Whelton, P. K., Kuller, L. H., & Klag, M. J. (1996). Diabetes mellitus, race, and socioeconomic status: A population-based study. *Annals of Epidemiology, 6,* 67–73.

Brancati, F. L., Whittle, J. C., Whelton, P. K., Seidler, A. J., & Klag, M. J. (1992). The excess incidence of diabetic end-stage renal disease among blacks. A population-based study of potential explanatory factors. *Journal of American Medical Association, 268,* 3079–3084.

Brinton, L. A., Berman, M. L., Mortel, R., Twiggs, L. B., Barrett, R. J., Wilbanks, G. D., Lannon, L., & Hoover, R. N. (1992). Reproductive, menstrual, and medical risk factors for endometrial cancer: Results from a case-control study. *American Journal of Obstetrics and Gynecology, 167,* 1317–1325.

Carey, D. G., Jenkins, A. B., Campbell, L. V., Freund, J., & Chisholm, D. J. (1996). Abdominal fat and insulin resistance in normal and overweight women. *Diabetes, 45,* 633–638.

Carter, J. S., Pugh, J. A., & Monterrosa, A. (1996). Non-insulin-dependent diabetes mellitus in minorities in the United States. *Annals of Internal Medicine, 125,* 221–232.

Clement, S. (1995). Diabetes self-management education. *Diabetes Care, 18,* 1204–1214.

Colditz, G. A., Willett, W. C., Stampfer, M. J., Manson, J. E., Hennekens, C. H., Arky, R. A., & Speizer, F. E. (1990). Weight as a risk factor for clinical diabetes in women. *American Journal of Epidemiology, 132,* 501–513.

Coonrod, B. A., Betschart, J., & Harris, M. I. (1994). Frequency and determinants of diabetes patient education among adults in the U.S. population. *Diabetes Care, 17,* 852–858.

Coustan, D. R. (1995). Gestational diabetes. In National Diabetes Data Group (Ed.), *Diabetes in America* (pp. 703–716). Washington, DC: National Institutes of Health, National Institute of Diabetes and Digestive and Kidney Diseases.

Cowie, C. C., & Eberhardt, M. S. (1995). Sociodemographic characteristics of persons with diabetes. In National Diabetes Data Group (Ed.), *Diabetes in America* (pp. 85–116). Washington, DC: National Institutes of Health, National Institute of Diabetes and Digestive and Kidney Diseases.

Cowie, C. C., Harris, M. I., Silverman, R. E., Johnson, E. W., & Rust, K. F. (1993). Effect of multiple risk factors on differences between blacks and whites in the prevalence of non-insulin-dependent diabetes mellitus in the United States. *American Journal of Epidemiology, 137,* 719–732.

Cowie, C. C., Port, F. K., Wolfe, R. A., Savage, P. J., Moll, P. P., & Hawthorn, V. M. (1989). Disparities in incidence of diabetic end-stage renal disease according to race and type of diabetes. *The New England Journal of Medicine, 321,* 1074–1079.

Dasmahapatra, A., Bale, A., Raghuwanshi, M. P., Reddi, A., Byrne, W., Suarez, S., Nash, F., Varagiannia, E., & Skurnick, J. H. (1994). Incipient and overt diabetic nephropathy in African Americans with NIDDM. *Diabetes Care, 17,* 297–304.

DeStefano, F., Ford, E. S., Newman, J. M., Wetterhall, S. F., Anda, R. F., & Vinicor, F. (1993). Risk factors for coronary heart disease mortality among persons with diabetes. *Annals of Epidemiology, 3,* 27–34.

Diabetes Control and Complications Trial Research Group. (1993). The effect of intensive treatment of diabetes on the development and progression of long-term complications in insulin-dependent diabetes mellitus. *The New England Journal of Medicine, 329,* 977–986.

Domel, S. B., Alford, B. B., Cattlett, H. N., & Gench, B. E. (1992). Weight control for black women. *Journal of the American Dietetic Association, 92,* 346–348.

Everhart, J. E., Pettitt, D. J., Bennett, P. H., & Knowler, W. C. (1992). Duration of obesity increases the incidence of NIDDM. *Diabetes, 41,* 235–240.

Fain, J. A. (1993). National trends in diabetes: An epidemiological perspective. *Nursing Clinics of North America, 28,* 1–7.

Feldman, H. I., Klag, M. J., Chiapella, A. P., & Whelton, P. K. (1992). End-stage renal disease in US minority groups. *American Journal of Kidney Disease, 19,* 397–410.

Fertig, B. J., Simmons, D. A., & Martin, D. B. (1995). Therapy for diabetes. In National Diabetes Data Group (Ed.), *Diabetes in America* (pp. 519–540). Washington, DC: National Institutes of Health, National Institute of Diabetes and Digestive and Kidney Diseases.

Fisher, J. E., Heins, J. M., Hiss, R. G., Lorenz, R. A., Marrero, D. G., McNabb, W. L., & Wylie-Rosett, J. (1994). *Metabolic control matters.* Washington DC: National Institutes of Health, National Institute of Diabetes and Digestive and Kidney Diseases.

Flatt, J. P. (1995). Integration of the overall response to exercise. *International Journal of Obesity, 19,* S31–S40.

Garrow, J. S. (1995). Exercise in the treatment of obesity: A marginal contribution. *International Journal of Obesity, 19*(Suppl. 4), S126–S129.

Gautier, J. F., Scheen, A., & Lefebvre, P. J. (1995). Exercise in the management of non-insulin-dependent (type 2) diabetes mellitus. *International Journal of Obesity, 19,* S58–S61.

Geiss L. S., Herman, W. H., Goldschmid, M. G., DeStefano, F., Eberhardt, M. S., Ford, E. S., German, R. R., Newman, J. M., Olson, D. R., Sepe, S. J., Stevenson, J. M., Vinicor, F., Wetterhall, S. F., & Will, J. C. (1993). Surveillance data for diabetes mellitus—United States, 1980–1989. *Morbidity and Mortality Weekly Reports, 42*(SS–2), 1–20.

Gerich, J. E. (1989). Oral hypoglycemic agents. *The New England Journal of Medicine, 321,* 1231–1245.

Goldschmid, M. G., Domin, W. S., Ziemer, D. C., Gallina, D. L., & Phillips, L. S. (1995). Diabetes in urban African-Americans. II. High prevalence of microalbuminuria and nephropathy in African-Americans with diabetes. *Diabetes Care, 18,* 955–961.

Gylys, J. A., & Gylys, B. A. (1974). Cultural influences and the medical behavior of low income groups. *Journal of the National Medical Association, 66,* 308–312.

Haffner, S. M., Valdez, R. A., Hazuda, H. P., Mitchell, B. D., Morales, P. A., & Stern, M. P. (1992). Prospective analysis of the insulin resistance syndrome (Syndrome X). *Diabetes, 41,* 715–722.

Harris, M. I. (1990). Non-insulin-dependent diabetes mellitus in black and white Americans. *Diabetes/Metabolism Reviews, 6,* 71–90.

Harris, M. I. (1993). Undiagnosed NIDDM: Clinical and public health issues. *Diabetes Care, 16,* 642–652.

Harris, M. I. (1995a). Classification, diagnostic criteria, and screening for diabetes. In National Diabetes Data Group (Ed.), *Diabetes in America* (pp. 15–36). Washington, DC: National Institutes of Health, National Institute of Diabetes and Digestive and Kidney Diseases.

Harris, M. I. (1995b). Summary. In National Diabetes Data Group (Ed.), *Diabetes in America* (pp. 1–13). Washington, DC: National Institutes of Health, National Institute of Diabetes and Digestive and Kidney Diseases.

Harris, M. I., Hadden, W. C., & Bennett, P. H. (1987). Prevalence of diabetes and impaired glucose tolerance and plasma glucose levels in U.S. population aged 20–74 yr. *Diabetes, 36,* 523–534.

Harris, M. I., Klein, R., Welborn, T. A., & Knuiman, M. W. (1992). Onset of NIDDM occurs at least 4–7 years before clinical diagnosis. *Diabetes Care, 15,* 815–819.

Harris, M. I., & Modan, M. (1994). Screening for NIDDM: Why is there no national program? *Diabetes Care, 17,* 440–444.

Heath, G. W., Wilson, R. H., Smith, J., & Leonard, B. E. (1991). Community-based exercise and weight control: Diabetes risk reduction and glycemic control in Zuni Indians. *American Journal of Clinical Nutrition, 53*(Suppl.), 642S–646S.

Helmrich, S. P., Ragland, D. R., Leung, R. W., & Paffenbarger, R. S. (1991). Physical activity and reduced occurrence of non-insulin-dependent diabetes mellitus. *New England Journal of Medicine, 325,* 147–152.

Henry, R. R., Wallace, P., & Olefsky, J. M. (1986). Effects of weight loss on mechanisms of hyperglycemia in obese non-insulin-dependent diabetes mellitus. *Diabetes, 35,* 990–998.

Herman, W. H., Smith, P. J., Thompson, T. J., Engelgau, M. M., & Aubert, R. E. (1995). A new and simple questionnaire to identify people at increased risk for undiagnosed diabetes. *Diabetes Care, 18,* 382–387.

Hiss, R. G. (1996). Barriers to care in non-insulin-dependent diabetes mellitus. The Michigan experience. *Annals of Internal Medicine, 124*(1, Pt. 2), 146–148.

Holm, R. P., Taussig, T., & Carlton, E. (1983). Behavioral modification in a weight-reduction program. *Perspectives in Practice, 83,* 170–174.

Hong, Y., Bots, M., Pan, X., Wang, H., Jing, H., Hofman, A., & Chen, H. (1994). Physical activity and cardiovascular risk factors in rural Shanghai, China. *International Journal of Epidemiology, 23,* 1154–1158.

Jakicic, J. M., & Leermakers, E. A. (1996). Commit to get fit: Exercise for life. *Diabetes Spectrum, 9,* 202–204.

Javitt, J. C., & Chiang, Y. (1995). Economic impact of diabetes. In National Diabetes Data Group (Ed.), *Diabetes in America* (pp. 601–611). Washington, DC: National Institutes of Health, National Institute of Diabetes and Digestive and Kidney Diseases.

Jeffery, R. W., & French, S. A. (1996). Socioeconomic status and weight control practices among 20-to-45-year-old women. *American Journal of Public Health, 86,* 1005–1010.

Jewler, D. (1991). Blacks and diabetes. *Diabetes Forecast, 44,* 49–51.

Jovanovic-Peterson, L., & Peterson, C. M. (1992). Pregnancy in the diabetic woman: Guidelines for a successful outcome. *Endocrinology and Metabolism Clinics of North America, 21,* 433–456.

Kahn, H. A., & Hiller, R. (1974). Blindness caused by diabetic retinopathy. *American Journal of Ophthalmology, 78,* 58–67.

Kanders, B. S., Ullman-Joy, P., Foreyt, J. P., Heymsfield, S. B., Heber, D., Elashoff, R. M., Ashley, J. M., Reeves, R. S., & Blackburn, G. L. (1994). The black American lifestyle intervention (BALI): The design of a weight loss program for working-class African-American women. *Journal of the American Dietetic Association, 94,* 310–312.

Kaplan, R. M., Hartwell, S. L., Wilson, D. K., & Wallace, J. P. (1987). Effects of diet and exercise interventions on control and quality of life in non-insulin-dependent diabetes mellitus. *Journal of General Internal Medicine, 2,* 220–227.

Kaye, S. A., Folsom, A. R., Sprafka, J. M., Prineas, R. J., & Wallace, R. B. (1991). Increased incidence of diabetes mellitus in relation to abdominal adiposity in older women. *Journal of Clinical Epidemiology, 44,* 329–334.

King, H., & Kriska, A. M. (1992). Prevention of type II diabetes by physical training: Epidemiological considerations and study methods. *Diabetes Care, 15*(Suppl. 4), 1794–1799.

King, H., & Rewers, M. (1994). Diabetes in adults is now a third world problem. *Ethnicity and Disease, 3*(Suppl.), S67–S74.

Klein, R., Klein, B. E. K., & Moss, S. E. (1993). Prevalence of microalbuminuria in older-onset diabetes. *Diabetes Care, 16,* 1325–1330.

Knowler, W. C., Pettitt, D. J., Savage, P. J., & Bennett, P. H. (1981). Diabetes incidence in Pima Indians: Contributions of obesity and parental diabetes. *American Journal of Epidemiology, 113,* 144–156.

Kumanyika, S. (1987). Obesity in black women. *Epidemiologic Reviews, 9,* 31–50.

Kumanyika, S. K., & Charleston, J. B. (1992). Lose weight and win: A church-based weight loss program for blood pressure control among black women. *Patient Education and Counseling, 19,* 19–32.

Kumanyika, S. K., Obarzanek, E., Stevens, V. J., Hebert, P. R., & Whelton, P. K. (1991). Weight-loss experience of black and white participants in NHLBI-sponsored clinical trials. *American Journal of Clinical Nutrition, 53,* 1631S–1638S.

Lasco, R. A., Curry, R. H., Dickson, V. J., Powers, J., Menes, S., & Merritt, R. K. (1989). Participation rates, weight loss, and blood pressure changes among obese women in a nutrition-excercise program. *Public Health Reports, 104,* 640–646.

Lewis, C. E., Raczynski, J. M., Heath, G. W., Levinson, R., Hilyer, J., James, C., & Cutter, G. R. (1993). Promoting physical activity in low-income African-American communities: The Parr project. *Ethnicity and Disease, 3,* 106–118.

Lipson, L. G., Kato-Palmer, S., Boggs, W. L., Moore, D., & Pope, A. (1988, September). Diabetes in black Americans. *Diabetes Forecast, 41,* 34–38.

Lipton, R. B., Liao, Y., Cao, G., Cooper, R. S., & McGee, D. (1993). Determinants of incident non-insulin-dependent diabetes mellitus among blacks and whites in a national sample. *American Journal of Epidemiology, 138,* 826–839.

Long, S. D., O'Brien, K., MacDonald, K. G. J., Leggett-Frazier, N., Swanson, M. S., Pories, W. J., & Caro, J. F. (1994). Weight loss in severely obese subjects prevents the progression of impaired glucose tolerance to type II diabetes: A longitudinal interventional study. *Diabetes Care, 17,* 372–375.

Maillet, N. A., Melkus, G., & Spollet, G. (1996). Using focus groups to characterize the health beliefs of black women with non-insulin-dependent diabetes. *The Diabetes Educator, 22,* 39–46.

Manson, J. E., & Spelsberg, A. (1994). Primary prevention of non-insulin-dependent diabetes mellitus. *American Journal of Preventive Medicine, 10,* 172–184.

Maynard, T. (1991). Exercise: Part I. Physiological response to exercise in diabetes mellitus. *The Diabetes Educator, 17,* 196–204.

Mazzuca, S. A., Moorman, N. H., Wheeler, M. L., Norton, J. A., Fineberg, N. S., Vinicor, F., Cohen, S. J., & Clark, C. M. (1986). The Diabetes Education Study: A controlled trial of the effects of diabetes patient education. *Diabetes Care, 9,* 1–10.

McNabb, W. L. (1994). Delivering more effective weight-loss programs for black American women. *Diabetes Spectrum, 7,* 332–333.

McNabb, W. L. (1997). Adherence in diabetes: Can we define it and can we measure it? *Diabetes Care, 20,* 215–218.

McNabb, W. L., Cook, S., & Quinn, M. T. (1996). A church-based health and wellness survey in urban African-American churches. *Diabetes, 45*(Suppl. 2), 337A.

McNabb, W. L., Quinn, M. T., & Rosing, L. S. (1993). Weight loss program for inner-city black women with non-insulin-dependent diabetes mellitus: PATHWAYS. *Journal of the American Dietetic Association, 93,* 75–77.

Melnyk, M. G., & Weinstein, E. (1994). Preventing obesity in black women by targeting adolescents: A literature review. *Journal of the American Dietetic Association, 94,* 536–540.

Metzger, B. E. (1991). Summary and recommendations of the third international workshop—Conference on gestational diabetes mellitus. *Diabetes, 40*(Suppl. 2), 197–201.

MMWR—Mortality and Morbidity Weekly Report. (1994). Prevalence of selected risk factors for chronic disease by education level in racial/ethnic populations—United States, 1991–1992. *MMWR—Morbidity and Mortality Weekly Report, 43,* 894–899.

Most, R. S., & Sinnock, P. (1983). The epidemiology of lower extremity amputations in diabetic individuals. *Diabetes Care, 6,* 87–91.

Murphy, F. G., & Elders, M. J. (1992). Diabetes and the black community. In R. L. Brathwaite & S. E. Taylor (Eds.), *Health issues in the black community* (pp. 121–131). San Francisco: Jossey-Bass.

Myers, H. F., Kagawa-Singer, M., Kumanyika, S. K., Lex, B. W., & Markides, K. S. (1995). Panel III: Behavioral risk factors related to chronic diseases in ethnic minorities. *Health Psychology, 14,* 613–621.

Nathan, D. M. (1993). Complications of diabetes mellitus. *New England Journal of Medicine, 328,* 1675–1684.

National Center for Health Statistics. (1981). Plan and operation of the Second National Health and Nutrition Examination Survey. *NCHS Vital and Health Statistics, Series 1*(15), 1–144.

National Center for Health Statistics. (1985). The National Health Interview Survey design 1973–1984 and procedures 1975–1983. *NCHS Vital and Health Statistics, Series 1*(18), 1–127.

National Diabetes Data Group. (1979). Classification and diagnosis of diabetes mellitus and other categories of glucose intolerance. *Diabetes, 28,* 1039–1057.

Neighbors, H. W. (1986). Ambulatory medical care among adult black Americans: The hospital emergency room. *Journal of the National Medical Association, 78,* 275–282.

Neil, A., Hawkins, M., Potok, M., Thorogood, M., Cohen, D., & Mann, J. (1993). A prospective population-based study of microalbuminuria as a predictor of mortality in NIDDM. *Diabetes Care, 16,* 996–1003.

Nolan, J. J., Ludvik, B., Beerdsen, P., Joyce, M., & Olefsky, J. (1994). Improvement in glucose tolerance and insulin resistance in obese subjects treated with troglitazone. *The New England Journal of Medicine, 331,* 1188–1193.

Pan, X., Li, G., & Hu, Y. (1995). Effect of dietary and/or exercise intervention on incidence of diabetes in 530 subjects with impaired glucose tolerance from 1986–1992. *Chinese Journal of Internal Medicine, 34,* 108–112.

Phelps, R. L., Sakol, P., Metzger, B. E., Jampol, L. M., & Freinkel, N. (1986). Changes in retinopathy during pregnancy. *Archives of Opthalmology, 104,* 1806–1810.

Pleas, J. (1988). Long-term effects of a lifestyle-change obesity treatment program with minorities. *Journal of the National Medical Association, 7,* 747–752.

Pugh, J. A., Medina, R. A., Cornell, J. C., & Basu, S. (1995). NIDDM is the major cause of diabetic end-stage renal disease. More evidence from a tri-ethnic community. *Diabetes, 44,* 1375–1380.

Rabb, M. F., Gagliano, D. A., & Sweeny, H. E. (1990). Diabetic retinopathy in blacks. *Diabetes Care, 13,* 1202–1206.

Raman, M., & Nesto, R. W. (1996). Heart disease in diabetes mellitus. *Endocrinology and Metabolism Clinics of North America, 25,* 425–438.

Rewers, M., & Hamman, R. F. (1995). Risk factors for non-insulin-dependent diabetes. In National Diabetes Data Group (Ed.), *Diabetes in America* (pp. 179–220). Washington, DC: National Institutes of Health, National Institute of Diabetes and Digestive and Kidney Diseases.

Rosenn, B., Miodovnik, M., Kranias, G., Khoury, J., Combs, C. A., Mimouni, F., Siddiqi, T. A., & Lipman, M. J. (1992). Progression of diabetic retinopathy in pregnancy: Association with hypertension. *American Journal of Obstetrics and Gynecology, 166,* 1214–1218.

Ruderman, N., Apelian, A. Z., & Schneider, S. H. (1990). Exercise in therapy and prevention of type II diabetes: Implications for blacks. *Diabetes Care, 13,* 1163–1168.

Sacks, D. B., & McDonald, J. M. (1996). The pathogenesis of type II diabetes mellitus. A polygenic disease. *American Journal of Clinical Pathology, 105,* 149–156.

Saris, W. H. M. (1995). Exercise with or without dietary restriction and obesity treatment. *International Journal of Obesity, 19*(Suppl. 4), S113–S116.

Selby, J. V., & Zhang, D. (1995). Risk factors for lower extremity amputation in persons with diabetes. *Diabetes Care, 18,* 509–516.

Siegel, P. Z., Brackbill, R. M., & Heath, G. W. (1995). The epidemiology of walking for exercise: Implications for promoting activity among sedentary groups. *American Journal of Public Health, 85,* 706–710.

Sørensen, T. I. A. (1995). Socio-economic aspects of obesity: Causes or effects? *International Journal of Obesity, 19*(Suppl. 6), S6–S8.

Soukup, J. T., Maynard, T. S., & Kovaleski, J. E. (1994). Resistance training guidelines for individuals with diabetes mellitus. *The Diabetes Educator, 20,* 129–137.

Stevens, V. J., Corrigan, S. A., Obarzanek, E., Bernauer, E., Cook, N. R., Hebert, P., Mattfeldt-Beman, M., Oberman, A., Sugars, C., Dalcin, A. T., & Whelton, P. K. (1993). Weight loss intervention in phase I of the trials of hypertension prevention. *Archives of Internal Medicine, 153,* 849–858.

Stolar, M. W. (1995). Clinical management of NIDDM patient. *Diabetes Care, 18,* 701–707.

Stunkard, A. J., & Sørensen, T. I. A. (1993). Obesity and socioeconomic status—A complex relation. *New England Journal of Medicine, 329,* 1036–1037.

Svec, F., Rivera, M., & Huth, M. (1990). Correlation of waist to hips ratio to the prevalence of diabetes and hypertension in black females. *Journal of the National Medical Association, 82,* 257–261.

Taylor, W. C., Beech, B. M., & Cummings, S. S. (1997). Increasing physical activity levels among youth: A public health challenge. In D. K. Wilson, J. R. Rodrigue, & W. C. Taylor (Eds.), *Health promoting and health compromising behaviors among minority adolescents* (pp. 107–128). Washington, DC: American Psychological Association.

Tinker, L. F. (1994). Diabetes mellitus—A priority health care issue for women. *Journal of the American Dietetic Association, 94,* 976–985.

Tremblay, A., & Buemann, B. (1995). Exercise-training, macronutrient balance and body weight control. *International Journal of Obesity, 19,* 79–86.

Tremblay, A., Després, J. P., Maheaux, J., Pouliot, M. C., Nadeau, A., Moorjani, S., Lupien, P. J., & Bouchard, C. (1991). Normalization of the metabolic profile in obese women by exercise and a low fat diet. *Medicine and Science in Sports and Exercise, 23,* 1326–1331.

Tull, E. S., & Roseman, J. M. (1995). Diabetes in African Americans. In National Diabetes Data Group (Ed.), *Diabetes in America* (pp. 613–630). Washington, DC: National Institutes of Health, National Institute of Diabetes and Digestive and Kidney Diseases.

U.S. Department of Health and Human Services. (1991). *Healthy people 2000: Executive summary.* Washington, DC: U.S. Government Printing Office.

Veal, Y. S. (1996). African Americans and diabetes: Reasons, rationale, and research. *Journal of the National Medical Association, 88,* 203–204.

Washburn, R. A., Kline, G., Lackland, D. T., & Wheeler, F. C. (1992). Leisure time physical activity: Are there black/white differences? *Preventive Medicine, 21,* 127–135.

Wassertheil-Smoller, S., Langford, H. G., Blaufox, M. D., Hawkins, M., Oberman, A., Levine, B., Cameron, M., Babcock, C., Pressel, S., Caggiula, A., Cutter, G., Curb, D., & Wing, R. (1985). Effective dietary intervention in hypertensives: Sodium restriction and weight reduction. *Journal of the American Dietetic Association, 85,* 423–430.

West, K. M., & Kalbfleisch, J. M. (1971). Influence of nutritional factors on prevalence of diabetes. *Diabetes, 20,* 99–108.

Wilson, D. K., Nicholson, S. C., & Krishnamoorthy, J. S. (1997). The role of diet in minority adolescent health promotion. In D. K. Wilson, J. R. Rodrigue, & W. C. Taylor (Eds.), *Health promoting and health compromising behaviors among minority adolescents* (pp. 129–152). Washington, DC: American Psychological Association.

Wing, R. R., & Anglin, K. (1996). Effectiveness of a behavioral weight control program for blacks and whites with NIDDM. *Diabetes Care, 19,* 409–413.

Wing, R. R., Epstein, L. H., Paternostro-Bayles, M., Kriska, A., Nowalk, M. P., & Gooding, W. (1991). Exercise in a behavioural weight control programme for obese patients with type 2 (non-insulin-dependent) diabetes. *Diabetologia, 31,* 902–909.

Wing, R. R., Nowalk, M. P., Marcus, M. D., Koeske, R., & Finegold, D. (1986). Subclinical eating disorders and glycemic control in adolescents with type I diabetes. *Diabetes Care, 9,* 162–167.

Wingard, D. L., & Barrett-Connor, E. (1995). Heart disease and diabetes. In National Diabetes Data Group (Ed.), *Diabetes in America* (pp. 429–448). Washington, DC: National Institutes of Health, National Institute of Diabetes and Digestive and Kidney Diseases.

World Health Organization. (1980). *Report of the expert committee on diabetes.* Geneva, Switzerland: Author.

World Health Organization. (1985). *Diabetes mellitus: Report of a study group.* Geneva, Switzerland: Author.

Wynder, E. L. (1996). Lifestyle medicine for the nineties. *Preventive Medicine, 25,* 82–83.

Ziemer, D. C., Goldschmid, M. G., Musey, V. C., Domin, W. S., Thule, P. M., Gallina, D. L., & Phillips, L. S. (1996). Diabetes in urban African Americans. III. Management of type II diabetes in a municipal hospital setting. *The American Journal of Medicine, 101,* 25–33.

WOMEN'S HEALTH: RESEARCH ON GENDER, BEHAVIOR, AND POLICY, 3(3&4), 301–314
Copyright © 1997, Lawrence Erlbaum Associates, Inc.

Health-Care-Related Attitudes and Utilization Among African American Women

Lonnie R. Snowden

*School of Social Welfare and Center for Mental Health Services Research
University of California at Berkeley*

Anne Libby

*Center for Mental Health Services Research
University of California at Berkeley*

Kathleen Thomas

Levy Economic Institute

This study examined attitudes of African American women toward medical care and health insurance. Data were analyzed from the National Medical Expenditure Survey, a large household survey conducted by the Agency for Health Care Policy and Research and focusing on insurance and health care utilization. The responses of African American women tended neither to downplay the importance of receiving health care as essential to health maintenance and recovery from illness, nor to minimize health insurance as a worthwhile investment. When African American women did give responses discounting the importance of health care, the attitude difference failed to account for race-related differences in utilization. There was no evidence in the data to indicate that attitudes lead African American women to neglect seeking medical care or acquiring health insurance, and solutions to the problem of medical care underutilization must be sought elsewhere.

Key words: African American women, health services, health care attitudes, insurance attitudes

---

Correspondence concerning this article should be addressed to Lonnie R. Snowden, SW 01, School of Social Welfare, University of California at Berkeley, 120 Haviland Hall #7400, Berkeley, CA 94720–7400.

The health status of African American women is a matter of legitimate and great concern. The death rate of African American women from 15 leading causes of death is greater than that of whites for all causes except two, and their death rate from heart disease, diabetes, liver and kidney disease, and AIDS is greater not only than that of whites, but also than that of African American men (O'Hare, Pollard, Mann, & Kent, 1991).

Contributing to the adverse health status of African American women is the relatively low rate at which they receive outpatient medical care. During pregnancy, African American women are less likely than their white counterparts to have early prenatal care, and the racial difference in prenatal care persists at every level of education (National Center for Health Statistics, 1996).

The gender-specific racial difference found in prenatal care mirrors general racial disparities found in aggregate outpatient treatment seeking. In 1991, the U.S. Department of Health and Human Services (DHHS) published a comprehensive literature review of findings from national studies conducted between 1964 and 1987. The DHHS report indicated that African American women and men reported fewer contacts with physicians than whites. Relying on data from a large household study, the National Health Interview Survey, the DHHS report further noted that African Americans were more than 20% less likely than whites to have seen a physician within the preceding year (DHHS, 1991). Similarly, in a 1986 national telephone survey of 10,130 persons living in the contiguous United States, Blendon, Aiken, Freeman, and Corey (1989) found African Americans to have poorer access to physician care than whites; African Americans had made significantly fewer ambulatory visits to physicians within the preceding year. Lewin-Epstein (1991) offered further evidence of race disparity in the utilization of health care in her findings from the 1987 Urban Family Life Survey of 3,016 parents living in poverty in Chicago.

Several factors appear to account for racial differences in outpatient medical care utilization. Although exceptions have been reported, most studies have found that socioeconomic differences alone fail to account for racial differences in health care utilization. For example, in the study by Blendon et al. (1989), African Americans were found to make fewer outpatient visits to physicians even after controlling for individual income as well as health status, age, and sex. Mutchler and Burr (1992) affirmed Blendon et al.'s findings in their 1984 panel survey of health in adults over 55 years of age. Mutchler and Burr considered not only personal income but also education, net financial worth, and private insurance coverage as indicators of socioeconomic status. Although education and net financial worth emerged as robust predictors of health status, race remained significant.

On the other hand Crawford, McGraw, Smith, McKinlay, and Pierson (1994) conducted a telephone interview of a random sample of 1,222 African Americans and 808 whites living in Boston, and found few racial differences either in coronary-related help seeking or in medical care. Socioeconomic status in the study was measured by aggregating three indicators: (a) high school completion, (b) problems with "paying for basics," and (c) whether or not respondents were employed at the time of assessment. Even in this study, selected racial differences were found: For example, African Americans proved less likely than whites to be referred to specialists.

In a comprehensive overview of the health of African American women, Leigh (1995) noted that travel time and the lack of minority clinicians also may obstruct African American women's use of health services. Leigh went on to point out that even after overcoming problems with access, African American women may enter health care environments that fail to affirm their importance as participants. The cultural competencies of providers, according to Leigh, can play a key role in alleviating this barrier by creating a mutually respectful atmosphere that accepts the "mores, language, and styles of the help seeking behaviors" of African American women (Leigh, 1995, p. 129).

In an effort to explain racial differences in receiving health care, many investigators and social critics have focused on differences in the financing of health care and in the structure of the health care delivery system. Figuring prominently in this analysis is the role of health insurance, and the fact that African Americans are less likely than whites to be insured (Short, Cornelius, & Goldstone, 1990). In 1987, African Americans were 1.67 times more likely than whites to have neither public nor private health insurance coverage, and the difference was attributable only in part to unemployment and poverty. In light of the considerable impact of insurance coverage on utilization, the lack of insurance coverage represents a notable barrier. Other characteristics of the health care delivery system believed to impede African American utilization include travel time to providers and a lack of minority clinicians (Leigh, 1995).

A smaller literature considers health-care-related attitudes and beliefs of African Americans and their possible impact on patterns of service utilization. To explain racial differences in symptom reporting rates, Strogatz (1990) hypothesized that African Americans might have less confidence than whites in the effectiveness of health care and might regard discussing their symptoms with a health care provider as futile. Strogatz's hypothesis is consistent with findings reported by Raczynski et al. (1994), indicating that African Americans who went untreated for diagnosed hypertension had relatively little confidence in the effectiveness of antihypertensive medication.

Other researchers have focused on racial differences in satisfaction with health care providers and with the health care system, and have discovered greater dissatisfaction among blacks. Blendon et al. (1989) reported that African Americans were less satisfied than whites with the physician–patient relationship they had experienced and were less satisfied also with their care overall. Similarly, Temkin-Greener (1986) found that African Americans rated their physicians as less humane than did whites and again were less satisfied overall with their care.

The research conducted thus far suggests that racial differences do exist in health-care-related attitudes and beliefs and that such differences might help to explain racial differences in utilization. The literature, however, is small, includes few community-based studies, and neglects fundamental attitudes toward health care and insurance coverage.

One kind of health-care-related attitude leads to minimizing the importance of health care to recovery from illness and to downplaying the value of insurance. Attitudes such as these reduce the likelihood of getting health insurance and of seeking outpatient medical care and would, if linked to race, help to explain race-related disparities. A history of racial discrimination and rejection from health care systems and a community tradition of self-reliance (Neighbors, Elliott, & Gant, 1990) might lead African Americans to hold such dismissive attitudes.

This study compared African American women with other race–gender groups on attitudes toward the importance of having health insurance and toward the necessity for health care in maintaining good health. The data came from a large community service that serves as a primary resource for understanding health care finance and utilization in the United States, the National Medical Expenditures Survey (NMES). The study enables us to understand for the first time the extent to which differential attitudes of African American women play a role in understanding differences in utilization.

METHOD

The data used for the study are from the 1987 NMES, specifically from the NMES Household Survey. The NMES is a project of the Center for General Health Services Intramural Research of the Agency for Health Care Policy and Research (AHCPR). The 1987 NMES was preceded by the 1977 National Medical Care Expenditure Survey and was guided by the need of the AHCPR Intramural Research Program to gather information on the health status of Americans and on health care financing and utilization.

The NMES Household Survey drew a national probability sample of the civilian, noninstitutionalized population. The sample was supplemented to achieve a greater representation than would otherwise have resulted of population groups of special interest, including the poor, the elderly, and African Americans and Hispanics. A parallel survey, the Survey of American Indian and Alaskan Natives, was conducted of American Indian and Alaska Native populations.

The Household Survey proceeded from a stratified, multistage area probability design with a total sample of roughly 36,400 adults and children (children were excluded from the analysis here). Families participating in the Household Survey were interviewed four times over 16 months, beginning in early 1987. Baseline data were collected on household composition, employment, and insurance, and the information was updated at each interview. Additional information was collected on illness, use of health services, and expenditures. The data were collected through face-to-face questioning, from calendars and diaries of medical events, and from a self-administered questionnaire, including attitude items used in this study, that was mailed and completed by respondents between Round 1 and Round 2 interviews. Data obtained from the Household Survey were partially corroborated and supplemented with data from the Medical Providers Survey and the Health Insurance Plan Survey that assessed, respectively, respondents' health care utilization as reported by their providers, and health insurance benefits as documented by their insurers.

Table 1 provides demographic information on the sample. Largely, the sample was comprised of married adults living above the poverty line with some form of health insurance.

The NMES reports attitudes toward health care and health insurance on a 5-point Likert scale, ranging from 1 (*strongly disagree*) to 5 (*strongly agree*) with a series of statements. For purposes of analysis, respondents were grouped dichotomously and considered to agree with an attitude statement if they indicated *agree somewhat* or *strongly agree*. Their responses were contrasted with those of persons who were *neutral,* or who indicated *disagree somewhat* or *strongly disagree*. This recoding was performed in order to avoid problems associated with the use of highly skewed response distributions. Table 2 presents items used in the survey.

The independent variables describe personal and regional characteristics. A set of dummy variables denote race and gender pairs, using African American women as the reference category. This highlights the differences between African American women and others. Other sets of dummy variables denote age, using younger adults 18 to 39 years old as the reference group; insurance coverage, using the uninsured as the reference group; region of residence, using the South as the reference group; and size of area of residence, using living in a small standard metropolitan statistical area as the reference group. In addition, variables were included to measure employment, education, language, marital status, and poverty status.

The analysis used logistic regression to model the effect of race and gender on each attitude statement, controlling for characteristics confounded with race and gender that might lead respondents to agree with the statement. This regression was weighted to adjust for survey design effects and nonresponse, and additional analyses were performed to adjust for the complex nature of the survey design.

A second round of logistic regression was conducted focusing on whether differences in attributes might translate into differences in outpatient medical care. The model included independent variables previously described, as well as attitude variables on which African American women rated health care or insurance as less important than other groups. The dependent variables were three indicators of health care where racial differences have been reported in the literature: (a) occurrence of any outpatient medical visit (physician or nonphysician, office or hospital), (b) occurrence of an outpatient physician visit, and (c) occurrence of a hospital emergency room visit. The purpose of the analysis was to determine whether attitude differences uncovered in the first phase of analysis might explain differences in utilization.

TABLE 1
National Medical Expenditures Survey: Sample Description

Participant Characteristics	%[a]
Race/Gender	
African American women	6.0
African American men	4.4
White women	43.4
White men	37.0
Other women	4.9
Other men	4.4
Age	
18–39	49.0
40–64	34.4
65 and over	17.7
Insurance (may have more than one)	
Any private	80.4
Public[b]	33.0
Uninsured	18.7
Region	
Northeast	20.4
Midwest	25.5
South	34.8
West	19.5
Urbanicity	
Large SMSA	26.1
Small SMSA	48.5
Not in SMSA	25.4
Employment	
Employed all year	53.8
Other	46.2
Income	
Lives in poverty	11.3
Other	88.7
Marital status	
Currently married	60.1
Other	39.9

Note. SMSA = Standard Metropolitan Statistical Area: Population center and adjacent communities as defined by Federal Office of Management and Budget.
[a]N = 18,432; children under 18 were excluded. [b]CHAMPUS, Medicare, Medicaid, other public assistance.

TABLE 2

Household Survey Adult Self-Administered Questionnaire

1. I'm healthy enough that I really don't need health insurance.

Disagree Strongly	Disagree Somewhat	Uncertain	Agree Somewhat	Agree Strongly
1	2	3	4	5

2. Health insurance is not worth the money it costs.

Disagree Strongly	Disagree Somewhat	Uncertain	Agree Somewhat	Agree Strongly
1	2	3	4	5

3. I'm more likely to take risks than the average person.

Disagree Strongly	Disagree Somewhat	Uncertain	Agree Somewhat	Agree Strongly
1	2	3	4	5

4. I can overcome most illness without help from a medically trained professional.

Disagree Strongly	Disagree Somewhat	Uncertain	Agree Somewhat	Agree Strongly
1	2	3	4	5

5. Home remedies are often better than drugs prescribed by a doctor.

Disagree Strongly	Disagree Somewhat	Uncertain	Agree Somewhat	Agree Strongly
1	2	3	4	5

6. If I get sick, it is my own behavior which determines how soon I get well again.

Disagree Strongly	Disagree Somewhat	Uncertain	Agree Somewhat	Agree Strongly
1	2	3	4	5

7. I understand my health better than most doctors do.

Disagree Strongly	Disagree Somewhat	Uncertain	Agree Somewhat	Agree Strongly
1	2	3	4	5

8. Luck plays a big part in determining how soon I will recover from an illness.

Disagree Strongly	Disagree Somewhat	Uncertain	Agree Somewhat	Agree Strongly
1	2	3	4	5

9. I think you can get medical care easily even if you don't have money with you.

Disagree Strongly	Disagree Somewhat	Uncertain	Agree Somewhat	Agree Strongly
1	2	3	4	5

RESULTS

Preliminary Bivariate Analysis

Table 3 presents results from bivariate analysis of the association between categories of gender and race, on the one hand, and, on the other hand, a belief in the importance of having insurance and obtaining health care for health-related problems. The table indicates the percentage of respondents expressing agreement or strong agreement with each item.

Inspection of Table 3 reveals that African American women were for the most part less likely than others to believe that recovery from illness is determined by personal behavior, χ^2 (1, $N = 18{,}432$) = 134.57, $p < .01$, that one knows one's health better than a doctor, χ^2 (1, $N = 18{,}432$) = 23.23, $p < .01$, and that one can get well without a doctor, χ^2 (1, $N = 18{,}432$) = 88.34, $p < .01$. On these items African American women, more than other groups, expressed attitudes affirming the importance of medical care and physicians. On the other hand, African American women were more likely than white women or men to believe that luck plays a big part in recovery from illness, χ^2 (1, $N = 18{,}432$) = 74.51, $p < .01$, indicating a fatalism that might undermine efforts at help seeking. African American women were less likely than men of either race, but more likely than white women, to describe

TABLE 3
Health Care Attitudes and Visits of Black and White Adult Men and Women

	Black Women	Black Men	White Women	White Men
Percentage agreeing with attitude				
Necessity for health care				
Own behavior determines recovery	50.81	50.32	63.74	63.62
Knows own health better than doctor	37.52	39.68	42.59	39.50
Luck is big part of recovery	12.69	16.06	8.29	9.93
Can get well without doctor	39.04	42.07	49.75	56.87
Home remedies better than prescriptions	32.80	28.12	26.41	23.83
Take more than average risks	20.26	27.49	16.92	33.00
Necessity for insurance				
Too healthy to need insurance	9.48	13.18	8.24	12.42
Health insurance not worth cost	19.96	21.24	18.36	22.81
Medical care available without cost	22.00	20.53	20.72	24.23
Percentage making visit in past year				
Any outpatient	74.09	54.19	83.84	69.15
Physician outpatient	65.71	45.92	79.29	62.69
Emergency room	21.32	17.62	14.87	14.25

Note. $N = 18{,}432$. *Agree Strongly* and *Agree Somewhat* responses were collapsed to yield 0% in overall agreement. Percentages are weighted. Differences between race/gender groups: All chi-square $p < .01$.

themselves as more than average risk-takers, χ^2 (1, N = 18,432) = 610.44, p < .01. Race- and poverty-related challenges may compel African American women more than white women to accept risk. Perhaps for cultural reasons discussed later, African American women were the most likely among the four groups to agree that, for medicinal purposes, home remedies are better than prescriptions, χ^2 (1, N = 18,432) = 50.84, p < .01.

In the realm of attitudes toward health insurance African American women proved less likely than white or black men, and only slightly less likely than white women, to believe that they were too healthy to need health insurance, χ^2 (1, N = 18,432) = 208.74, p < .01, or that insurance was not worth the cost, χ^2 (1, N = 18,432) = 51.82, p = .01. Thus, African American women relative to other groups saw little reason to go without insurance. On the other hand, African American women were less likely than only white men to believe that medical care was easily available without cash χ^2 (1, N = 18,432) = 31.70, p < .01. The difference may reflect African American womens' need for resourcefulness in finding sources of health care despite limited financial resources.

Multivariate Analysis of Attitudes: Logistic Regression

Results from multivariate analysis (see Table 4) altered somewhat the pattern of results. Controlling for sociodemographic and other differences between the groups, African American women continued to be less likely than white women (β = .44, SE = .07, odds ratio [OR] = 1.55, p < .01) or white men (β = .38, SE = .07, OR = 1.46, p < .01) to believe that personal behavior determines recovery from illness, and that one can recover from illness without the intervention of physicians (for white women, β = .44, SE = .07, OR = 1.55, p > .01; for white men, β = .65, SE = .07, OR = 1.92, p < .01). In these respects, African American women again were more likely than whites of either gender to affirm the importance of physicians and health care. African American women proved less likely than only white women to indicate that individuals know their own state of health better than physicians (β = .23, SE = .07, OR = 1.26, p < .01). The greater caution displayed by African American women than other groups did not remain statistically signifi-cant in controlled analysis. African American women continued to be less likely than black or white men, but were no different from white women, in identifying themselves as risk-takers (for black men, β = .41, SE = .11, OR = 1.51, p < .01); for white men, β = .84, SE = .09, OR = 2.33, p < .01). The apparently greater adventurousness of African American than white women suggested in bivariate analysis was attributable to socioeconomic, marital, or other differences con-founded with race. African American women were once again more likely than white women (β = −.31, SE = −.11, OR = .73, p <.01), but not more likely than white men, to indicate that luck plays a big part in recovery from illness. As in

TABLE 4
Race and Gender Associated With Health Care Attitudes: Multivariate Analysis

Attitudes	Black Men vs. Black Women			White Women vs. Black Women			White Men vs. Black Women		
	β	SE	OR	β	SE	OR	β	SE	OR
Necessity for medical care									
1. Own behavior determines recovery	-.08	.09	.92	.44**	.07	1.55	.38**	.07	1.46
2. Knows own health better than doctors	-.07	.10	1.07	.23*	.07	1.26	.07	.07	1.07
3. Luck is big part of recovery	.35**	.14	1.43	-.31**	.11	.73	-.04	.11	.96
4. Can get well without doctors	.01	.10	1.01	.44*	.07	1.55	.65**	.07	1.92
5. Home remedies better than prescriptions	-.24*	.10	.79	-.25**	.07	.78	-.41**	.08	.67
6. More than average risk taker	.41**	.11	1.51	-.04	.09	.96	.84**	.09	2.33
Necessity for insurance									
7. Too healthy to need insurance	.33*	.15	1.39	.03	.12	1.03	.50**	.17	1.65
8. Health insurance not worth cost	-.05	.12	1.06	-.01	.00	1.00	.25**	.09	1.28
9. Medical care available without cost	-.06	.12	.95	-.11	.08	.89	.09	.08	1.09

$*p < .05.$ $**p < .01.$

bivariate analysis, African women were more likely than any of the other race- and gender-defined groups to describe home remedies as superior to prescription medications for medicinal purposes (for black men, $\beta = -.24$, $SE = .25$, OR = .79, $p < .01$; for white women, $\beta = -.25$, $SE = .07$, OR = .78, $p < .01$; for white men, $\beta = -.41$, $SE = .08$, OR = .67, $p < .01$).

With respect to attitudes toward health insurance, African American women again tended not to deny its importance. They proved no different from white women, but less likely than African American men ($\beta = .33$, $SE = .15$, OR = 1.39, $p < .01$) or white men ($\beta = .50$, $SE = .17$, OR = 1.65, $p < .01$) to describe themselves as too healthy to need insurance, and less likely than white men to indicate that health insurance was not worth the cost ($\beta = .25$, $SE = .09$, OR = 1.28, $p < .01$). There was no difference between African American women and other groups in likelihood of agreement that health care was available without money.

Logistic Regression: Racial Differences in Utilization Controlling for Selected Attitudes

In controlled analysis, African American women endorsed two attitudes that might impede health care utilization relative to whites: a greater belief than white women that luck plays a big part in recovery from illness, and a greater faith than members of other race- and gender-defined groups in the superior effectiveness of home remedies. Items indicating these attitudes were included in models used previously to examine race-related differences in health care utilization. As a starting point, uncontrolled differences were calculated and are presented in Table 3. In percentage of persons receiving any outpatient care, χ^2 (1, $N = 18,432$) = 799.96, $p < .01$, physician outpatient care, χ^2 (1, $N = 18,432$) = 900.53, $p < .01$, and emergency room care, χ^2 (1, $N = 18,432$) = 50.59, $p < .01$, the race- and gender-defined groups differed from each other significantly. However, underrepresentation of African American women in outpatient care and overrepresentation in emergency care occurred only in relation to white women.

Logistic regression was used to examine whether differences in health care utilization would disappear when attitudes deterring use were controlled. Results from this analysis are presented in Table 5. These results mirrored earlier findings, despite taking into account the differential belief of African American women that home remedies are better than prescriptions and that luck plays a significant role in recovery. African American women remained less likely than white women to have made an outpatient visit ($\beta = .42$, $SE = .08$, OR = 1.52, $p < .01$), or a physician visit ($\beta = .50$, $SE = .08$, OR = 1.65, $p < .01$), and more likely to have visited the emergency room ($\beta = -.26$, $SE = .09$, OR = .77, $p < .01$). Taking account of the attitudes held by African American women that might deter health care utilization failed to explain racial differences in health services use.

TABLE 5
Racial Differences in Health Care Controlling for Health-Care Related Attitudes:
White Versus African American Women

	Home Remedies			Luck		
Health Services	β	SE	OR	β	SE	OR
Any outpatient	.42**	.08	1.52	.44**	.09	1.55
Physician outpatient	.50**	.08	1.65	.52**	.08	1.65
Emergency room	−.26**	.09	.77	−.26**	.09	.77

Note. Dummy coding: white women = 1, African American women = 0.
*$p < .05$. **$p < .01$.

DISCUSSION

Overall, African American women were rarely more likely than African American men or than white women and men to demonstrate a lack of faith in health care providers and procedures. In controlled analysis, African American women proved more likely than white women to believe that luck plays a big part in recovering from illness, and more likely than all other race- and gender-defined groups to believe that folk remedies are better than medicines. Otherwise, African Americans were no more likely than the other race and gender groups to downplay the importance of health care and insurance, and often were less likely to do so than other groups.

An interesting exception to the general pattern of findings was the response of African American women indicating that home remedies are superior to prescription medications. African American women, as noted previously, were more likely than others to affirm this belief.

This finding can be readily explained in light of a tradition in African American communities of indigenous practitioners and beliefs. Anthropologists have noted distinctive concepts of illness and explanatory principles (Snow, 1993). For example, in an ethnomedical study, Camino (1989) investigated "nerves" in an African American community in the southern United States. In describing nerves Camino indicated:

> First, nerves constitutes an illness syndrome that carries substantial symptomatology.
> Second, complaints of nerves serve as idioms of distress that communicate powerful messages about physiological, social, and emotional distress of its sufferers. Third, the frequency of nerves is documented to be higher among women than men, no matter what the cultural group. (p. 204)

Folk remedies have evolved along with indigenous disorders. Folk preparations combine substances believed on principle and from years of experience to have significant medicinal properties. Recipes and preferred methods of administration are handed down in a tradition born principally by women. It is reasonable to believe, then, that a belief in home remedies reflects the impact of African American history and culture on beliefs about healing practices among African American women today.

When African American women did discount the importance of health care, the attitude difference failed to explain racial disparities in health services utilization. Neither a greater faith in home remedies nor a greater belief in the role of luck explained race-related differences in health care. After attitude differences were taken into account, African American women continued to receive less outpatient medical treatment than white women, and to use more emergency care.

African American women were not more likely than other groups to downplay the importance of health insurance. They failed to reject insurance as necessary for them because they were too healthy or because it was not worth its cost. They declined more than other groups to endorse an expectation that medical care could be obtained without money. Rather, it was white men who most often endorsed these views.

The NMES was carefully designed and rigorously conducted, but suffers from important limitations for understanding the problem at hand. Like all household surveys, it omits from consideration persons who are homeless and, like the census, underrepresents hard-to-reach groups like the inner-city poor. As African American women are overrepresented among both groups, the inclusion of the homeless and inner-city poor might alter the results that were obtained in this study. Nevertheless, the NMES permits the most rigorous assessment of differential race- and gender-related attitudes toward health care and health insurance currently available.

Results from the study give no cause to believe that low levels of outpatient medical care and low rates of insurance coverage among African American women can be attributed to a belief that medical care and insurance are unnecessary. The data indicate equal if not greater receptivity among African American women as among other race- and gender-defined groups. The possibility remains that attitudes unlike those measured in this study—dissatisfaction and mistrust of a more specific character, arising perhaps from particular, aversive health-care-related experiences—might serve as psychological barriers to treatment seeking.

These findings suggest that attempts to increase access to health care and wider insurance coverage will not be thwarted by medical care and insurance-related beliefs among African American women. It appears that a proper emphasis for intervention ought to primarily remain structural, promoting programs and financing mechanisms that overcome barriers to access.

REFERENCES

Blendon, R. J., Aiken, L. H., Freeman, H. E., & Corey, C. R. (1989). Access to medical care for black and white Americans. *Journal of American Medical Association, 261,* 278–281.

Camino, L. A. (1989). Nerves, worriation and black women: A community study in the American south. In D. L. Davis & S. M. Low (Eds.), *Gender, health and illness: The case of nerves*. New York: Hemisphere.

Crawford, S. L., McGraw, S. A., Smith, K. W., McKinlay, J. B., & Pierson, J. E. (1994). Do blacks and whites differ in the use of health care for symptoms of coronary heart disease? *American Journal of Public Health, 84,* 957–964.

Leigh, W. A. (1995). The health of African American women. In D. C. Adams (Ed.), *Health issues for women of color: A cultural diversity perspective* (pp. 295–314). Thousand Oaks, CA: Sage.

Lewin-Epstein, N. (1991). Determinants of regular source of health care in black, Mexican, Puerto Rican, and non-Hispanic white populations. *Medical Care, 29,* 543–557.

Mutchler, J. E., & Burr, J. A. (1992). Racial differences in health and health care service utilization in later life: The effect of socioeconomic status. *Journal of Health and Social Behavior, 32,* 342–356.

National Center for Health Statistics. (1996). *Health, United States, 1995.* Hyattsville, MD: Public Health Service.

Neighbors, H. W., Elliott, K. A., & Gant, K. M. (1990). Self help and Black Americans: A strategy for empowerment. In T. J. Powell (Ed.), *Working with self-help* (pp. 189–217). Silver Spring, MD: National Association of Social Workers Press.

O'Hare, W. P., Pollard, K. M., Mann, T. L., & Kent, M. M. (1991). African Americans in the 1990s. *Population Bulletin, 46,* 1–40.

Raczynski, J. M., Taylor, H., Cutter, G., Hardin, M., Rappaport, N., & Oberman, A. (1994). Diagnoses, symptoms, and attribution of symptoms among black and white inpatients admitted for coronary heart disease. *American Journal of Public Health, 84,* 951–956.

Short, P. F., Cornelius, L. J., & Goldstone, D. E. (1990). Health insurance of minorities in the United States. *Journal of Health Care for the Poor and Underserved, 1,* 9–24.

Snow, F. L. (1993). *Walkin' over medicine*. Boulder, CO: Westview.

Strogatz, D. S. (1990). Use of medical care for chest pain: Differences between blacks and whites. *American Journal of Public Health, 80,* 290–294.

Temkin-Greener, H. (1986). Medicaid families under managed care: Anticipated behavior. *Medical Care, 24,* 721–732.

U.S. Department of Health and Human Services. (1991). *Health status of minorities and low-income groups* (3rd ed.). Washington, DC: Bureau of Health Professions, Division of Disadvantage Assistance.

WOMEN'S HEALTH: RESEARCH ON GENDER, BEHAVIOR, AND POLICY, 3(3&4), 315–348

Intimate Violence and Black Women's Health

Nancy Felipe Russo and Jean E. Denious

Department of Psychology
Arizona State University

Gwendolyn P. Keita

American Psychological Association, Washington, DC

Mary P. Koss

University of Arizona

After reviewing the literature on health effects of intimate violence, we report secondary analyses of responses of 439 black women who participated in the Commonwealth Fund's national survey on women's health. Lower income women were more likely to experience partner violence but not childhood abuse; and income group was related to self-esteem, depressive symptoms, and perceived health status. Childhood physical and sexual abuse and partner violence were intercorrelated; both abuse history and partner violence were related to greater risk for depressive symptoms, lower life satisfaction, and lower perceived health care quality. Partner violence was also related to lower self-esteem and perceived health status. Sexually abused women had more difficulties in interpersonal relationships, including lower perceived health care quality even with self-esteem and depressive symptoms controlled. Implications for prevention, training, and future research as well as methodological issues in research on violence against black women are discussed.

Key words: black, battering, abuse, health care perceptions, mental health, sexual abuse, victimization

Correspondence concerning this article should be addressed to Nancy Felipe Russo, Department of Psychology, Box 871104, Arizona State University, Tempe, AZ 85287–1104. E-mail: nancy.russo@asu.edu.

Intimate violence—including physical and sexual abuse in childhood, rape, and battering—is a pervasive threat to black[1] women's health. Although statistics depend on definitions used, it is clear that such violence is a daily fact of life for women in the United States, regardless of race or ethnicity (for reviews of this literature, see Crowell & Burgess, 1996; Gelles & Straus, 1989; Koss et al., 1994; Tjaden & Thoenees, 1997).

We focus here on health-related effects of physical and sexual abuse in childhood, particularly sexual abuse, and violence from a male partner. These are the prevalent forms of intimate violence in black women's lives. Black women report high rates of childhood sexual abuse, rates similar to their white peers. For example, in one of the most thorough studies, based on a community sample, 40% of black women reported coercive contact of a sexual nature before age 18 (Wyatt, 1985). Black women also report high rates of partner violence. Estimates from the Second National Family Violence Survey suggest that at a rate of 174 per 1,000 couples, 603,000 black women experience partner violence each year, and 244,000 experience severe violence. Rates of severe partner violence for low income black women are particularly high—144 per 1,000, compared to 58 per 1,000 for higher income black women (Hamptom & Gelles, 1994). The finding that partner violence experienced by poor women is more likely to be severe and life threatening than that experienced by higher income women has been reported by others as well (Belle, 1990; Neff, Holamon, & Schluter, 1995; Steele et al., 1982).

Socioeconomic status has wide-ranging health effects that go beyond those associated with increased risk for intimate violence (Adler, 1997; Adler et al., 1994; Adler & Coriell, 1997). Lack of economic resources is associated with a variety of stressful living conditions and events that take their own toll on physical and mental health and on well-being, as well as reflect and cause disruption in interpersonal relationships (Belle, 1990; Lyons, Salganicoff, & Rowland, 1996; Russo & Zierk, 1992). In addition, access to economic resources can mitigate the effects of physical and sexual abuse and violence against women to some extent (e.g., Burgess & Holmstrom, 1978). For one thing, economic resources can be translated into other coping resources, including increased access to quality health care. The combination of higher exposure to stressful life events and lack of access to resources to deal with those events is expected to have direct health-related effects as well as to compound the negative effects of intimate violence. In other words, stress and powerlessness are expected to be a deadly combination (Guttentag, Salasin, & Belle, 1980).

---

[1]We use the term *black* because it is the label most often used in previous research, and it best represents the current state of knowledge. We interpret it as a broad social category that encompasses African Americans (an American ethnic group) as well as recent immigrants from Africa, the Caribbean, and other countries who classify themselves as Black. It should be recognized that it is a crude classification at best, and its power to predict important social and health behaviors is itself a comment on the power of racism in American society.

After providing a more general summary of the literature on the health effects of intimate violence, we present data on the health-related effects of childhood abuse and partner violence for lower income as compared to higher income black women. We conclude with a discussion of the implications of the research findings for health prevention and intervention programs, training, and research, with special consideration of methodological issues in survey research on violence against black women.

HEALTH-RELATED EFFECTS OF VIOLENCE

Over the past decade, a substantial literature has begun to document links between intimate violence and a host of negative health outcomes that extend beyond immediate effects of death and direct injury (Abbott, Johnson, Koziol-McLain, & Lowenstein, 1995; Astin, Lawrence, Ogland-Hand, & Foy, 1993; Beitchman et al., 1992; Cascardi, Langhinrichsen, & Vivian, 1992; Goodman, Koss, & Russo, 1993a, 1993b; Koss et al., 1994; Koss & Heslet, 1992; Mitchell & Hobson, 1983; Shepard & Pence, 1988). This research, which is sometimes based on samples that include black women, suggests that intimate violence has a wide-ranging and long-lasting impact on physical and mental health, with profound implications for our health care system (Abbott et al., 1995; Bergman, Brismal, & Nordin, 1992; Eby, Campbell, Sullivan, & Davidson, 1995; Ingram, Corning, & Schmidt, 1996; Laws & Golding, 1996). In fact, severely victimized women not only report more distress and lower well-being, they make physician visits twice as frequently and incur outpatient costs that are more than double those of nonvictims. Further, this higher health care usage does not predate victimization (Koss, Koss, & Woodruff, 1991).

Childhood Abuse and Rape

Although survivors of intimate violence are remarkably healthy considering their experiences, potential long-term consequences of childhood sexual abuse include anxiety, anger, eating disorders, depression, dissociation, impairment of self-concept, interpersonal problems, obsessions and compulsions, posttraumatic stress responses, revictimization, self-mutilation, precocious sexual experience (including earlier onset of masturbation and sexual intercourse), sexual problems, somatization, substance abuse, and suicidality (Beitchman et al., 1992; Briere & Runtz, 1987; Brown & Anderson, 1991; Golding, 1996; Golding & Taylor, 1996; Green, 1993; Laws & Golding, 1996; Moeller, Bachman, & Moeller, 1993; Neumann, Houskamp, Pollock, & Briere, 1996; Stein, Golding, Siegel, Burnam, & Sorenson, 1988; Wilsnack, Klassen, & Vogeltanz, 1994). Higher rates of childhood sexual abuse are found for women seeking treatment for substance abuse problems as compared to women who are in the general population or who are receiving other mental health services (Gutierres, Russo, & Urbanski, 1994; Miller & Downs, 1993; Miller, Downs, Gondoli, & Keil, 1987; Rohsenow, Corbett, & Devine, 1988). This finding persists even after demographic characteristics and parental alcohol problems are controlled (Miller, Downs, & Testa, 1993).

In addition to direct physical and psychological trauma, the experience of victimization can affect health through indirect pathways. Childhood sexual abuse in particular has been linked to high-risk sexual behaviors, which are of particular concern for black women given the spread of AIDS in ethnic minority communities (Cunningham, Stiffman, & Dore, 1994; Koss, Heise, & Russo, 1994). Abused girls have been found to be less likely to use birth control at first intercourse, and more likely to have sex earlier, use alcohol and drugs, be battered, and have traded sex for food, money, shelter, or drugs (Berenson, San Miguel, & Wilkinson, 1992; Boyer & Fine, 1992; Finkelhor, 1987; Meyerding, 1977; Nagy, Adcock, & Nagy, 1994; Nelson, Higginson, & Grant-Worley, 1995; Paone, Chavkin, Willets, Friedman, & Des Jarlais, 1992). Sexual abuse has been linked to teenage pregnancy and motherhood (Wyatt, Guthrie, & Notgrass, 1992) and negligent parenting (Ethier, Lacharite, & Coutoure, 1995). Women experiencing sexual assault in childhood have been found to be three times more likely to become pregnant before age 18 as compared to nonvictimized women (Zierler et al., 1991).

In one of the few studies examining the effects of child sexual abuse among African American women, Wyatt (1990) found African American and Caucasian American women in a community sample to be similar with regard to initial response and short-term effects of the experience, with both groups showing lasting sexual problems. Although this study did not examine a wide range of outcomes, the similarity in responses on the measures used suggests that the range of negative health outcomes of child sexual abuse identified in the literature at large indeed apply to black women.

Research has also identified multiple physical and mental health consequences of rape, and these too can be long-lasting. More than one third of rape victims report sustaining serious physical injury, and more than one half seek medical treatment (Beebe, 1991). In addition to sexually transmitted diseases, gastrointestinal disorders, headaches, and psychogenic seizures, rape victims are more likely to experience chronic pelvic pain and premenstrual symptoms (Golding, 1996; Golding & Taylor, 1996; Koss & Heslet, 1992). Common presenting symptoms of rape victims include anxiety, depression, substance abuse, chronic headaches, abdominal pain, joint and muscle pain, disorders of sleeping and eating, sexual dysfunction, and recurrent vaginal infections (Randall, 1990, 1991). Psychological sequelae of rape include higher risk for major depressive episode, substance abuse disorders, and anxiety disorder (see Crowell & Burgess, 1996; Goodman, Koss, & Russo, 1993a, 1993b). Research comparing the impact of sexual assault on black women and on white women suggests that the physical, psychological, and sexual effects of the experience are similar for both groups (Wyatt, 1992).

Partner Violence

Battering by an intimate partner is the single most common cause of injuries to women requiring medical intervention, accounting for more injuries than automobile accidents, muggings, and rapes combined. An estimated 1 million women each year seek medical assistance for injuries resulting from such battering (see Goodman, Koss, & Russo, 1993a). Injuries vary widely, and can include black eyes, cuts, bruises, concussions, bites, burns, bone fractures, damage to hearing and vision, and knife and bullet wounds (Browne, 1992; Goodman, Koss, & Russo, 1993a). Other health consequences include anxiety, depression, substance abuse, complaints of sexual dysfunction, recurrent vaginal infections, sleeping and eating disorders, and suicide attempts. Victims of violence are also more likely to suffer pain in the form of chronic headaches as well as abdominal, joint, and muscle pain (see Koss & Heslet, 1992; Stark & Flitcraft, 1996).

The idea that psychological and behavioral outcomes are consequences and not simply correlates of battering was explored in a study that compared medical profiles of battered and nonbattered women before and after their first reported episode of injury. Battered and nonbattered women were similar on all factors before their first reported episode of injury except for alcohol abuse, which was found to be higher among battered women. After the first episode, however, battered women were more likely to experience psychosocial problems, alcohol abuse, drug abuse, psychiatric disorders, and suicide attempts, and to use mental health services (Stark & Flitcraft, 1996). These findings suggest a causal role of battering in battered women's higher risk for depression, drug abuse, and other psychological problems.

In 1985, the Surgeon General of the United States recommended that routine prenatal assessments include evaluation for battering (Koop, 1985). There is good reason for this recommendation: Women are at highest risk for battering in their childbearing years, and pregnant women are more likely to experience violence than other women (Gelles, 1988). Women who have a history of being beaten by their husbands are three times more likely to sustain injuries during pregnancy than women who are not battered (Helton, McFarlane, & Anderson, 1987; Hillard, 1985; Stark & Flitcraft, 1988). Women battered during pregnancy are more likely to have miscarriages and stillbirths and deliver low-birthweight infants (Bullock & McFarlane, 1989; Helton et al., 1987; McFarlane, 1989; McFarlane, Parker, Soeken, & Bullock, 1992; Satin, Hemsell, Stone, Theriot, & Wendel, 1991). Other negative health outcomes include rupture of membranes; placental separation; premature labor; antepartum hemorrhage; fetal fractures; and rupture of the uterus, liver, or spleen (Saltzman, 1990). Likelihood of violence during pregnancy is higher for women who are of lower socioeconomic status, have a history of depression, use alcohol and drugs, receive less emotional support from others for the pregnancy, and are involved with partners who use illicit drugs (Amaro, Fried, Cabral, &

Zuckerman, 1990). When other factors are controlled, ethnicity does not appear to predict level of violence during pregnancy. History is the most important predictor: Women with histories of partner violence are three times more likely to sustain injuries during pregnancy than other women (Helton et al., 1987; Hillard, 1985; Stark & Flitcraft, 1988). Although we were not able to explore these effects in our study, no review of the partner violence literature would be complete without mentioning them.

Partner violence is associated with high-risk health behaviors, including risky sexual behavior (Koss et al., 1991; Nelson et al., 1995). Rates of violence are higher among women whose pregnancies are unwanted or mistimed (i.e., unintended pregnancies), regardless of race. One study found that among women who reported that their husband or partner had "physically hurt" them during the 12 months before delivery, 70% also reported their pregnancy was unintended. Among black women, the proportion of women experiencing physical violence during an unwanted pregnancy, 11.7%, was twice that of black women who experienced violence during an intended pregnancy, 6.3% (Gazmararian et al , 1995).

Unfortunately, there is little research on the health-related effects of partner violence that specifically focuses on black women (Coley & Beckett, 1988; Koss et al., 1994; Uzell & Peebles-Wilkins, 1989). In general, the knowledge base documenting links between violence and health outcomes has significant limitations, for research reports often either fail to mention the ethnicity of the women in the sample, include only white women, or include women of diverse ethnic groups, but not in proportions sufficient for between-group comparisons (Asbury, 1987). Although some scholars have explored causes of partner violence against black women on the part of black men (Gooden, 1980; Liebow, 1967; Ucko, 1994), examining the consequences of such violence to black women, including physical and mental health outcomes, has been neglected (Barbee, 1992).

Hamptom and Gelles (1994) conducted one of the few studies specifically examining the links between partner violence toward black women and health outcomes. Their findings are based on a nationally representative sample of 797 black households including adults 18 years of age or older who were either (a) married or cohabiting, (b) divorced or separated within the past 2 years, or (c) single parents with a child under 18 years of age living in the household. Partner violence was measured by the Conflict Tactics Scales (Straus, 1979). These scales present a list of behaviors, or "conflict tactics," that can then be used to construct a dichotomous index indicating whether any violence has occurred at least once in the past 12 months. The items can also be classified into minor or severe violence categories. Respondents are asked to indicate how often they used each tactic when they had a disagreement or were angry with a family member, both in the past year and over the course of the relationship. Items classified as minor violence include: threw something at other; pushed, grabbed, or shoved other; and slapped or spanked other. Severe violence items include: kicked, bit, hit with fist; hit or tried to hit other with an object; beat up the other; choked other; threatened with knife or gun; used knife or fired a gun.

Partner violence, particularly severe forms of such violence, was found to be highly associated with reported stress and somatic and depressive symptoms. For example, 41.4% of women experiencing severe violence reported having headaches or pain in the head fairly or very often, compared to 14.9% of women who reported no violence. Such women were also more than three times more likely to be bothered by feelings of sadness or depression than women experiencing no violence (31.0% vs. 9.6%), and eight times more likely to have suicidal thoughts (3.4% vs. 0.4%, respectively). This research underscores the importance of documenting the links between partner violence and health outcomes in black women (Hamptom & Gelles, 1994).

Research is needed on factors that mediate and moderate the links between partner violence and negative health outcomes. One potential factor is the patient–physician relationship. Given that less severe forms of violence escalate into more severe and deadly ones, insensitivity on the part of health care providers and lack of responsiveness in the health care system may compound health risks. Thus, lack of access or discomfort with their health care provider may put black women, particularly lower income black women, at even higher risk for negative health outcomes from experiencing escalating partner violence.

Medical Response to Victims of Intimate Violence

Medical response to victims of intimate violence has been severely criticized (Koss et al., 1994). Rape victims are often unidentified, and evidence suggests that large proportions of those who are identified do not receive full emergency care (e.g., pregnancy and HIV testing) recommended by rape protocols (National Victims Center, 1992). The medical records of battered women have been found to contain pseudopsychiatric labels (e.g., "multiple symptomatology with psychosomatic overlay"; Stark & Flitcraft, 1996, p. 13). Battered women are also often unidentified, their problems labeled as "psychiatric." This may be why battered women are more likely to be given tranquilizers as compared to nonbattered women. One study of women receiving emergency care found 24% of the battered women received prescriptions for minor tranquilizers or pain medication, compared to 9% of nonbattered women (Stark & Flitcraft). The fact that battered women are more likely to report a variety of painful symptoms may also contribute to a higher rate of prescriptions for pain medication.

The fact that sexually abused women have difficulties forming mutual, equitable relationships (Wyatt, 1990; Wyatt et al., 1992) may have implications for their doctor–patient relationships. Both intimate partner and doctor–patient relationships share the need for trust, communication, and mutual respect, and these may be particularly difficult to establish if the physician does not have knowledge of and sensitivity to the issues involved. Intimate violence in general, and childhood sexual abuse and partner violence in particular, may also interfere with a woman's ability to establish trusting relationships with others by increasing risk for depression. Depression-related cognitions may lower perceived quality of the doctor–patient relationship. However, we believe the impact of sexual abuse on self-concept and interpersonal relationships involves changes in interpersonal responses that go beyond effects associated with depression. Although we were not able to test our hypotheses directly and fully by analyzing this preexisting data set, we present evidence congruent with our hypotheses and point to the need for future research.

In summary, a wide range of physical and mental health correlates and consequences of intimate violence have been reported, but few studies have specifically focused on the lives of black women. In the next section we present data related to several questions: Does intimate violence in the lives of black women lower their self-esteem and increase their risk for depression? Does such violence affect perceived health status and life satisfaction? Is intimate violence associated with increased use of unhealthy substances? Does childhood abuse undermine ability to establish good intimate relationships? Do black women who feel they experienced physical and sexual abuse in childhood or partner violence report poorer relationships with and lower perceived quality on the part of their doctors, and is this perception related to the mental health effects of those experiences? Does having a lower income affect the links between various forms of intimate violence and its outcomes?

To answer such questions, we conducted secondary analyses on data obtained from The Commonwealth Fund's 1993 survey, *The Health of American Women* (Bell et al., 1994; Falik & Collins, 1996). After examining the data set to determine which items had sufficient base rates to be usable for testing specific hypotheses, we developed a set of predictions related to our questions of interest, listed earlier. These are detailed in the results section.

A survey research approach on the topic of violence has several limitations, including underreporting bias and underrepresentation of poor women. Further, using an existing data set means that research questions are limited to those that can be tested by the available data. Nonetheless, we believe that the data set's combination of information about history of physical and sexual abuse, partner violence, and perceptions of and experience with the health care system make it worthwhile for analyzing black women's experiences in more depth, as long as limitations are recognized and caution is taken in generalizing the results.

In reviewing the data set, we decided against making cross-race comparisons with white women. First, we believe black women's health is important to study in its own right, and given space limitations we prefer to devote our efforts to exploring the effects of economic diversity among black women. We believe stereotyping black culture as "violent" can lead to a misattribution of effects of poverty to culture in interpreting research on the effects of violence on black women's health. As Landrine and Klonoff (in press) so eloquently observed, "poverty, low education, and unemployment ... never have been aspects ... of anyone's culture." Documenting how the relations of violence to health-related variables differ for lower income black women as compared to higher income black women is a step toward building the knowledge base needed to understand the diverse factors affecting black women's health.

Further, we do not consider it appropriate to make cross-race comparisons unless relevant social and economic variables can be controlled (Lockhart & White, 1989). For example, the literature on partner violence suggests that in addition to income, rates of violence vary with age, social class, husband's employment status, and degree of social-network embeddedness, as indicated by number of years in the neighborhood, number of children, and number of nonnuclear family members in the household (Cazenave & Straus, 1979; Hamptom & Gelles, 1994). In particular, black women who have unemployed husbands have particularly high rates of severe partner violence—189 per 1,000 (Hamptom & Gelles, 1994). All of these variables are correlated with race, and making cross-race comparisons without controlling for them could produce a very misleading picture. Because we are working with a preexisting data set, we are not able to control all of the relevant variables needed to make meaningful cross-race comparisons. For example, black women who have one child have substantially lower rates of violence than women with two or more children (65 per 1,000 vs. 146 per 1,000, respectively; Hamptom & Gelles, 1994). Unfortunately, the survey used to gather the data here only asked whether the woman had any children, not how many children she had. Finally, examining cross-race effects in a meaningful way would require a sample size large enough to detect interaction effects with sufficient power. Given the low base rates of many behaviors of interest, the relevant cell sizes were simply not large enough to conduct those analyses.

In this study, the relatively low number of women in the sample who report experiencing violence means that small but nonetheless important effects of violence may not achieve statistical significance. Thus, nonsignificant findings may simply reflect the fact that the study has insufficient power to detect small or medium-sized effects (Cohen, 1992). Given this context, the fact that we obtained so many significant findings in support of our hypotheses is testimony to the profound impact of the experience of intimate violence on black women's lives.

METHOD

The results reported here are based on secondary analyses of *The Health of American Women,* a random household survey of more than 2,500 women and 1,000 men 18 years or older residing in the continental United States. Telephone interviews were conducted in February and March 1993 by Louis Harris and

Associates, asking respondents about their experience with physical and sexual abuse, rape and partner violence, health care, self-esteem, depressive symptoms, and demographic characteristics, among other variables (Bell et al., 1994; Falik & Collins, 1996). All interviews were conducted by female interviewers. More detailed information about the survey and summaries of overall findings can be found in Falik and Collins (1996). Analyses that specifically focus on violence in the larger sample are found in Plichta (1996). The analyses reported here differ in that they focus on black women, control for income, and explore different questions. Analyses of black women's use of preventative health services can be found in Lillie-Blanton, Bowie, and Ro (1996). They do not consider issues related to intimate violence, however.

Sample

The subsample drawn for this study consisted of the 439 women who identified themselves as either Black (60.1%) or African American (39.9%). The median age range was 35 to 39 years old; 40.1% were married ($n = 176$), 18.9% were separated or divorced ($n = 89$), and 41% were single ($n = 174$). Almost half of the sample were mothers, with 43.3% ($n = 190$) reporting having at least one child. The median family income range was $25,000 to $35,000; 22.6% ($n = 99$) of the sample reported incomes of $7,500 or less, and over 36.5% ($n = 160$) of the sample reported incomes that fell below $15,000. The majority of participants reported having at least completed high school (81.5%, $n = 358$), and half of the sample reported educational experience beyond high school (50.1%).

Not all of the analyses could be performed on the entire sample ($N = 439$), as not everyone was asked every question. Only women who had a regular doctor were asked about their perceptions of their doctor–patient relationship ($n = 370$), and only women who were married or living "as a couple" with someone were asked about partner violence ($n = 195$).

Variables

Demographic variables included age, income, marital status, and parental status. Lower income was defined as having a total family income of less than $15,000 or receiving some form of financial assistance, or both. Responses to the question "In the last year, when you have asked him to, has your partner ever refused to wear a condom, or not?" provided a crude measure of potential exposure to unprotected sexual intercourse. Responses to the question "Have you ever had an abortion, or not?", were considered a crude indicator of unintended pregnancy. Replies to both questions were coded as 1 (*yes*) and 0 (*no*).

The sample size was too small to analyze relations between violence and use of specific drugs in a meaningful way. Therefore, a measure of "unhealthy substance use," defined by use of tobacco, alcohol, or other mind-altering drugs, was created. If a woman reported ever using tobacco (86 women), alcohol (165 women), marijuana (73 women), tranquilizers (28 women), or "crack or cocaine, heroin, speed, or downers" (4 women), the variable was coded as 1. If she did not use any of these substances, her answer was coded as 0.

Health care variables.   Respondents were asked a series of questions about their health care experience, including if they ever declined to get care because they felt too embarrassed, anxious, or scared; and whether their doctor ever talked down to them, told them a medical condition they had was "all in their head," or made comments or gestures of an inappropriate sexual nature. Each of these questions was treated as a single-item measure with answers coded as 1 (*yes*) and 0 (*no*). Base rates for specific health conditions (e.g., hypertension, cancer) were so low that they could not be profitably used to test specific physical health-related hypotheses.

Women who indicated they had a regular doctor, or "one place in particular" they usually went to when sick or wanting advice about health, were asked several questions to assess the perceived quality of their doctor–patient relationship. Perceived quality was measured by seven items that asked the women "How would you rate your regular doctor on the job he or she is doing to ..." in seven areas: provide you with good health care overall, be knowledgeable and competent to treat your illnesses, really care about you and your health, personally spend enough time with you, make a special effort to get you to explain your symptoms completely, answer your questions honestly and completely, and make sure you understand what you've been told about your medical problems or medications. Rating for these items ranged from 1 (*poor*) to 4 (*excellent*), with higher scores indicating a more positive perception of doctor–patient relationship quality. The possible range of scores for this variable was 7 to 28 ($\alpha = .93$).

Violence variables.   Violence variables included one-item measures of childhood physical and sexual abuse. Participants were asked if, when they were growing up, they ever felt physically abused or sexually abused. Answers for each question were coded 1 (*yes*) or 0 (*no*). These questions were used to construct variables to represent experience of childhood physical and sexual abuse. In addition to the one-item measures, the variable "abuse level" was constructed. It ranged from 0 to 2, 0 indicating no reported history of physical or sexual abuse, 1 indicating a report of either physical or sexual abuse, and 2 indicating a report of both types of abuse. The construction of this variable assumes that experiencing both types of abuse is a more intense abuse experience than experiencing one type of abuse, all other things being equal. Unfortunately, the number of times abuse was experienced and the nature of the abuse acts is unknown. There is no reason to believe, however, that individuals who experience both physical and sexual abuse in childhood experience that abuse less frequently or in less severe form than individuals who experience only one type of abuse. Thus, it was decided to examine the properties of this variable before condensing it to a simpler "abused" versus "nonabused" dichotomy, even though the dichotomous variable would provide larger sample sizes for testing interaction effects. We want to emphasize that the childhood abuse variables are based on reported feelings that participants were abused while growing up, not reports of specific behaviors that an outside observer might define as abusive.

Eleven items that were based on a modified version of the Conflict Tactics Scale (Straus, 1979) were used to construct variables related to partner violence. Only women who were married or had lived as a couple were given these items. They were asked whether, in the past 12 months, their partner had ever: (a) insulted or swore at you; (b) stomped out of the room or house or yard; (c) threatened to hit you or throw something at you; (d) threw or smashed or hit or kicked something; (e) threw something at you; (f) pushed, grabbed, shoved, or slapped you; (g) kicked, bit, or hit you with a fist or some other object; (h) beat you up; (i) choked you; (j) threatened you with a knife or gun; or (k) used a knife on you. As only four women reported being physically forced to have sexual relations with their partners, the effects of partner rape were not analyzed separately. This item was added to those from the Conflict Tactics Scale as Item 12. For each of these items, the women answered 1 (*yes*) or 0 (*no*). When summed, higher scores indicate that more kinds of partner abuse were experienced. In keeping with the violence literature (Straus, 1979), type of violence was defined as having three levels: 1 (*no violence*), not answering yes to Items 3 through 12; 2 (*minor violence*), answering yes only to Items 3 through 6; and 3 (*severely violent*), answering yes to Items 7 through 12. Most analyses reported here focus on effects by type of violence.

A continuous variable representing physical violence was also created, which summed only items that involved physical or physically threatening behavior (Items 3–12); the possible range of scores for this variable was 0 to 9 ($\alpha = .78$). Level of severe violence was assessed by summing Items 7 though 12. Having a violent partner, coded 1 (*yes*) or 0 (*no*), was defined as answering yes at least once on Items 3 through 12.

Mental health variables.   These included measures of self-esteem, indicators of depression (depressive symptoms, suicide attempts, tranquilizer use, and doctor's diagnosis of anxiety or depression), perceived health status, and life satisfaction. Self-esteem was measured by the 10-item Rosenberg Self-Esteem Scale, which includes statements such as "I am a person of worth," "I am inclined to feel that I am a failure," "I have a number of good qualities," and "I sometimes think I am 'no good' at all" (see Rosenberg, 1965). Respondents indicate whether they strongly disagree, disagree, agree, or strongly agree with each statement. The items were coded 1 to 4, with negatively worded statements reverse-coded so that a higher score indicates higher self-esteem. The range for this variable is 10 to 40 ($\alpha = .74$).

Depressive symptoms were measured by six items taken from the Center for Epidemiological Studies Depression Scale (Radloff, 1977). Respondents were asked to indicate how often (never, rarely, some of the time, most of the time) they had experienced symptoms in the past week: "I felt depressed," "My sleep was restless," "I enjoyed life," "I had crying spells," "I felt sad," and "I felt that people disliked me." Coding was similar to self-esteem, resulting in a possible range of scores of 0 to 18 on the measure, with higher scores reflecting greater depressive symptomatology ($\alpha = .76$).

Additional depression-related single-item measures, coded 1 (*yes*) and 0 (*no*), were constructed from questions that asked whether or not the woman had actually thought about ending her life in the past year, whether in the past 5 years a doctor had told her that she had anxiety or depression, and whether she had taken tranquilizers in the past 12 months.

Perceived health status was assessed by a one-item measure that asked the women to indicate whether their health was "excellent, very good, good, fair, or poor." Responses were coded from 1 (*poor*) to 5 (*excellent*). Life satisfaction was assessed by a one-item measure that asked women to indicate how satisfied they were with their life: "very satisfied, somewhat satisfied, not very satisfied, or not satisfied at all." Responses were coded from 1 (*not satisfied at all*) to 4 (*very satisfied*).

Procedure

In addition to descriptive statistics for the sample reported earlier in this article, two sets of analyses were performed, the first focusing on perceptions of childhood abuse and the second on partner violence. Multivariate analyses of variance (MANOVAs) were used when possible to examine effects on the major continuous variables of interest. Although we were testing specific directional predictions, significance levels reported are two-tailed unless otherwise specified.

Set I: Childhood physical and sexual abuse.   Most of the analyses that focused on relations between feeling physically or sexually abused and mental health variables were based on the entire sample of 439 black women drawn from the larger study. Differences in these relations by income group (lower income vs. higher income) were also explored. In addition, this section includes analyses that examine the relation of sexual abuse to partner violence, based on the subsample of 195 partnered women, as described earlier.

Although some health care questions were asked of the entire sample, analyses that focus on the relations of childhood abuse and perceived quality of the doctor–patient relationship are primarily based on the experiences of the 370 women in the sample who reported a source of regular health care. Only women who answered yes when asked if there was "one place in particular you usually go when you are sick or want advice about your health, or isn't there?" were asked about their relationships with their health care provider.

Set II: Partner violence.   Because only women who were married or living with someone as a couple were asked about partner violence, the analyses of the effects of partner violence are based on responses from 195 partnered women who were asked those questions. Analyses parallel to those in Set I were conducted, but with a focus on the relation of partner violence to mental health and health care variables.

RESULTS

Set I: Childhood Physical and Sexual Abuse

Childhood physical and sexual abuse were highly correlated. A total of 76 women reported experiencing physical or sexual abuse in childhood, with 46 reporting feeling either physically or sexually abused, and 30 reporting both types of abuse. Of the 55 women who felt they experienced sexual abuse, 55% also reported physical abuse, and of the 51 women reporting physical abuse, 59% reported experiencing sexual abuse, $r(438) = .51$, $p = .000$. Income was not correlated with abuse level, $r(403) = -.06$, $p = .28$; or type of abuse, $r(403) = -.07$, $p = .16$ for physical abuse, and $r(403) = -.03$, $p = .59$ for sexual abuse.

Other correlational analyses not reported here found that being currently married, having a higher income, and more years of education were all significantly related to each other. However, abuse level was not related to being currently married, annual income, level of education, or having a particular place to go for health care. It should be noted that the sample size is sufficient to detect medium-, but not small-sized effects of these variables with this statistic, but in all cases, $r^2 < .004$, which would represent an extremely small effect in any case (Cohen, 1992).

To simplify the presentation of the results, the hypotheses and major findings for each set of analyses are presented first, followed by a description of the analyses used to test them.

Mental Health Variables

Hypothesis 1.   The experience of childhood abuse is positively associated with indicators of anxiety and depression, and negatively associated with self-esteem, life satisfaction, and perceived health status, particularly for lower income women.

Findings.   A 3 × 2 MANOVA was conducted to examine the relation of abuse level (no abuse, physical or sexual abuse, physical and sexual abuse) and income group (lower income, higher income) to self-esteem, depressive symptoms, perceived health status, and life satisfaction variables. The overall Fs for abuse level and income group were significant. Table 1 contains the means, standard deviations, univariate F, and η^2 results for these analyses for the direct effects of abuse level

TABLE 1
Weighted Means and Standard Deviations for Self-Esteem, Depressive Symptoms, Perceived Health Status, and Life Satisfaction by Abuse and Income Group

Variable	M	SD	F Value[a] η^2	Group Comparison[b]
Self-esteem				
No abuse	36.10	4.22	2.01	1 < 2, 3
Physical or sexual abuse	35.71	4.27	.02	
Both	33.85	6.32		
Lower income	34.01	5.04	23.45**	1 < 2
Higher income	37.15	3.45	.06	
Depressive symptoms				
No abuse	5.02	3.49	6.91**	1 < 2, 3
Physical or sexual abuse	6.71	3.57	.04	
Both	7.33	3.85		
Lower income	6.59	3.78	12.10**	1 > 2
Higher income	4.56	3.24	.03	
Perceived health status				
No abuse	3.38	1.07	.03	
Physical or sexual abuse	3.41	.95	.000	
Both	3.22	1.34		
Lower income	3.06	1.15	9.90*	1 < 2
Higher income	3.58	.97	.03	
Life satisfaction				
No abuse	4.31	.90	5.68*	1 > 3
Physical or sexual abuse	3.98	1.01	.03	
Both	3.78	1.15		
Lower income	4.12	.87	.83	
Higher income	4.31	1.05	.002	

Note. Table gives weighted means from 3 × 2 (Abuse Level × Income Group) multivariate analysis of variance.
[a]Pillais multivariate $F = 2.62$, $p = .008$ for abuse level; for income group, $F = 7.09$, $p = .000$. [b]Group 1 = no abuse, $N = 306$; Group 2 = physical or sexual abuse, $N = 41$; Group 3 = both, $N = 27$. Lower income, $N = 149$; Higher income, $N = 225$. Degrees of freedom for univariate Fs = 2, 368 and 1, 368 for abuse level and income group, respectively. Group comparisons made with Tukey's honestly significant difference test.
*$p < .005$. **$p < .001$.

and income group. The interactive effects of abuse level and income group were not significant ($F = .45$, $p = .89$), so only the results for direct effects are presented.

Partial correlations controlling for income group were computed to examine the relation of abuse experience to the dichotomous indicators of anxiety and depression. Even with income group controlled, abuse level was significantly and positively related to the depression variables, including suicidal thoughts in the past year, $r(412) = .15$, $p = .002$; a woman being told she had anxiety or depression by a doctor in the past 5 years, $r(412) = .20$, $p = .000$; and having taken tranquilizers in the past 12 months, $r(411) = .11$, $p = .023$.

In summary, abuse level was significantly associated with lowered life satisfaction and increased risk for depressive symptomatology and indicators of anxiety and depression, but was not significantly related to self-esteem or perceived health status. These findings held regardless of income group, as the interactive effects of abuse and income group were not significant for any of the variables.

Hypothesis 2.   Income will have direct and interactive effects on self-esteem, depression, life satisfaction, and perceived health status.

Findings.   Income had a direct effect on self-esteem, depression, and perceived health status, but not on life satisfaction (see Table 1).

Comparisons of the means in Table 1 revealed that in most cases, the significant results reflected the difference between nonabused women and the other two groups. Thus, the dichotomous variable "abuse history" (abused vs. nonabused) was created and used for the remaining analyses. Table 2 contains the *n*s, percentages, chi-square results, and partial correlations (with income controlled) for the analyses of the single-item depression-related measures.

Hypothesis 3.   The relation of abuse to depression goes beyond its relation to self-esteem.

TABLE 2
Percentages and Partial Correlations of Responses to Dichotomous Variables by Abuse History

Variable	No Abuse (%)	Abuse (%)	χ^2	r^a
Suicidal thoughts[b]	3.0	9.2	6.07*	.12*
Doctor said had anxiety or depression[c]	8.6	25.0	16.78***	.20***
Used tranquilizers in past year[d]	4.7	13.3	7.95*	.14**

Note. $df = 1$ for all comparisons.
[a]Partial correlation controlling for income group. [b]$n = 438$. [c]$n = 438$. [d]$n = 436$.
*$p < .05$. **$p < .01$. ***$p < .001$.

Findings.   Self-esteem and depression, $r(391) = -.60$, $p = .000$, are highly correlated, raising the question of whether abuse history makes an independent contribution to depression beyond its relation to self-esteem. A multiple regression analysis on depressive symptoms that entered self-esteem before abuse history determined that abuse predicted depressive symptoms independently from its relation to self-esteem, F-change $(2, 387) = 13.82$, $p = .0002$. Thus, when self-esteem was controlled, abuse history continued to make an independent contribution to the variance of depressive symptoms. In fact, the partial correlation of abuse history and depressive symptoms only changed from .19 to .18 when both self-esteem and income group were controlled.

Health Behaviors

Hypothesis 4.   Women with an abuse history, particularly lower income women, will be more likely to use unhealthy substances.

Findings.   Abuse history was correlated with unhealthy substance use, $r(408) = .15$, $p = .003$, with income group controlled. Seventy-three percent of women who reported a history of abuse also reported using unhealthy substances, compared to 54% of women who did not report such a history, $\chi^2(1, N = 434) = 9.70$, $p = .002$. Abuse history was also correlated with number of substances used, $r(408) = .17$, $p = .001$, controlling for income. The proportion of women reporting childhood abuse who used two or more unhealthy substances was nearly double that of women who did not report such abuse (36% vs. 19%).

Income group was negatively correlated with using unhealthy substances, $r(412) = -.12$, $p = .008$. In other words, lower income women were less likely to use unhealthy substances: 49% of lower income women reported no use of the substances listed, compared with 37% of upper income women. Closer examination of the items suggests this finding is due to the fact that lower income black women are substantially less likely to use alcohol than are higher income black women, 28% versus 46%, respectively, $\chi^2(1, N = 412) = 14.08$, $p = .000$.

Sexual Abuse and Interpersonal Relationships

Hypothesis 5.   Sexually abused women, particularly those with lower incomes, are more likely to have conflict in their partner relationships than other women.

Findings.   Sexually abused women were more than twice as likely than other women to have a violent partner, 36% versus 17%, $\chi^2(1, N = 193) = 5.25$, $p = .02$, and this was true regardless of income. The relation works both ways: Women with a violent partner were nearly two and a half times as likely to report feeling sexually abused in childhood than were other women, 24% versus 10%. Because of the high correlations between physical and sexual abuse and between income group and partner violence, the relation between partner violence and sexual abuse was examined while controlling for physical abuse and income group. The partial correlation between level of partner violence and sexual abuse continued to be significant, $r(181) = .21$, $p = .004$. An analysis of variance (ANOVA) was conducted to examine the interactive effects of income group and sexual abuse on level of partner violence, controlling for physical abuse. Both main effects were significant (both $Fs > 4.8$, $p < .03$ in both cases), but the interaction was not ($F = 2.06$, $p = .15$; $\eta^2 = .01$). Even if the sample size were larger, the small η^2 suggests that if there is an interaction effect, it is minimal. The importance of controlling for income when examining data on partner violence was underscored by the finding that lower income women were more than twice as likely to have a violent partner than higher income women (32% vs. 15%, respectively), $\chi^2(1, N = 185) = 7.54$, $p < .006$, and this pattern held regardless of whether or not they had a history of sexual abuse.

In summary, sexual abuse was correlated with increased risk for partner violence, regardless of income and physical abuse, and lower income women were more likely to experience partner violence than higher income women.

Hypothesis 6.   Sexually abused women are more likely to experience unprotected sexual intercourse, particularly lower income sexually abused women.

Findings.   Sexually abused women were more likely to report having a partner who refused to wear a condom, partial $r(250) = .14$, $p = .022$, controlling for income group and physical abuse. Specifically, 17% of sexually abused women reported having a partner who refused to use a condom, compared to 6% of other women, $\chi^2(1, N = 262) = 6.59$, $p = .010$. We expected these relations to be stronger for lower income women. When the correlation between sexual abuse and partner refusal to wear a condom was analyzed separately by income group, however, the relation held only for higher income women. For poor women, no relation between sexual abuse and partner refusal to wear a condom was found, $r(94) = .08$, $p = .47$, controlling for physical abuse, whereas for higher income women, the relation was relatively more substantial, $r(159) = .22$, $p = .006$. Using an r to z transformation, the difference between the correlations for the two groups was not found to be significant when physical abuse was controlled ($z = 1.16$, $p > .05$).

This possible difference by income group needs to be explored by future research. It may partially reflect the differential rates of refusal for the two groups. Among poor women, about 12% had partners who refused to wear a condom, regardless of whether they reported feeling sexually abused. Among higher income women, sexually abused women were more than six times more likely than their nonabused peers to have partners who refused to wear a condom (19% vs. 2.3%). Thus, income group may make a difference with regard to the relation of sexual abuse to condom use, but in the reverse direction of what we expected.

Hypothesis 7.   Sexually abused women are more likely to experience un-wanted pregnancy, as indicated by having an abortion, particularly lower income women.

Findings.   Sexually abused women were more likely to report having an unwanted pregnancy, as indicated by having an abortion, $r(412) = .17$, $p = .008$, controlling for income group and physical abuse. In fact 40% of sexually abused women reported having an abortion as compared to 14% of other women, $\chi^2(1, N = 437) = 23.79$, $p = .000$. Looking at the data another way, 30% of women reporting an abortion also had a history of sexual abuse. Although the pattern held regardless of income group, the proportion of higher income abused women reporting an abortion was particularly substantial (50% compared to 28% for low-income abused women).

In summary, these findings suggest links between sexual abuse and partner violence, partner refusal to wear a condom, and abortion. They underscore the complexity of the difficulties sexually abused women have in their interpersonal relationships, difficulties that may also occur in their doctor–patient relationships.

Health Care Variables

Hypothesis 8.   Abused women, particularly sexually abused women, report more difficulties in their relationships with their doctors than do nonabused women.

Findings.   Abused women (i.e., women who experienced either physical or sexual abuse) were more likely than other women to report they had been talked down to by their doctors (39.5% vs. 14.9%), $r(438) = .24$, $p = .000$; and to have been told a medical condition was "all in their head" (30.3% vs. 13.0%), $r(437) = .18$, $p = .000$. Abused women were also more likely to report having problems or needs they would have liked to discuss with their doctor, but did not because either they or their doctor felt uncomfortable (19.4% vs. 10.3%), $r(369) = .11$, $p = .033$; and to have a doctor make comments or act in ways of a sexual nature that were inappropriate or offensive, $r(411) = .11$, $p = .027$. Income group is controlled in these analyses.

The relationship problems represented by these responses may be why only 14 (20%) of the women who experienced physical or sexual abuse, or both, reported ever discussing any abuse incidents with a doctor. Of the women who did discuss an incident with a doctor, 43% said that the doctor was not helpful.

Partial correlations were computed between sexual abuse and these measures. With physical abuse and income group controlled, sexually abused women were still more likely than other women to report they had been talked down to by their doctors, $r(411) = .10, p = .038$; and to report having problems or needs they would have liked to discuss with their doctor but did not, $r(352) = .11, p = .031$. However, sexual abuse was not significantly correlated with having been told a medical condition was "all in their head," $r(411) = .07, p = .19$, when income group and physical abuse were controlled.

Revictimization issues make the finding that sexual abuse is significantly correlated with having a doctor make inappropriate comments or behaviors of a sexual nature particularly interesting. With income group and physical abuse controlled, $r(411) = .11, p = .027$, lower income women were not more likely to have doctors who acted in sexually inappropriate ways (2.3% of poor women vs. 3.4% of other women). However, when the relation between experience of sexual abuse in childhood and acts of an inappropriate or sexual nature on the part of doctors was examined separately by income group, it was found that the relation held only for lower income women, $r(176) = .26, p = .000$. The relation was not significant for higher income women, $r(287) = .07, p = .29$. Using an r to z transformation, the difference between the correlations for the two groups was significant ($z = 2.10, p < .05$).

Perceived Quality of Doctor–Patient Relationship

The relation of abuse history to the perceived quality of the doctor–patient relationship, held by the 370 women in the sample who reported having one particular place to go when they were sick or wanted advice about their health, was examined; 67 women in this subsample had histories of physical or sexual abuse, or both. Having a health care provider was not significantly related to abuse history in this case.

Hypothesis 9.   Abused women, particularly lower income abused women, report lower perceived quality in their doctor–patient relationships.

Findings.   A 2 × 2 ANOVA was used to examine the direct and interactive effects of abuse history and income group on perceived quality of doctor–patient relationship. Abused women reported a lower perceived quality of doctor–patient relationship, regardless of income. Abuse was associated with lower perceived quality, $F(1, 351) = 5.39, p = .021; \eta^2 = .015$. Over 30% of abused women averaged less than "good" in their ratings of perceived quality of the doctor–patient relationship, compared to 20% of nonabused women. The figure was highest for sexually abused women, 34%. Neither the direct ($F = 1.45$. $df = 1, 351, p = .229$; $\eta^2 = .004$) nor interactive ($F = .40, p = .525$; $\eta^2 = .001$) effects of income were significant.

Hypothesis 10.   Sexual abuse will have a significant impact on perceived quality of the doctor–patient relationship, and this impact will not be fully accounted for by self-esteem and depressive symptoms associated with abuse history.

Findings.   Perceived quality of doctor–patient relationship was positively correlated with self-esteem, $r(342) = .23, p = .000$; and negatively correlated with depressive symptoms, $r(351) = -.15, p = .004$, and abuse history, $r(353) = -.12, p = .029$. However, multiple regression analyses separating the effects of physical and sexual abuse revealed that sexual abuse made an independent contribution to perceived quality over and above its relation to self-esteem and depression, with physical abuse and income group controlled. When self-esteem, depressive symptoms, and then sexual abuse were entered in separate blocks before physical abuse, physical abuse did not make an additional contribution to the equation (F-change $= .45, p = .50$). When the order of physical and sexual abuse was reversed, with sexual abuse entered in the last block of the regression, the F-change for sexual abuse was significant (F-change $= 5.40, p = .02$). In the final equation (which, of course, was the same for both analyses), both self-esteem and sexual abuse had independent relations to perceived quality ($T = 3.5, p = .004$ and $T = -2.32, p = .021$, for self-esteem and sexual abuse, respectively).

Given our earlier findings on the link between abuse history and partner violence, and our belief that partner abuse would also prove to be an important predictor of perceived quality, we then controlled for level of partner abuse. Multiple regression analyses revealed that sexual abuse no longer made an additional contribution to the equation when having a violent partner was added before sexual abuse (F-change $= .067, p = .797$; partial correlation $= .003, p = .972$). However, the independent relation of self-esteem to perceived quality of care persisted when physical abuse, sexual abuse, partner violence, and depressive symptoms were all controlled ($T = 2.08, p = .039$).

Set II: Partner Violence

A total of 195 women who were either married or cohabiting with a partner were asked about their experiences with partner violence. In this subsample, 37 women (19%) reported experiencing partner violence. This figure is similar to the 17% figure of Hamptom and Gelles (1994). Of the 37, 13 reported experiencing severe violence (i.e., being kicked, bitten, hit with fist or other object; beaten up; choked; threatened with knife or gun; partner used knife or fired a gun; suffered forcible or attempted forcible intercourse against her will).

Mental Health Variables

Hypothesis 11.   Type of partner violence will be significantly and negatively related to self-esteem, perceived health status, and life satisfaction, and positively related to depressive symptoms and indicators, particularly for lower income women.

Findings.   A 3×2 MANOVA examined the relation between type of partner violence (none, minor, severe) and income group (lower, higher) to self-esteem, depressive symptoms, perceived health status, and life satisfaction. Multivariate Fs were significant for type of violence ($F = 5.57, p = .000$) and income group ($F = 3.47, p = .010$), but not for the interaction of the two ($F = 1.47, p = .167$). Table 3 contains the means, standard deviations, univariate Fs, and η^2 results for these analyses.

The hypothesis was supported for the direct effect of type of partner violence (see Table 3). Further, these analyses established that income was significantly and positively related to self-esteem and negatively related to depression, but not related to perceived health status or life satisfaction when partner violence was controlled.

Given that the effect of type of violence primarily reflected the difference between women with severely violent partners and the other two groups, the MANOVAs were supplemented by correlational analyses that examined the relation between having a severely violent partner and the mental health variables of interest. With income group controlled, having a severely violent partner was significantly and negatively correlated with self-esteem, $r(179) = -.18, p = .018$; perceived health status, $r(182) = -.17, p = .021$; and life satisfaction, $r(182) = -.33, p = .000$. It was positively correlated with depressive symptoms, $r(182) = .34, p = .000$; and having suicidal thoughts in the past year, $r(182) = .20, p = .006$. Looking at this relation another way, 23% of women experiencing severe violence in the past year had thought about taking their own life, compared to 4% of other women. Neither the type of violence nor having a severely violent partner was related to women being told they had anxiety or depression by a doctor in the past 5 years, or using tranquilizers in the past 12 months. It is noted that the sample size is sufficient to detect medium-, but not small-sized effects of these variables (Cohen, 1992).

Health Behaviors

Hypothesis 12.   Women with violent partners will be more likely to use unhealthy substances, particularly lower income women.

Findings.   The partial correlation between having a violent partner and unhealthy substance use, with income group controlled, was not significant, $r(182) = .09, p = .206$. For women having a severely violent partner, the correlation was higher and in the predicted direction, but did not reach acceptable levels of statistical

TABLE 3
Weighted Means, Standard Deviations, and Group Comparisons for Self-Esteem, Depressive Symptoms, Perceived Health Status, and Life Satisfaction by Violence Type and Income Level

Variable	M	SD	F Value[a] η^2	Group Comparisons[b]
Self-esteem				
No violence	36.23	4.57	4.59**	1, 2 > 3
Minor violence	36.89	2.45	.05	
Severe violence	32.17	5.91		
Lower income	33.57	5.74	12.40***	
Higher income	36.94	3.71	.07	
Depressive symptoms				
No violence	4.97	3.37	12.76***	1, 2 < 3
Minor violence	4.47	2.74	.13	
Severe violence	10.17	3.97		
Lower income	6.51	4.07	6.01*	
Higher income	4.82	3.30	.03	
Perceived health status				
No violence	3.45	1.00	3.28*	1 > 3
Minor violence	3.42	1.07	.04	
Severe violence	2.58	1.08		
Lower income	3.11	1.15	.96	
Higher income	3.50	.97	.005	
Life satisfaction				
No violence	4.38	.80	16.10***	1, 2 > 3
Minor violence	4.11	.88	.16	
Severe violence	3.00	1.28		
Lower income	4.28	.90	.01	
Higher income	4.25	.95	.0003	

Note. Table shows weighted means from 3 × 2 (Type of Violence × Income) control group. [a]Pillais multivariate $F = 5.57$, $p = .000$ for type of violence; for income group, $F = 3.47$, $p = .01$. Univariate $df = 2, 166$. [b]Group 1 = No violence; $N = 141$. Group 2 = Minor violence; $N = 19$. Group 3 = Severe violence; $N = 12$. Group comparisons made with Tukey's honestly significant difference test. *$p < .05$. **$p < .01$. ***$p < .001$.

significance, $r(182) = .13$, $p = .09$, two-tailed, controlling for income group. Given the size of the correlation, it is likely that with a larger sample size and more sensitive measures of violent behaviors, the reliability of these effects would be confirmed.

Health Care Variables

Only two of the women who experienced partner violence reported ever discussing those incidents with a doctor, but they reported those visits as very helpful.

The relation of partner violence to health care experiences of the 178 married or cohabiting women who reported having one particular place to go when they were sick or wanted advice about their health was examined in more detail to supplement the analyses of partner violence included in the section on childhood abuse.

Hypothesis 13.   Partner violence will be associated with lower perceived quality of health care, particularly for lower income women.

Findings.   Partial correlation analyses controlling for income group found both type and level of partner violence to be negatively correlated with perceived quality of care, $r(174) = -.17, p < .021$, and $r(174) = -.20, p < .008$, respectively. A 2×2 ANOVA was conducted to examine the direct and interactive effects of having a violent partner by income group. Having a violent partner had a direct main effect, $F(1, 167) = 6.22, p = .014, \eta^2 = .036$, but income group did not, $F(1, 167) = .84, p = .36, \eta^2 = .005$, and the interaction effect was not significant, $F(1, 167) = 1.04, p = .31, \eta^2 = .006$. The power to detect effects of income group, directly and in interaction was small (.178 and .178, respectively), but the effect sizes appeared minimal, in any case.

Other Comparisons Between Lower Income Women and Other Women

The cut-offs for low-income women used here differ slightly from those used by Hamptom and Gelles (1994), $15,000 versus $10,000, respectively. Results were similar in that women who were lower income (again, defined as having an annual income of less than $15,000 or receiving some form of governmental financial assistance, or both) were more likely than higher income women to experience both minor violence (18.9% vs. 9.8%) and severe violence (13.2% vs. 4.5%), $\chi^2(2, N = 185) = 7.98, p = .018$. The projected rate of severe violence for low-income women, 132 per 1,000, is slightly lower than the 144 per 1,000 estimated by Hamptom and Gelles for low-income women, which would be expected given that the cut-off used in this study was $5,000 higher.

DISCUSSION

This research documents links between violence against black women and their mental health and well-being, perceived health status and health behavior, and perception of the quality of their health care. Physical abuse, sexual abuse, and partner violence tend to be intercorrelated, but both separately and in combination they are variously associated with lower self-esteem, perceived health status, and life satisfaction, and with higher risk for depressive symptoms, unhealthy behaviors, and difficulties in interpersonal relationships. Taken as a whole, these results construct a portrait of intimate violence that takes multiple forms and has multiple effects on black women's health and well-being.

These findings have several implications for the design of health prevention and intervention programs, training, research, and service provision. First, these results suggest health prevention and intervention programs designed to address a variety of black women's health concerns—including sexually transmitted diseases, unwanted pregnancy, and unhealthy substance use—will not be maximally effective unless they start early and address issues of intimate violence over the life cycle.

With regard to training, the fact that nearly one out of four women with a violent partner reported sexual abuse underscores the need for health care providers of battered women to be trained to deal with issues arising from childhood sexual abuse. Sexually abused women were not only more likely to have violent partners—they were more likely to report having a partner who refused to wear a condom, and to have had an abortion. Indeed, 40% of sexually abused women reported having an abortion, and 30% of women reporting an abortion had a history of sexual abuse. These findings suggest that service providers in reproductive health and family planning programs have a particular need for understanding the causes and consequences of intimate violence, as well as a special role to play in prevention and intervention efforts.

The design of health prevention and intervention programs, training curricula, and research studies must recognize black women's economic and social diversity, however. Income group had a substantial relation to self-esteem, depressive symptoms, and perceived health status. Given that lower income women were more likely to have a violent partner, these findings confirm the importance of using caution when generalizing about black women across income groups and of controlling for income group when studying the impact of violence on black women's lives. The widespread impact of income group as a direct effect, combined with the fact that small cell sizes often resulted in little power to detect interactive effects, suggests that future research exploring the interactive effects of poverty and violence on health variables, using larger samples and more refined measures, would be worthwhile.

Although the various forms of intimate violence had overlapping effects, the effects were not uniform (e.g., partner violence predicted self-esteem, whereas abuse history did not). This may reflect measurement incomparability or differential effects. Research that explores the physical and mental health outcomes of various forms of intimate violence—alone and in combination with others—is urgently needed.

The finding that the relation of abuse level to depressive symptoms is independent from its relation to self-esteem is congruent with the hypothesis that the damaging effects of childhood abuse result from its impact on feelings of instrumentality, which in turn leads to depression and other negative health outcomes. An alternative interpretation is that depressive cognitions result in women interpreting their childhood experiences as abusive. But if so, then self-esteem would be expected to have a stronger correlation with reports of childhood abuse. The answer to this question has implications for prevention and intervention programs, and is a particularly interesting area for future research.

Although few interactive effects between income group and violence experience were found, the findings are nonetheless suggestive. Particularly intriguing was the finding that upper income black women who did not report a history of sexual abuse rarely had a partner who refused to wear a condom (2.3%); but when such women had a history of sexual abuse, then nearly one out of five (19%) had such partners. In contrast, abuse history had little relation to condom refusal for low-income women. This finding leads to an interesting hypothesis: Could it reflect the impact of childhood sexual abuse on instrumentality (i.e., agency, or self-efficacy)? Upper income black women, who may be high in feelings of instrumentality, may be in a good position to successfully negotiate condom use with their partners. However, if those feelings are eroded by a history of childhood sexual abuse, they may be less able to protect themselves. For lower income women, abuse might be but one of numerous factors that erode feelings of instrumentality (Belle, 1990). Future research must widen its lens beyond the relation of intimate violence to self-esteem and also examine the role that instrumentality plays in mediating and moderating the health outcomes of such violence.

Health providers have critical roles to play in the prevention, detection, intervention, and amelioration of the effects of violence in the lives of women (Koss et al., 1994; Plichta, 1996). But without specific attention to improving the quality of the doctor–patient relationship, the promise of that role will be unfulfilled. The findings with regard to perceived quality of the doctor–patient relationship suggest that proactive steps need to be taken to train physicians to communicate more effectively with abused women, particularly women who have been sexually abused. Doctors were perceived as patronizing and unhelpful, and in the case of lower income women who had been sexually abused, viewed as acting in sexually inappropriate ways. Although perceived quality of doctor–patient relationship was correlated with self-esteem and depression, regression analyses revealed that the relation was not fully explained by these variables. It may be that childhood sexual abuse interferes with establishing relationships requiring mutual trust and respect in ways that go beyond those related to self-esteem and depression. The fact that adding partner violence to the equation reduces the correlation between sexual abuse and perceived quality to nonsignificance is congruent with this hypothesis. It may be that instrumentality is involved, or it may be something else. Finding out exactly how a history of childhood sexual abuse may affect a woman's ability to establish and negotiate close relationships is an important research priority.

Many other factors contribute to difficulties between doctors and patients who have histories of violence and abuse. In addition to limitations of time and support staff, screening for violence is sometimes neglected because of fear of offending the patient and uncertainty about what to do with the information when it is obtained (Sugg & Inui, 1992). Health problems such as chronic pain, for example, are difficult to diagnose and treat. In addition to considering characteristics of the patient, a comprehensive examination of contributors to quality of the doctor–patient relationship would consider attributes of the doctor in relation to problems presented (Dutton, Haywood, & El-Bayoumi, 1997). Similarly, effective treatment of victims of violence requires that health providers take a broader view; help victims understand the links between their health status and the violence they experience; consider issues of safety and prevention; and be able to provide information about a variety of psychological, legal, and social services (Dutton et al. 1997; Koss et al., 1994; Plichta, 1996).

Dealing with issues related to perceived quality of health care providers is clearly needed, but designing programs to intervene in and ameliorate the health effects of violence must reflect understanding of social and cultural diversity among women in general and black women in particular (Landrine & Klonoff, in press; Wyatt, 1994). For example, some research suggests that having a strong network of family and friends plays a more important role in mediating the effects of violence for black women than for white women (Cazaneve & Strauss, 1979). Belief systems, cultural values, and cross-cutting social identities (e.g., those linked to social categories of race, ethnicity, nationality, regionality, age, sexual orientation, and disability) are just a few of the intersecting factors contributing to women's diversity that need to be considered.

Directly addressing issues of racism is also needed. For example, black women are less likely to turn to shelters for battered women than are white women. This may reflect a general lack of resources such as shelters for violence victims in black communities. It may also reflect a perception that the shelter movement has been run by and for white women (Asbury, 1987). Research suggests that African American women who do turn to shelters are likely to be poor, unemployed, and in need of a variety of health and social services (Sullivan & Rumptz, 1994). Insofar as turning to battered women's shelters may reduce likelihood of severe injury and death, confronting racism and developing a culturally sensitive shelter network is an important component for any comprehensive prevention and intervention plan targeting intimate violence.

A comprehensive strategy that recognizes and builds on the strengths of black women in their communities also recognizes that ministers in black churches serve as "health providers" for many black women. That is, they are consulted about physical symptoms as well as psychological problems, provide social support and health information, and have a powerful influence on health behaviors and decisions (Landrine & Klonoff, in press; Watson, 1984). Developing prevention and intervention programs that draw on the strengths of black communities requires involving black churches in their design, and training church leaders in the causes and consequences of intimate violence in all of its forms.

Methodological Issues

Needless to say, all of the standard cautions for survey research apply: The data are cross-sectional and correlational, making causal inferences speculative. Self-report, particularly with regard to potentially stigmatizing experiences, may be inaccurate, and at best is subject to the limitations of memory. In addition, this study illustrates some basic problems that need to be addressed in survey research that focuses on violence against women in general, and black women in particular. In one sense, the fact that these findings were obtained despite some substantial limitations of method is testimony to the power of childhood abuse and partner violence to have profound and long-lasting effects. How to define the variables is a central issue. Critical features of childhood abuse, including age at first victimization, time period involved, nature and severity of the experience, duration of the abuse, the abuser–victim relationship, whether threat or force was involved, and the response of significant others to learning of the abuse were not able to be examined. Only one-item measures of abuse were used, and such measures have been found to underestimate abuse prevalence (Koss, 1993; Peters, Wyatt, & Finkelhor, 1986). Construction of multi-item measures of abuse experiences, as well as health-related behaviors and outcomes would both increase reliability and enhance understanding of complexities in the relations. Nonetheless, stress and coping research (Lazarus & Folkman, 1984) suggests that cognitive appraisal, or "feeling" that one is abused, should be a key factor in whether abuse experiences have severe and negative psychological effects, so that exploring the relation of such feelings to mental health as we have done here is warranted. It should be recognized that the focus is on the subjective experience of feeling abused while growing up, however. Further, the results reported here should not be used to project rates of abusive behavior in the larger population. Such behaviors were not measured.

It is also unfortunate that number, spacing, and age of children, and whether or not they were planned, wanted, or both, could not be ascertained. The fact that women having one versus repeated abortion experiences could not be separated was also a problem, given research that suggests that these two groups have different psychological and social characteristics (Russo & Zierk, 1992). Exploring the relation of abuse and battering to unwanted births and abortion is an extremely important, but neglected, research area.

Other problems include the relatively small sample size (which made it impossible to explore relations to rape, substance abuse, and other health behaviors with low base rates), the underreporting that is expected with a telephone survey method, and the retrospective nature of the questions. Again, correlation is not causation: With no independent means of verifying the verbal reports, it could be argued that people who are more depressed are simply more likely to remember negative incidents and to interpret them as abusive. The fact that the findings of this study are congruent with findings in the field mitigates these criticisms to some extent. Nonetheless, research based on a larger sample, using more reliable and in-depth measurement, personal interviews that build more rapport, and more detailed definitions of violence and abuse, would allow exploration of other relations not possible here.

Sampling issues are also of concern in this research. The fact that this survey was based on a national sample is an important strength. However, it is important to remember that the racism black people have historically experienced and continue to experience may lead to distrust of researchers in general and health care researchers in particular, which may produce a selective response rate (Landrine & Klonoff, in press). Further, black women are more likely to be poor and homeless than other women, and thus less likely to have telephones. The effects of income reported here would be expected to be even stronger in a study that could include the poorest of women in the sample.

Another sampling issue stems from the fact that black women are much more likely to be never married than either white or Hispanic women. In 1988, 50% of black women 25 to 29 years of age were never married, compared to about 26% for white and for Hispanic women; 54% of black female-headed families were maintained by women who were never married, compared to 17% of white women and 32% of Hispanic women (Saluter, 1989). In this study, only respondents who reported they were married or lived as a couple with someone were asked about their experience with partner violence. This is an improvement over studies that have only included married couples. Nonetheless, the wording of the item, which focuses on couples who are living in the same household together, means that black women who have intimate relationships but do not live with their partner under the same roof are not included in the results. Indeed, the time that a woman is most likely to be killed by her partner is after she has separated from him (Browne, 1987).

CONCLUSION

Although the findings from this study provide an important piece of the picture, it is only one piece of a very complex portrait that has yet to be adequately drawn. Hopefully, it will serve as a catalyst for research—quantitative and qualitative—that will articulate the social and cultural factors that moderate the links between intimate violence and diverse health behaviors and outcomes. Research on how black women conceptualize what has happened to them, how they view their options for responding, and how they assess the possibilities in their futures are needed to inform service provision and make service more culturally appropriate and empathic. Such research must be framed in a way that will empower women rather than blame or pathologize them, and emphasize the responsibility of all of us to work to change the social systems that foster and maintain violence against women as well as fail to ameliorate its effects.

ACKNOWLEDGMENTS

We thank Angela duMont for her assistance in the literature search. We also express our deep appreciation and admiration to the Commonwealth Fund for providing important leadership on women's health issues, as well as for making their important database available to us.

REFERENCES

Abbott, J., Johnson, R., Koziol-McLain, J., & Lowenstein, S. R. (1995). Domestic violence against women: Incidence and prevalence in an emergency department population. *Journal of the American Medical Association, 273,* 1763–1767.

Adler, N. E. (1997). Socioeconomic status and women's health. In S. J. Gallant, G. P. Keita, & R. Royak-Schaler (Eds.), *Health care for women: Psychological, social, and behavioral influences* (pp. 11–24). Washington, DC: American Psychological Association.

Adler, N. E., Boyce, T., Chesney, M. A., Cohen, S., Folkman, S., Kahn, R. L., & Syme, S. L. (1994). Socioeconomic status and health: The challenge of the gradient. *American Psychologist, 49,* 15–24.

Adler, N. E., & Coriell, M. (1997). Socioeconomic status and women's health. In S. J. Gallant, G. P. Keita, & R. Royak-Schaler (Eds.), *Health care for women* (pp. 11–24). Washington, DC: American Psychological Association.

Amaro, H., Fried, L. W., Cabral, H., & Zuckerman, B. (1990). Violence during pregnancy and substance abuse. *American Journal of Public Health, 80,* 575–579.

Asbury, J. (1987). African-American women in violent relationships: An exploration of cultural differences. In R. Hamptom (Ed.), *Violence in the Black family* (pp. 86–106). Lexington, MA: Lexington.

Astin, M. C., Lawrence, J. J., Ogland-Hand, S. M., & Foy, D. W. (1993). Posttraumatic stress disorder among battered women: Risk and resiliency factors. *Violence & Victims, 8,* 17–28.

Barbee, E. (1992). African American women and depression: A review and critique of the literature. *Archives of Psychiatric Nursing, 6*(5), 257–265.

Beebe, D. K. (1991). Emergency management of the adult female rape victim. *American Family Physician, 43,* 2041–2046.

Beitchman, J. H., Zucker, K. L., Hood, J. E., DaCosta, G. A., Akman, D., & Cassavia, E. (1992). A review of the long-term effects of child sexual abuse. *Child Abuse and Neglect, 16,* 101–118.

Bell, R., Duncan, M., Eilenberg, J., Fullilove, M., Hein, D., Innes, L., Mellman, L., & Panzer, P. (1994). *Violence against women in the United States: A comprehensive background paper.* New York: The Commonwealth Fund.

Belle, D. (1990). Poverty and women's mental health. *American Psychologist, 49,* 384–389.

Berenson, A. B., San Miguel, V. V., & Wilkinson, G. S. (1992). Prevalence of physical and sexual assault in pregnant adolescents. *Journal of Adolescent Health, 13,* 466–469.

Bergman, B., Brismal, B., & Nordin, D. (1992). Utilisation of medical care by abused women. *British Medical Journal, 305,* 27–28.

Boyer, D., & Fine, D. (1992). Sexual abuse as a factor in adolescent pregnancy and child maltreatment. *Family Planning Perspectives, 24,* 4–10.

Briere, J., & Runtz, M. (1987). Post-sexual abuse trauma: Data and implications for clinical practice. *Journal of Interpersonal Violence, 2,* 367–379.

Brown, G. R., & Anderson, B. (1991). Psychiatric morbidity in adult inpatients with childhood histories of sexual and physical abuse. *American Journal of Psychiatry, 148,* 55–61.

Browne, A. (1987). *When battered women kill.* New York: Macmillan/Free Press.

Browne, A. (1992). Violence against women: Relevance for medical practitioners. Council on Scientific Affairs, American Medical Association. *Journal of the American Medical Association, 267,* 3184–3189.

Bullock, L., & McFarlane, J. (1989). The birthweight/battering connection. *American Journal of Nursing,* 1153–1155.

Burgess, A. W., & Holmstron, L. L. (1978). Recovery from rape and prior life stress. *Research on Nursing and Health, 1,* 165–174.

Cascardi, M., Langhinrichsen, J., & Vivian, D. (1992). Marital aggression: Impact, injury, and health correlates for husbands and wives. *Archives of Internal Medicine, 152,* 1178–1184.

Cazenave, N. A., & Straus, M. A. (1979). Race, class, network embeddedness and family violence: A search for potent support systems. *Journal of Comparative Family Studies, 10,* 280–300.

Cohen, J. (1992). A power primer. *Psychological Bulletin, 112,* 115–159.

Coley, S. A., & Beckett, J. O. (1988). Black battered women: A review of empirical literature. *Journal of Counseling and Development, 66,* 266–270.

Crowell, N., & Burgess, A. W. (Eds.). (1996). *Understanding violence against women.* Washington, DC: National Academy Press.

Cunningham, R. M., Stiffman, A. R., & Dore, P. (1994). The association of physical and sexual abuse with HIV risk behaviors in adolescence and young adulthood: Implications for public health. *Child Abuse & Neglect, 18,* 233–245.

Dutton, M., Haywood, Y., & El-Bayoumi, G., (1997). Impact of violence on women's health. In S. J. Gallant, G. P. Keita, & R. Royak-Schaler (Eds.), *Health care for women: Psychological, social, and behavioral influences* (pp. 41–71). Washington, DC: American Psychological Association.

Eby, K. K., Campbell, J. C., Sullivan, C. M., & Davidson, W. S. (1995). Health effects of experiences of sexual violence for women with abusive partners. *Health Care for Women International, 16,* 563–576.

Ethier, L. S., Lacharite, C., & Coutoure, G. (1995). Childhood adversity, parental stress, and depression of negligent mothers. *Child Abuse & Neglect, 19,* 619–632.

Falik, M. M., & Collins, K. S. (Eds.). (1996). *Women's health: The Commonwealth Fund survey.* Baltimore: The Johns Hopkins University Press.

Finkelhor, D. (1987). The sexual abuse of children: Current research reviewed. *Psychiatric Annals, 17,* 233–241.

Gazmararian, J. A., Adams, M. M., Saltzman, L. E., Johnson, C. H., Bruce, F. C., Marks, J. S., & Zahniser, S. C. (1995). The relationship between pregnancy intendedness and physical violence in mothers of newborns. *Obstetrics & Gynecology, 85,* 1031–1038.

Gelles, R. (1988). Violence and pregnancy: Are pregnant women at greater risk for abuse? *Journal of Marriage and the Family, 50,* 841–847.

Gelles, R. J., & Straus, M. A. (1989). *Intimate violence: The causes and consequences of abuse in the American family.* New York: Simon & Schuster.

Golding, J. M. (1996). Sexual assault history and women's reproductive and sexual health. *Psychology of Women Quarterly, 20,* 101–121.

Golding, J. M., & Taylor, D. L. (1996). Sexual assault history and premenstrual distress in two general population samples. *Journal of Women's Health, 5,* 143–152.

Gooden, W. E. (1980). *The adult development of Black men* (Vols. 1 & 2). Ann Arbor, MI: University Microfilms.

Goodman, L. A., Koss, M. P., & Russo, N. F. (1993a). Violence against women: Physical and mental health effects. Part I: Research findings. *Applied & Preventive Psychology: Current Scientific Perspectives, 2,* 79–89.

Goodman, L. A., Koss, M. P., & Russo, N. F. (1993b). Violence against women: Physical and mental health effects, Part II: Conceptualizing post-traumatic stress. *Applied & Preventive Psychology: Current Scientific Perspectives, 2,* 123–130.

Green, A. H. (1993). Child sexual abuse: Immediate and long-term effects and intervention. *Journal of the American Academy of Child and Adolescent Psychiatry, 32,* 890–902.

Gutierres, S. E., Russo, N. F., & Urbanski, L. (1994). Sociocultural and psychological factors in American Indian drug use: Implications for treatment. *International Journal of the Addictions, 29,* 1761–1786.

Guttentag, M., Salasin, S., & Belle, D. (Eds.). (1980). *The mental health of women.* New York: Academic.

Hamptom, R. L., & Gelles, R. J. (1994). Violence toward Black women in a nationally representative sample of Black families. *Journal of Comparative Family Studies, 25,* 105–119.

Helton, A., McFarlane, J., & Anderson, E. T. (1987). Battered and pregnant: A prevalence study. *American Journal of Public Health, 77,* 1337–1339.

Hillard, P. J. (1985). Physical abuse in pregnancy. *Obstetrics & Gynecology, 6,* 185–190.

Ingram, K. M., Corning, A. F., & Schmidt, L. D. (1996). The relationship of victimization experiences to psychological well-being among homeless women and low-income housed women. *Journal of Counseling Psychology, 43,* 218–227.

Koop, C. E. (1985). *The Surgeon General's workshop on violence and public health.* Washington, DC: U.S. Government Printing Office.

Koss, M. P. (1993). Detecting the scope of rape: A review of prevalence research methods. *Journal of Interpersonal Violence, 8,* 198–222.

Koss, M. P., Goodman, L., Browne, A., Fitzgerald, L., Keita, G. P., & Russo, N. F. (1994). *No safe haven: Male violence against women, at home, at work, and in the community.* Washington, DC: American Psychological Association.

Koss, M. P., Heise, L., & Russo, N. F. (1994). The global health burden of rape. *Psychology of Women Quarterly, 18,* 509–530.

Koss, M. P., & Heslet, L. (1992). Somatic consequences of violence against women. *Archives of Family Medicine, 1,* 53–59.

Koss, M. P., Koss, P. G., & Woodruff, W. J. (1991). Deleterious effects of criminal victimization on women's health and medical utilization. *Archives of Internal Medicine, 151,* 342–357.

Landrine, H., & Klonoff, E. A. (in press). Cultural diversity and health psychology. In A. Baum, T. Revenson, & J. Singer (Eds.), *Handbook of health psychology.* Mahwah, NJ: Lawrence Erlbaum Associates, Inc.

Laws, A., & Golding, J. M. (1996). Sexual assault history and eating disorder symptoms among white, Hispanic, and African-American women and men. *American Journal of Public Health, 86,* 579–582.

Lazarus, R. S., & Folkman, S. (1984). *Stress, appraisal, and coping.* New York: Springer.

Liebow, E. (1967). *Tally's corner: A study of streetcorner men.* Boston: Little, Brown.

Lillie-Blanton, M., Bowie, J., & Ro, M. (1996). African American women: Social factors and the use of preventive health services. In M. M. Falik & K. S. Collins (Eds.), *Women's health: The Commonwealth Fund survey* (pp. 99–122). Baltimore, MD: The Johns Hopkins University Press.

Lockhart, L., & White, B. (1989). Understanding marital violence in the Black community. *Journal of Interpersonal Violence, 4*(4), 3–4.

Lyons, B., Salganicoff, A., & Rowland, D. (1996). Poverty, access to health care, and Medicaid's critical role for women. In M. M. Falik & K. S. Collins (Eds.), *Women's health: The Commonwealth Fund survey* (pp. 273–295). Baltimore: The Johns Hopkins University Press.

McFarlane, J. (1989). Battering during pregnancy: Tip of an iceberg revealed. *Women & Health, 15,* 69–84.

McFarlane, J., Parker, B., Soeken, K., & Bullock, L. (1992). Assessing for abuse during pregnancy: Severity and frequency of injuries and associated entry into prenatal care. *Journal of the American Medical Association, 267,* 3176–3178.

Meyerding, J. (1977). Early sexual experience and prostitution. *American Journal of Psychiatry, 134,* 1381–1385.

Miller, B. A., & Downs, W. R. (1993). The impact of family violence on the use of alcohol by women. *Alcohol, Aggression, and Inquiry: Alcohol Health & Research World, 17,* 137–143.

Miller, B. A., Downs, W. R., Gondoli, D. M., & Keil, A. (1987). The role of childhood sexual abuse in the development of alcoholism in women. *Violence and Victims, 2,* 157–171.

Miller, B. A., Downs, W. R., & Testa, M. (1993). Interrelationships between victimization experiences and women's alcohol use. *Journal of Studies on Alcohol, 11*(Suppl.), 109–117.

Mitchell, R., & Hobson, C. (1983). Coping with domestic violence: Social support and psychological health among battered women. *American Journal of Community Psychology, 11,* 629–654.

Moeller, T. P., Bachman, G. A., & Moeller, J. R. (1993). The combined effects of physical, sexual, and emotional abuse during childhood: Long-term health consequences for women. *Child Abuse & Neglect, 17,* 623–640.

Nagy, S., Adcock, A. G., & Nagy, M. C. (1994). A comparison of risky health behaviors of sexually active, sexually abused, and abstaining adolescents. *Pediatrics, 93,* 570–575.

National Victims Center. (1992). *Rape in America: A report to the nation.* Arlington, VA: Author.

Neff, J. A., Holamon, B., & Schluter, T. D. (1995). Spousal violence among Anglos, Blacks, and Mexican Americans: The role of demographic variables, psychosocial predictors, and alcohol consumption. *Journal of Family Violence, 10,* 1–21.

Nelson, D. E., Higginson, G. K., & Grant-Worley, J. A. (1995). Physical abuse among high school students. Prevalence and correlation with other health behaviors. *Archives of Pediatric Adolescent Medicine, 149,* 1254–1258.

Neumann, D. A., Houskamp, B. M., Pollock, V. E., & Briere, J. (1996). The long-term sequelae of childhood sexual abuse in women: A meta-analytic review. *Child Maltreatment, 1*(1), 6–16.

Paone, D., Chavkin, W., Willets, I., Friedman, P., & Des Jarlais, D. (1992). The impact of sexual abuse: Implications for drug treatment. *Journal of Women's Health, 1,* 149–153.

Peters, S. D., Wyatt, G. E., & Finkelhor, D. (1986). In D. Finkelhor (Ed.), *A sourcebook on child sexual abuse* (pp. 15–59). Beverly Hills, CA: Sage.

Plichta, S. B. (1996). Violence and abuse: Implications for women's health. In M. M. Falik & K. S. Collins (Eds.), *Women's health: The Commonwealth Fund survey* (pp. 237–272). Baltimore: The Johns Hopkins University Press.

Radloff, L. (1977). The CES-D Scale: A self-report depression scale for research in the general population. *Applied Psychological Measurement, 1,* 385–401.

Randall, T. (1990). Domestic violence begets other problems of which physicians must be aware to be effective. *Journal of the American Medical Association, 264,* 940–943.

Randall, T. (1991). Hospital-wide program identifies battered women; offers assistance. *Journal of the American Medical Association, 266,* 1177–1179.

Rohsenow, D. J., Corbett, R., & Devine, D. (1988). Molested as children: A hidden contribution to substance abuse? *Journal of Substance Abuse Treatment, 5,* 13–18.

Rosenberg, M. (1965). *Society and the adolescent self-image.* Princeton, NJ: Princeton University Press.

Russo, N. F., & Zierk, K. L. (1992). Abortion, childbearing, and women's well-being. *Prefessional Psychology: Research and Practice, 23,* 269–280.

Saltzman, L. E. (1990). Battering during pregnancy: A role for physicians. *Atlanta Medicine, 64,* 45–48.

Saluter, A. (1989). Singleness in America. In U.S. Bureau of the Census, *Studies in marriage and the family* (Current population reports, Series P–23, No. 162). Washington, DC: U.S. Government Printing Office.

Satin, A. J., Hemsell, D. L., Stone, I. C., Theriot, S., & Wendel, G. D. (1991). Sexual assault in pregnancy. *Obstetrics and Gynecology, 77,* 710–714.

Shepard, M., & Pence, E. (1988). The effect of battering on the employment status of women. *Affilia, 3,* 55–61.

Stark, E., & Flitcraft, A. (1988). Women and children at risk: A feminist perspective on child abuse. *International Journal of Health Services, 18*(1), 97–118.

Stark, E., & Flitcraft, A. (1996). *Women at risk.* Thousand Oaks, CA: Sage.

Steele, E., Mitchell, J., Graywolf, E., Belle, D., Chang, W., & Schuller, R. B. (1982). The human cost of discrimination. In D. Belle (Ed.), *Lives in stress: Women and depression* (pp. 109–119). Beverly Hills, CA: Sage.

Stein, J. A., Golding, J. M., Siegel, J. M., Burnam, M. A., & Sorenson, S. B. (1988). Long-term psychological sequelae of child sexual abuse: The Los Angeles Epidemiologic Catchment Area Study. In G. E. Wyatt & G. J. Powell (Eds.), *Lasting effects of child sexual abuse* (pp. 135–154). Newbury Park, CA: Sage.

Straus, M. A. (1979). Measuring intrafamily conflict and violence: The Conflict Tactics (CT) Scales. *Journal of Marriage and the Family, 41,* 75–88.

Sugg, N. K., & Inui, T. (1992). Primary care physicians' response to domestic violence. *Journal of the American Medical Association, 267,* 3157–3160.

Sullivan, C. M., & Rumptz, M. H. (1994). Adjustment and needs of African-American women who utilized a domestic violence shelter. *Violence and Victims, 9,* 275–286.

Tjaden, P., & Thoenees, N. (1997, January 16). *Stalking in America: Findings from the National Violence Against Women Survey.* Presented at the National Institute of Justice Research in Progress Seminar, Washington, DC.

Ucko, L. G. (1994). Culture and violence: The interaction of Africa and America. *Sex Roles, 31*(3–4), 185–204.

Uzell, O., & Peebles-Wilkins, W. (1989). Black spouse abuse: A focus on relational factors and intervention strategies. *Western Journal of Black Studies, 13,* 10–16.

Watson, W. (1984). *Black folk healing.* New Brunswick, NJ: Transaction Books.

Wilsnack, S. C., Klassen, A. D., & Vogeltanz, N. D. (1994, May). *Childhood sexual abuse and women's substance abuse: National survey findings.* Paper presented at the conferences on Psychosocial and Behavioral Factors in Women's Health: Creating an Agenda for the 21st Century, Washington, DC.

Wyatt, G. E. (1985). The sexual abuse of Afro-American and White American women in childhood. *Child Abuse and Neglect, 8,* 507–519.

Wyatt, G. E. (1990). The aftermath of child sexual abuse of African American and White American women: The victim's experience. *Journal of Family Violence, 5,* 61–81.

Wyatt, G. E. (1992). The sociocultural context of rape. *Journal of Social Issues, 48,* 77–91.

Wyatt, G. E. (1994). The sociocultural relevance of sex research. *American Psychologist, 49,* 748–754.

Wyatt, G. E., Guthrie, D., & Notgrass, C. M. (1992). Differential effects of women's child sexual abuse and subsequent sexual revictimization. *Journal of Consulting and Clinical Psychology, 60,* 167–172.

Zierler, S., Feingold, L., Laufer, D., Velentgas, P., Kantorwitz-Gordon, S. B., & Mayer, K. (1991). Abuse and subsequent risk of HIV infection. *American Journal of Public Health, 81,* 572–575.

WOMEN'S HEALTH: RESEARCH ON GENDER, BEHAVIOR, AND POLICY, *3*(3&4), 349–366

HIV Risk Behaviors Among Inner-City African American Women

Kathleen J. Sikkema, Timothy G. Heckman, Jeffrey A. Kelly,
and the Community Housing AIDS Prevention Study Group
Center for AIDS Intervention Research (CAIR)
Department of Psychiatry and Behavioral Medicine
Medical College of Wisconsin

This study examined the prevalence and predictors of HIV risk behaviors among a sample of 875 low-income, African American women residents of inner-city housing developments. The women completed an anonymous questionnaire that revealed that one third of them were at high risk for HIV either because they had multiple partners or because of the high-risk behaviors of their regular partner. HIV risk was highest among women who accurately perceived themselves to be at increased HIV risk, reported weak behavioral intentions to reduce risk, and held stronger beliefs about psychosocial barriers to condom use. Women at high risk were also younger, reported higher rates of substance use, and indicated that their housing development lacked social cohesiveness. These findings suggest that HIV prevention efforts for this population should focus on strengthening women's risk reduction behavioral intentions and self-efficacy through skill development, overcoming psychosocial barriers to condom use, managing the risk related to substance use, and incorporating approaches that take into account the social, psychological, and relationship barriers to change among economically impoverished African American women.

Key words: HIV risk, HIV prevention, Black women, women's health

The incidence of new HIV infections and AIDS cases is rising at alarming rates among American women. Women are the fastest growing subgroup of AIDS cases, accounting for 19% of all new AIDS cases during 1995 (Centers for Disease Control and Prevention [CDC], 1996). Similar to the historical pattern of HIV infection

Correspondence concerning this article should be addressed to Kathleen J. Sikkema, Center for AIDS Intervention Research (CAIR), Medical College of Wisconsin, 1201 North Prospect Avenue, Milwaukee, WI 53202.

among men, risk for becoming infected is not equally distributed across all women, but is disproportionately high among economically impoverished minority women in inner cities. Approximately 76% of female AIDS cases diagnosed in the United States in 1995 occurred among African American and Hispanic women (16 and 7 times higher rates than for white women, respectively), although African American and Hispanic women make up only 21% of all U.S. women (CDC, 1996). In addition, the majority of children with AIDS in the United States are African American. Among women with HIV infection, heterosexual transmission, rather than a woman's own injection drug use, now accounts for the majority of new infections ("Update: Acquired immunodeficiency syndrome—United States," 1993).

There has been limited research documenting the prevalence, patterns, and determinants of HIV risk-related sexual behavior among women (Ickovics & Rodin, 1992; Morrill, Ickovics, Golubchikov, Beren, & Rodin, 1996). Normative beliefs concerning condom use have been identified as salient influences on minority women's intentions to use condoms (Jemmott & Jemmott, 1991), whereas substance use, greater severity of competing life stressors and concerns, high levels of depression, and low self-esteem were determinants of increased HIV risk behavior among homeless and drug-addicted minority women (Nyamathi, Bennett, Leake, Lewis, & Flaskerud, 1993). Indices of social norm perception, strength of behavioral intentions to reduce risk, and beliefs about self-efficacy of behavior change (Sikkema et al., 1995), as well as accuracy of perception of personal HIV risk, psychosocial barriers to condom use, age, and substance use have been shown to differentiate levels of sexual risk behavior among women living in inner-city housing developments (Sikkema, Heckman, et al., 1996). These differences indicated that women at greatest risk were those who did not perceive safer sex as socially normative, who held weak intentions and had little confidence in their ability to convince partners to use condoms, and were young and used substances at high levels. Predictors of high rates of condom use among the same sample of women included the woman's use of safer sex negotiation strategies, stronger risk-reduction intentions, perception of few barriers to condom use, and having multiple sex partners (Heckman et al., 1996). Based on a longitudinal prospective study examining factors predictive of the maintenance or initiation of heterosexual women's safer sexual behavior, relationship involvement and attitudes toward condoms were important factors in both the initiation and maintenance of safer behavior (Morrill et al., 1996). HIV counseling and testing, partner risk, and optimism were also related to the initiation of safer sexual behavior; depression, health locus of control, and outcome efficacy beliefs made significant contributions to the maintenance of safer sexual behavior.

Few researchers consider the impact of gender roles in studying HIV prevention issues among women (Amaro, 1995). Social and cultural factors such as patterns of traditional sex role socialization, social and economic dependence on a male partner, power imbalance in relationships, and male partner resistance to sexual negotiation and condom use create barriers to women's ability to reduce risk of sexually transmitted HIV infection (Kalichman, Hunter, & Kelly, 1992; Marin, 1989; Mays & Cochran, 1988). Condom use may be determined by a number of characteristics of women themselves or of their relationships with men. These characteristics include the type of relationship that exists between the sexual partners, the HIV risk status of a main or primary partner, one's number of different sexual partners, a woman's childbearing intentions or desires, and quality and extent of communication within the relationship (Santelli et al., 1996). In contrast to patterns observed in men in which sexual HIV risk is often due to having sex with a large number of different partners, women with a single partner may be more frequently at risk due to his drug use or sexual activity outside of their relationship. Recently, studies have begun to explore the contribution of partner type and relationship characteristics to HIV risk among heterosexual, inner-city women (Morrill et al., 1996; Santelli et al., 1996; Wagstaff et al., 1995).

Among women at risk for HIV infection, economically impoverished African American women are at disproportionately high risk. The purpose of this study was to delineate the prevalence of HIV risk factors among low-income, African American women residents of inner-city housing developments, and to highlight the extent to which characteristics of the women's sexual relationships played a role in their risk. Specifically, we examined the proportion of women at risk for HIV because they have multiple partners, as opposed to the high-risk behavior of a single primary partner, and the relationship of psychosocial factors to these sexual relationship characteristics. Within this population of women, variability in levels of HIV risk was expected, with some women at little or no risk and others at very high risk. Therefore, the final purpose of this study was to determine whether psychological and social characteristics such as HIV risk knowledge, perceived HIV risk, behavioral intention to reduce risk, perceptions of safer sex norms, beliefs about barriers to condom use, substance use, and community cohesiveness predicted HIV risk behavior in community samples of African American, low-income women.

METHOD

Setting and Participants

This study was conducted in 1994 and 1995 in 18 low-income, inner-city housing developments in Roanoke, Virginia; Rochester, New York; Cleveland, Ohio; Milwaukee, Wisconsin; and Seattle and Tacoma, Washington. These cities were selected because they are typical of middle-sized cities in the United States now witnessing an increase in HIV infections among women. The housing developments were located in inner-city areas with high rates of crime, poverty, and drug use. Data were collected from women ages 18 and older living in the developments, and we report here only data from African American women in the sample.[1] Female research staff recruited women into the study over a 6-week period; approximately 80% of all women living in the housing developments agreed to participate. Women received $15 for completing the assessment.

Assessment Measure

Women completed the assessment instrument in small groups in community rooms within each housing development. Because data collected through face-to-face interviews may result in inaccurate reports of sexual or drug use behavior (Catania, Gibson, Chitwood, & Coates, 1990), each woman received a printed questionnaire on which to anonymously record her responses. To ensure that the assessment instrument was understood by women with limited reading skills, and to provide an opportunity to explain each question in more detail if necessary, research staff displayed a facsimile of the instrument using an overhead projector and read each item aloud to guide survey completion. Content of the questionnaire was adapted from previous research on factors related to HIV risk (Kelly et al., 1994; Sikkema et al., 1995). One hundred women from similar, but nonparticipating, housing developments assisted with pilot testing and ensured that questions were easily understood. The instrument took approximately 30 min to complete and assessed the following.

Demographic characteristics. Women reported their age, ethnicity, education level, income, and current relationship status. Each woman also indicated if she had been treated for a sexually transmitted disease (STD) in the past 2 months, whether she had been tested for antibodies to HIV, and—if tested—the result of her most recent test.

HIV risk behavior knowledge scale. Practical understanding of HIV risk behavior was assessed using a 12-item true–false scale (sample item: "Latex is the best material a condom can be made of for protection against the AIDS virus.") This scale demonstrated adequate internal consistency ($\alpha = .73$, $N = 859$).

Sexual and substance use behavior. Women were asked to report their number of male sexual partners in the past 2 months, the number of times they had

---

[1]These data were collected as part of a multisite trial evaluating the effectiveness of a community-level HIV risk-reduction intervention for women living in low-income housing developments. Other research has been published describing HIV risk characteristics of a smaller subsample of women in this sample (Heckman et al., 1996; Heckman, Kelly, Sikkema, Cargill, et al., 1995; Sikkema, Heckman, et al., 1996; Wagstaff et al., 1995). The data presented in this study are based on African American women respondents ($n = 875$) from a full sample of 1,259 women. Six women were deleted from the sample due to extreme measures on several indexes of sexual behavior.

intercourse in the past 2 months, and the number of times they used condoms in the past 2 months. The format to assess sexual risk behavior was pilot-tested extensively, and the "past 2 months" time frame was utilized because it has been shown to elicit reliable reports of sexual behavior (Kauth, St. Lawrence, & Kelly, 1991). Women described their sexual behavior on these measures for both their regular sexual partner and any other sexual partners. A regular partner was defined as a man with whom the respondent had a current and long-term relationship, and other partners were defined as any other men with whom the respondent had sex in the past 2 months. Each woman also provided the number of days in the past 2 months when she used alcohol, marijuana, cocaine, or injected drugs.

Risk levels of male sexual partners.   Women may be at risk for HIV infection not only if they have multiple sexual partners or inject drugs, but also if they have an exclusive sexual relationship with a man who either injects drugs or has unprotected sex with someone else. Therefore, women completed items assessing the HIV risk of their regular sexual partner and, if applicable, other sexual partners. Using 4-point Likert scales ranging from 1 (*sure he did not*) to 4 (*sure he did*), women indicated how sure they were that their sexual partner(s) injected drugs or had sex with someone else in the past year. From this measure, it was possible to calculate the number of women who were sure or pretty sure their partner engaged in HIV risk behaviors.

Personal risk estimation.   Women were asked "Based on your behavior over the past two months, how high is your own risk for getting the AIDS virus?" Response options ranged from 1 (*no risk at all*) to 5 (*a lot of risk*). In addition to its face validity, this measure has exhibited predictive validity in previous investigations of HIV risk (Heckman, Kelly, Sikkema, Roffman, et al., 1995; Kelly et al., 1995).

Risk reduction behavioral intentions scale.   Women completed a three-item measure assessing intentions to use condoms during the next intercourse occasion. Each item consisted of a statement (sample statement: "I will use a condom the next time I have sex with a male partner") and a 4-point Likert scale to indicate level of agreement from 1 (*strongly disagree*) to 4 (*strongly agree*). This summated scale yielded scores ranging from 3 to 12, with higher scores indicative of stronger risk-reduction intentions. The measure demonstrated satisfactory internal consistency ($\alpha = .81$, $N = 845$).

Safer sex peer norm scale.   Respondents completed a four-item measure assessing perceptions of peer norms concerning condom use. Each item consisted of a statement (sample statement: "Most of my closest women friends use condoms when they have sex with a man") and a 4-point Likert scale to indicate level of agreement from 1 (*strongly disagree*) to 4 (*strongly agree*). This scale produced scores ranging from 4 to 16, with higher scores indicative of a safer sex norm among one's peer group; this scale showed satisfactory internal consistency ($\alpha = .81$, $N = 830$).

Condom barrier beliefs.   Four items were employed to assess women's attributions about barriers or negative aspects associated with condom use. Women provided their level of agreement with each statement using a 4-point Likert scale from 1 (*strongly disagree*) to 4 (*strongly agree*). The four condom barrier beliefs were: "Sex is not as good with a condom," "Using condoms means you don't trust your partner," "I do not have a need to use condoms," and "My partner would react badly if I suggested the use of a condom." This scale produced scores ranging from 4 to 16, with higher scores indicative of increased psychosocial barriers to condoms use ($\alpha = .64$, $N = 825$).

Conversations about condoms and AIDS concerns.   To assess women's efforts to reduce their HIV risk, as well as their personal interest in the threat of HIV and AIDS, each woman reported the number of times in the past 2 months that she talked to her male sexual partners about (a) condoms and (b) AIDS concerns. Women also reported how often they talked with other women in the housing development about AIDS concerns.

Housing cohesiveness scale.   Women completed a three-item measure designed to assess their perceptions of community or social cohesiveness within each housing development. Women indicated their level of agreement with each item using a 4-point Likert scale ranging from 1 (*strongly disagree*) to 4 (*strongly agree*). The three items comprising the scale were "This housing development is a safe place to live," "If there is a problem in this development, I can count on my neighbors to help me out," and "I trust most of the people living in this housing development." The scale, designed specifically for the current study, demonstrated adequate internal consistency ($\alpha = .70$, $N = 862$).

RESULTS

Sample Characteristics

The current study's sample consisted of 875 African American women living in low-income housing developments. The women had a mean age of 34.3 years (*SD* = 12.6, range = 15–84 years), had completed a mean of 11.5 years of education (*SD* = 2.0, range = 1–17 years), and had an average of 3.1 children (*SD* = 2.0, range = 0–14 children). Most women were economically impoverished; 81% of women reported an annual household income less than $1,000 per month.

Women consumed alcohol a mean of 5.5 days in the previous 2 months, used marijuana an average of 2.4 days (SD = 8.3, range = 0–60 days) in the past 2 months, and used cocaine an average of .52 days (SD = 4.0, range = 0–60 days) in the past 2 months; no woman reported using injection drugs. Twelve percent of the women had been treated for an STD in the past 2 months. Sixty-two percent of the women said they had been tested for HIV at some time in the past; 21% of all the women had been tested more than 1 year ago; only 5 women in the sample (0.6%) said they had tested positive for HIV.

HIV Risk Behavior Knowledge

The women exhibited substantial variation in their understanding about HIV risk behavior. On average, women answered correctly 71% of the 12 items comprising the HIV risk behavior knowledge scale; 19% of women answered one half or fewer of the items correctly. As shown in Table 1, women demonstrated having several important misconceptions about AIDS risk behavior. For example, 45% of women did not know that Vaseline and other oils should not be used to lubricate condoms, 54% did not know that latex condoms afford the greatest degree of protection against HIV, 58% incorrectly believed that most people infected with HIV look and feel unhealthy, and over one fourth of the women believed that condoms cause men pain.

TABLE 1

Proportion of Women Answering Each HIV Risk Behavior Knowledge Test Item Correctly

Item	% Answering Correctly
Birth control pills protect against the AIDS virus (F)	89
If a man pulls out right before orgasm (cumming), condoms don't need to be used to protect against the AIDS virus (F)	88
Most people who have the AIDS virus look sick (F)	76
Vaseline and other oils should not be used to lubricate condoms (T)	55
Latex is the best material a condom can be made of for protection against the AIDS virus (T)	46
Cleaning injection needles with water is enough to kill the AIDS virus (F)	88
Most people who carry the AIDS virus look and feel healthy (T)	42
Hand lotion is not a good lubricant to use with a condom (T)	59
A woman is not likely to get the AIDS virus from having sex with a man unless he is gay/bisexual (F)	85
Condoms cause men physical pain (F)	73
If you're seeing a man and if he agrees not to have sex with other people, it is not important to use a condom (F)	84
Always leave some room or slack in the tip of a condom when putting it on (T)	62

Relationship Characteristics

As shown in Table 2, 16% of the women reported that they had multiple sexual partners in the previous 2 months; 23% reported that they had a regular sexual partner whom they knew or believed engaged in high HIV risk behavior; 38% had a regular sexual partner who they knew or believed did not inject drugs or have sex with other people; and 23% reported they were not sexually active in the past 2 months. Thus, almost 40% of the women in the sample were at potentially elevated risk either because they had multiple partners or had sex with a single and steady but high-risk male partner. Among the entire sample, the women reported an average of .93 male sexual partners in the past 2 months ($SD = .85$, range = 0–11 partners) and an average of 7.1 intercourse occasions over the past 2 months (median = 4.0, $SD = 10.5$, range = 0–64 occasions).

Among the sexually active women, 34% used a condom during their most recent intercourse occasion, and 37% ($SD = 46\%$, range = 0–100%) of all intercourse occasions in the past 2 months were condom protected. For intercourse occasions involving regular sexual partners, 36% were condom protected. During intercourse occasions involving other sexual partners, 61% of intercourse occasions were condom protected.

HIV Risk By Relationship Status

A series of one-way analyses of variance (ANOVAs) and chi-square tests for association were conducted to determine if HIV risk behavior and characteristics were associated with relationship status. As shown in Table 3, relationship status was significantly associated with several indexes of HIV risk. A chi-square analysis revealed that condom use during the last intercourse occasion varied by relationship status. Women who had multiple sexual partners in the past 2 months were more likely to have used a condom during their most recent intercourse occasion (50%),

TABLE 2

Proportion and Number of African American Women in 18 Low-Income Housing Developments, By Sexual Behavior in the 2 Months Prior to the Survey

Sexual Behavior and Perception of Partner	%	n
Multiple partners	15.9	139
Regular, risky partner	22.5	197
Partner believed to have had other sexual partners in past year	20.9	183
Partner believed to have ever injected drugs	1.6	14
Regular, low-risk partner	36.7	321
Not sexually active	23.7	207
Missing data	1.2	11
Total	100.0	892

TABLE 3
Mean Scores and Proportions Assessing Women's Sexual Behavior and HIV Risk-Related Characteristics in Past 2 Months

Measure	Multiple Partners (1)	Exclusive, Risky Partner (2)	Exclusive, Low-Risk Partner (3)	Not Sexually Active (4)	χ^2	F	p <	Pairwise Comparisons
Used condom at last intercourse (%)	50	37	25	33	79.7		.0001	1 > 2; 1 > 4; 1 > 3; 2 > 3
Treated for an STD in past 2 months (%)	30	11	8.2	7.3	49.5		.0001	1 > 2; 1 > 3; 1 > 4
Mean perceived risk for HIV infection	2.06	2.06	1.61	1.24		32.6	.001	4 < 3; 4 < 2; 4 < 1; 3 < 1; 3 < 2
Mean condom use intentions	9.93	9.87	9.28	10.39		6.7	.0001	3 < 4
Mean condom use barriers	8.14	7.91	8.74	9.04		4.4	.005	2 < 3

followed by women with a single, regular but high-risk male sexual partner (37%), women who were not sexually active in the 2 months (33%), and, finally, women with a single, regular partner not known or believed to be at high risk (25%).

STD treatment history also varied by relationship status. Thirty percent of women with multiple sexual partners were treated for an STD in the past 2 months compared to lower rates among women with a single, regular high-risk male sexual partner (11%), women with a single, regular low-risk partner (8.2%), and women reporting no sexual activity in the past 2 months (7.3%). Regarding the latter percentage, some women who were not sexually active in the past 2 months before the survey reported treatment for an STD during that period. Such reports may reflect ongoing treatment of a chronic STD or treatment of infections that were contracted prior to and detected within the 2-month retrospective recall period.

We next examined if continuously measured factors related to HIV risk varied by relationship status. A two-group multivariate analysis of variance (MANOVA) was used to determine if the set of dependent variables (i.e., risk-reduction intentions, perceived risk estimation, and condom barrier beliefs) varied by relationship status. The MANOVA indicated that women's responses to the combined set of dependent measures varied by relationship status, Wilks's lambda = .86, $F(9, 1922) = 13.5$, $p <$ .001. Univariate ANOVAs were then conducted to identify individual variables that varied by relationship status. As also shown in Table 3, women with multiple sexual partners or those who had a high HIV risk male sexual partner correctly perceived themselves to be at greater risk for contracting HIV infection, $F(3, 846) = 32.5$, $p <$ .001. Post hoc multiple comparisons (Tukey's a) indicated that women who did not have sexual intercourse during the past 2 months believed themselves to be at significantly lower personal risk than did women in the other three groups. In addition, women with a regular, nonrisky partner reported significantly lower risk estimation scores than did women with multiple sexual partners and women with a risky partner.

A one-way ANOVA revealed that risk-reduction behavioral intentions varied by relationship status, $F(3, 833) = 51.3$, $p < .002$. Women who were not sexually active reported higher risk- reduction behavioral intentions ($M = 10.4$) than did women with a regular, nonrisky sexual partner ($M = 9.28$). No other post hoc pairwise comparisons were significant. Condom barrier beliefs also varied by relationship status, $F(3, 812) = 4.41$, $p < .005$. Women who were not sexually active and women with an exclusive, low-risk partner perceived significantly more barriers and negative consequences to condom use than did women with a single, regular but risky male sexual partner.

Univariate Regression Analyses Identifying Predictors of HIV Risk Levels Among African American Women

To identify psychological and behavioral predictors of high HIV risk among the sample, respondents were classified into high- or low-risk groups, and the classification was modeled with logistic regression. Women at high risk were defined as those who (a) had multiple sexual partners in the past 2 months, and reported any unprotected intercourse; (b) had unprotected intercourse with a partner believed to have injected drugs or to have had sex with other people in the past year; (c) had unprotected intercourse with an HIV-positive man; (d) had used injected drugs in the past 2 months; (e) had been treated for an STD in the past 2 months, and reported any unprotected intercourse; or (e) had unprotected intercourse with a regular partner with whom she had been sexually involved for less than 1 year, and was uncertain whether that partner had injected drugs or had sex with other people. Women at low risk were those who reported no intercourse, those who reported completely consistent condom use, or those involved in a mutually monogamous relationship with a man who had tested negative for HIV and whom the woman believed did not inject drugs or have sex with other people. This classification scheme yielded 447 low-risk women and 253 women at high risk. The remaining 85 women could not be reliably categorized and thus were not included in these analyses.

Corroborative analyses supported the validity of this classification scheme. Women at high HIV risk reported more than twice as many male sexual partners ($M = 1.44$) as low HIV risk women ($M = 0.6$). Further, whereas only 9% of low HIV risk women had been treated for an STD in the past 2 months, 24% of women at high HIV risk were treated for an STD in the previous 2 months, $\chi^2(1, N = 695) = 28.6, p < .0001$.

As shown in Table 4, univariate logistic regression analyses identified several variables associated with high HIV risk. Women at high risk for HIV infection were more likely to (a) be younger, (b) accurately perceive themselves to be at higher risk for HIV infection, (c) more frequently talk with their sexual partner(s) about condom use, (d) more frequently talk to their male sexual partner(s) about AIDS, (e) report a greater number of days in the past 2 months on which they used alcohol or illegal substances, (f) report lower safe sex peer norms, (g) report lower risk-reduction intentions, (h) report higher psychosocial condom barrier beliefs, (i) perceive their housing development to be less cohesive, and (j) have been tested for HIV at sometime in the past.

Multiple Logistic Regression Analysis Modeling HIV Risk Classification

Given the substantial intercorrelations among many of the predictor variables as shown by the correlation matrix in Table 5, a forward stepwise logistic regression analysis was performed to evaluate all variables that were significant in univariate logistic regression analyses and that were conceptually related to HIV risk. As shown in Table 6, six variables provided significant and unique contributions to HIV risk classification: (a) personal risk estimation score, (b) risk-reduction behavioral intentions, (c) number of days in past 2 months alcohol and drugs were used,

TABLE 4
Univariate Predictors of Level of HIV Risk Among African American Women in Low-Income
Housing Developments

Variable	Odds Ratio	p <	95% Confidence Interval
Education	0.94	ns	.87–1.02
Age (in decades)	0.66	.0001	.57–.76
HIV risk behavior knowledge	1.61	ns	.75–3.42
Personal risk estimation	2.06	.0001	1.73–2.48
Number of conversations with sexual partner about condoms[a]	1.56	.05	1.01–2.41
Number of conversations with sexual partner about AIDS[a]	2.01	.001	1.32–3.06
Number of days in past 2 months used drugs or illegal substances[a]	2.51	.001	1.86–3.38
Safer sex peer norms	0.91	.0001	.88–.95
Risk reduction behavioral intentions	0.84	.0001	.79–.89
Number of conversations with other women about AIDS[a]	1.02	ns	.68–1.52
Condom barrier beliefs	1.05	.03	1.02–1.08
Housing cohesiveness score	0.88	.0001	.83–.93
Been tested for HIV	1.40	.05	1.02–1.97

[a]$Log_{10}(X + 1)$ transformation applied to variable.

(d) participant's age, (e) condom barrier beliefs, and (f) housing development cohesiveness index. Women who were at high risk for HIV infection accurately perceived themselves to be at greater risk, reported weaker intentions to use condoms during sex, and tended to be younger. Women at high risk for HIV also reported stronger psychosocial barriers to condom use, such as beliefs that sex is not as good if condoms are used and that using condoms means you do not trust your partner. Finally, women at high HIV risk indicated that their housing development lacked social cohesiveness, reflecting the view that their housing situation was not safe and that there were few women who lived in their development whom they could trust. Number of conversations with sexual partners about AIDS, number of conversations with sexual partners about condoms, and safer sex peer norm scores did not enter the final logistic regression model. Additional analyses revealed that none of the significant predictor variables in the multivariate analysis were involved in any higher order interactions.

Overall, the six-variable model correctly classified 75.1% of the women in the regression analysis into their respective risk category, $\chi^2(6, N = 498) = 129.1, p < .0001$. The model was particularly successful in classifying women who were at low risk for HIV (i.e., 87% classification accuracy), but performed less well for women at high HIV risk, correctly classifying only 55% of these women.

TABLE 5
Correlation Matrix Showing Intercorrelations Among Important Predictor Variables

	Risk Estimation	Peer Norms	Risk Reduction Intentions	Barriers to Condoms	Conversations About AIDS	Conversations About Condoms	Drug Use
Risk estimation	1.0	-.13**	-.11**	-.05	.16**	.19**	.18**
Safer sex peer norms		1.0	.49**	.05	.01	.01	-.06
Risk reduction intentions			1.0	-.09**	.01	.12**	-.06
Barriers to condom use				1.0	-.06	-.15**	-.08*
Conversations about AIDS					1.0	.55**	.14**
Conversations about condoms						1.0	.12**
Drug use							1.0

*p < .05. **p < .01.

TABLE 6
Stepwise Multiple Logistic Regression Analysis Modeling HIV Risk Among Women Living in
Low-Income Inner-City Housing Developments

Variable	Ratio	95% Confidence Interval	p <
Step 1: Personal risk estimation	2.15	1.69–2.74	.0001
Step 2: Risk reduction behavioral intentions	0.86	.79–.93	.0002
Step 3: Number of days alcohol and drugs used, past 2 months[a]	1.91	1.34–2.75	.0004
Step 4: Age (in decades)	0.76	.62–.92	.007
Step 5: Condom barrier beliefs	1.11	1.04–1.17	.004
Step 6: Housing cohesiveness scale	0.90	.84–.98	.03

Note. Results shown are for variables entered into the final model.
[a]$Log_{10}(X + 1)$ transformation applied to variable.

DISCUSSION

Many African American women living in inner-city, low-income housing developments are at risk for contracting HIV infection because of their multiple sexual partners or because of their involvement in sexual relationships with regular partners who inject drugs or have sex outside of their primary relationships. However, fewer women (16%) in this sample had sex with multiple partners than had a single, regular relationship with a man known to have had extrarelationship sex (21%). High rates of recent treatment for STD and low rates of condom use with regular but high-risk partners substantiated the risk for HIV infection among this latter group of women. Condom use was more likely among women with multiple partners than among women with single, but risky, partners. Condoms were not used in two thirds of the intercourse occasions with men who were known or believed to be risky partners. Eleven percent of women in a single, regular relationship with a high-risk male partner required treatment for an STD in the past 2 months. Thus, women in this sample were at risk for HIV both when they had unprotected sex in single, regular relationships with high-risk men, and also when they had unprotected intercourse with multiple male partners. However, not all women in this sample were at risk; a large number of women were not sexually active in the past 2 months, had only one regular partner not known or believed to be engaging in risk behavior, or consistently used condoms.

Women in this sample demonstrated relatively high overall levels of HIV risk behavior knowledge, but with misconceptions in specific areas such as proper condom and lubricant use, and misconceptions about the physical appearance of most people with HIV. Educational efforts in these targeted areas of misconception are still needed.

Our findings concerning predictors of HIV risk level in this sample underscore the importance of addressing several key issues in HIV prevention efforts among low-income, inner-city African American women at risk for HIV and AIDS. These include strengthening intentions to take action to reduce risk and developing ways to handle barriers to condom use that may involve the woman's own negative attributions about condoms but also involve expected resistance from the man. The associations between younger age and higher levels of substance use with elevated HIV risk indicate that interventions should be especially focused on young women, address substance use as a potential risk cofactor, and perhaps integrate HIV prevention into substance-use treatment. Interestingly, we did not find that women high in HIV risk underestimated their vulnerability. The development of skills, competencies, problem-solving strategies, and supports needed to effect behavior change appear to be more important intervention elements than increasing awareness about AIDS.

These findings are consistent with social–cognitive (Bandura, 1994) and reasoned action (Fishbein & Ajzen, 1975) theories applied to HIV risk reduction, and support HIV prevention approaches that emphasize strengthening of women's risk-reduction behavioral intentions and self-efficacy through skill development. Some of the skill areas especially pertinent for low-income, inner-city African American women involve proper condom use and sexual communication tailored for women. Culturally and personally relevant prevention messages that emphasize cultural pride, community concern, and family responsibility may be especially useful. Sexual negotiation and communication skills require tailoring to cultural, gender, and relationship context. Women with multiple partners, women who trade sex for money or drugs, and women with single, high-risk partners have qualitatively different relationships that present different risk circumstances and barriers, and therefore require different approaches to behavior change. Intervention approaches must be tailored to the interpersonal context of sexual behavior, distinguishing between the emotional and social factors related to casual and committed sexual relationships. Group interventions that focus on enhancing perceptions of HIV risk, motivating risk-behavior change, identifying and managing factors (such as substance use) related to high-risk behavior, developing women's problem-solving and sexual communication skills, and providing social and peer support for behavior-change efforts show promise as effective interventions for inner-city African American women at risk for HIV infection (DiClemente & Wingood, 1995; Hobfoll, Jackson, Lavin, Britton, & Shepherd, 1994; Kelly et al., 1994).

A challenge to HIV behavior change interventions is to incorporate prevention approaches that take into account the social, psychological, economic, and relationship barriers to change among many low-income, inner-city African American women. For example, the finding that women's perception of lack of cohesiveness and safety in their housing developments is associated with HIV-risk behavior suggests the need for broader based approaches to HIV risk reduction. Inner-city housing developments are an appropriate and important setting for HIV prevention programs targeting adult and adolescent women at risk for HIV infection. Preliminary findings from a community-level intervention that combined the utilization of opinion leaders, skills-training workshops, and community mobilization strategies implemented with women in housing developments have proven promising and have produced significant increases in condom use (Sikkema, Kelly, et al., 1996). Housing developments and other community settings constitute venues for reaching at-risk communities of low-income African American women and provide an opportunity to integrate HIV prevention with other health, social service, and residential activities in housing development communities.

The sample studied in this research was low-income, inner-city African American women. However, it is also clear that the challenge of protecting women from HIV requires more than women's efforts alone. Interventions for men, particularly high-risk heterosexual men, are also needed. Most barrier protections against HIV are male controlled, and men's attitudes toward condoms can influence whether condoms will be used, especially in power-imbalanced relationships and those in which the woman is economically dependent. HIV prevention efforts for women require interventions for women. They also require more vigorous research to understand and then intervene to change the behavior of men who place their female partners at risk for HIV.

ACKNOWLEDGMENTS

This research was supported by National Institute of Mental Health Center Grant P30–MH52776 awarded to Jeffrey A. Kelly and Grant R01–42908 from the National Institute of Mental Health awarded to Kathleen J. Sikkema. Members of the Community Housing AIDS Prevention Study Group who contributed significantly to this article include David A. Wagstaff, Richard A. Winett, Laura J. Solomon, Roger A. Roffman, Victoria Cargill, Eileen S. Anderson, Melissa J. Perry, Ann D. Norman, Denise A. Crumble, and Mary Beth Mercer. We also extend appreciation to R. Wayne Fuqua, Brenda Alston, Jill Baroni, Renee Brown, Brenda Coley, Crystal Copeland, Catherina Galdabini, Colleen Keane, Lisa Noel, Christine Russ, Zestian Smith, Deborah Tate, and Paula Wood.

REFERENCES

Amaro, H. (1995). Love, sex and power: Considering women's realities in HIV prevention. *American Psychologist, 50,* 437–447.
Bandura, A. (1994). Social cognitive theory and exercise of control over HIV infection. In R. J. DiClemente & J. L. Peterson (Eds.), *Preventing AIDS: Theories and methods of behavioral interventions* (pp. 25–59). New York: Plenum.

Catania, J. A., Gibson, D. R., Chitwood, D. D., & Coates, T. J. (1990). Methodological problems in AIDS behavioral research: Influence on measurement error and participant bias in studies of sexual behavior. *Psychology Bulletin, 108,* 339–362.

Centers for Disease Control and Prevention. (1996). U.S. AIDS Cases reported through December, 1995. *HIV/AIDS Surveillance Reports, 7,* 1–39.

DiClemente, R. J., & Wingood, G. M. (1995). A randomized controlled trial of an HIV sexual risk-reduction intervention for young African-American women. *Journal of the American Medical Association, 274,* 1271–1276.

Fishbein, M., & Ajzen, I. (1975). *Belief, attitude, intention, and behavior: An introduction to theory and research.* Reading, MA: Addison-Wesley.

Heckman, T. G., Kelly, J. A., Sikkema, K. J., Cargill, V., Norman, A. D., Fuqua, R. W., Wagstaff, D. A., Solomon, L. J., Roffman, R. A., Crumble, D. A., Perry, M. J., Winett, R. A., Anderson, E. S., Mercer, M. B., & Hoffmann, R. (1995). HIV risk characteristics of young adult, adult, and older adult women who live in inner-city housing developments: Implications for prevention. *Journal of Women's Health, 4,* 397–406.

Heckman, T. G., Kelly, J. A., Sikkema, K. J., Roffman, R. A., Solomon, L. J., Winett, R. A., Stevenson, L. Y., Perry, M. J., & Norman, A. D. (1995). Differences in HIV risk characteristics between bisexual and exclusively gay men. *AIDS Education and Prevention, 7,* 504–512.

Heckman, T. G., Sikkema, K. J., Kelly, J. A., Fuqua, R. W., Mercer, M. B., Hoffmann, R. G., Winett, R. A., Anderson, E. S., Perry, M. J., Roffman, R. A., Solomon, L. J., Wagstaff, D. A., Cargill, V., Norman, A. D., & Crumble, D. A. (1996). Predictors of condom use and human immunodeficiency virus test seeking among women living in inner-city public housing developments. *Sexually Transmitted Diseases, 23,* 357–365.

Hobfoll, S. E., Jackson, A. P., Lavin, J., Britton, P. J., & Shepherd, J. B. (1994). Reducing inner-city women's AIDS risk activities: A study of single, pregnant women. *Health Psychology, 13,* 397–403.

Ickovics, J., & Rodin, J. (1992). Women and AIDS in the United States: Epidemiology, natural history, and mediating mechanisms. *Health Psychology, 11,* 1–16.

Jemmott, L. S., & Jemmott, J. B., III. (1992). Applying the theory of reasoned action to AIDS risk behavior: Condom use among Black women. *Nursing Research, 40,* 228–234.

Kalichman, S. C., Hunter, T. L., & Kelly, J. A. (1992). Perceptions of AIDS susceptibility among minority and nonminority women at risk for HIV infection. *Journal of Consulting and Clinical Psychology, 60,* 725–732.

Kauth, M. R., St. Lawrence, J. S., & Kelly, J. A. (1991). Reliability of retrospective assessments of sexual HIV risk behavior: A comparison of biweekly, three-month, and 12-month self-reports. *AIDS Education and Prevention, 3,* 207–214.

Kelly, J. A., Murphy, D. A., Washington, D. C., Wilson, T. S., Koob, J. J., Davis, D. R., Ledezma, G., & Davantes, B. (1994). The effects of HIV/AIDS intervention groups for high-risk women in urban clinics. *American Journal of Public Health, 84,* 1918–1922.

Kelly, J. A., Sikkema, K. J., Winett, R. A., Solomon, L. J., Roffman, R. A., Heckman, T. G., Stevenson, L. Y., Perry, M. J., Norman, A. D., & Desiderato, L. J. (1995). Factors predicting continued high-risk behavior among gay men in small cities: Psychological, behavioral, and demographic characteristics related to unsafe sex. *Journal of Consulting and Clinical Psychology, 63,* 101–107.

Marin, G. (1989). AIDS prevention among Hispanics: Needs, risk behaviors, and cultural values. *Public Health Reports, 104,* 411–415.

Mays, V. M., & Cochran, S. D. (1988). Issues in the perception of AIDS risk and risk reduction activities by Black and Hispanic/Latina women. *American Psychologist, 43,* 949–957.

Morrill, A. C., Ickovics, J. R., Golubchikov, V. V., Beren, S. E., & Rodin, J. (1996). Safer sex: Social and psychological predictors of behavioral maintenance and change among heterosexual women. *Journal of Consulting and Clinical Psychology, 64,* 819–828.

Nyamathi, A., Bennett, C., Leake, B., Lewis, C., & Flaskerud, J. (1993). AIDS-related knowledge, perceptions, and behaviors among impoverished minority women. *American Journal of Public Health, 83,* 65–71.

Santelli, J. S., Kouzis, A. C., Hoover, D. R., Polacsek, M., Burwell, L. G., & Celentano, D. D. (1996). Stage of behavior change for condom use: The influence of partner type, relationship and pregnancy factors. *Family Planning Perspectives, 28,* 101–107.

Sikkema, K. J., Heckman, T. G., Kelly, J. A., Anderson, E. S., Winett, R. A., Solomon, L. J., Wagstaff, D. A., Roffman, R. A., Perry, M. J., Cargill, V., Crumble, D. A., Fuqua, R. W., Norman, A. D., & Mercer, M. B. (1996). HIV risk behaviors among women living in low-income, inner-city housing developments. *American Journal of Public Health, 86,* 1123–1128.

Sikkema, K. J., Kelly, J. A., Heckman, T. G., Solomon, L. J., Winett, R. A., Cargill, V. C., Roffman, R. A., Wagstaff, D. A., Perry, M. J., Norman, A. D., Crumble, D. A., Mercer, M. B., & Anderson, E. S. (1996, November). *Outcomes of a community-level HIV risk reduction intervention for inner city women.* Paper presented at the 124th annual meeting of the American Public Health Association, New York.

Sikkema, K. J., Koob, J. J., Cargill, V. C., Kelly, J. A., Desiderato, L. L., Roffman, R. A., Norman, A. D., Shabazz, M., Copeland, C., Winett, R. A., Steiner, S., & Lemke, A. L. (1995). Levels and predictors of HIV risk behavior among women living in low-income public housing developments. *Public Health Reports, 110,* 707–713.

Update: Acquired immunodeficiency syndrome—United States. (1993). *Morbidity and Mortality Weekly Report, 42,* 547–551.

Wagstaff, D. A., Kelly, J. A., Perry, M. J., Sikkema, K. J., Solomon, L. J., Heckman, T. G., Anderson, E. S., & the Community Housing AIDS Prevention Study Group. (1995). Multiple partners, risky partners and HIV risk among low-income urban women. *Family Planning Perspectives, 27,* 241–245.

WOMEN'S HEALTH: RESEARCH ON GENDER, BEHAVIOR, AND POLICY, 3(3&4), 367–381
Copyright © 1997, Lawrence Erlbaum Associates, Inc.

Conclusions: The Future of Research on Black Women's Health

Hope Landrine

Public Health Foundation
City of Industry, California

Elizabeth A. Klonoff

Behavioral Health Institute
California State University–San Bernardino

The preponderance of studies on Black women's health cited in the eight articles of this special issue were published in medical and public health journals, rather than in health psychology journals. Health psychology stands conspicuously apart from other health disciplines in this neglect and exclusion of Blacks and Black women. On the other hand, although there are many studies of Black women's health published in medical and public health journals, these studies have neglected a variety of important cultural and social–contextual variables, and often are methodologically inadequate. Hence, we conclude that studies on Black women's health that examine neglected variables and employ rigorous methods are needed in health psychology, behavioral medicine, and the other health disciplines as well. Specific variables and hypotheses that might be addressed in such future research are highlighted.

Key words: Black women, health, health psychology, behavioral medicine, preventive medicine

In the introductory article, we highlighted the virtual absence of research on Black women in health psychology and behavioral medicine and noted that more studies of white rats than of Black women's three major health problems have been

Correspondence concerning this article should be addressed to Hope Landrine, Senior Research Scientist, Public Health Foundation, 13200 Crossroads Parkway North, Suite 135, City of Industry, CA 91746.

published in the past 14 years in the two leading health psychology journals. Simultaneously, the eight articles in this special issue contained lengthy literature reviews detailing the findings of an abundance of health studies that included Black women as participants, or indeed, focused on Black women's health alone. This apparent contradiction stems from the fact that very few of the 615 studies cited in the articles here were published in *Health Psychology* ($n = 7$, or 1.1%), *Journal of Behavioral Medicine* ($n = 2$, or .3 %), or indeed in any psychology journal. Instead, the preponderance of the studies cited throughout this special issue ($n = 606$, or 98.54%) were published in medical, public health, and social science journals—most notably *American Journal of Public Health, Journal of the American Medical Association, Preventive Medicine,* and *Social Science and Medicine.* Thus, the authors of the articles in this special issue found a wealth of studies on or related to Black women's health in health journals, but not in health psychology journals. This summary is supported by Hoffman-Goetz and Mills (this issue) who noted that, in their thorough search of the literature for studies of Black women and cancer, they found 300 citations in CancerLine (medical and public health journals) but only 8 in PsychInfo (psychology journals).

From this analysis of the 615 references cited in the eight articles here and the results of the Goetz and Mills search, we conclude that many disciplines study the health of Blacks and of Black women, but that health psychology simply is not one of them. The health of Blacks and of Black women is not neglected by health researchers in general, but instead is neglected by health psychology researchers alone. The question then is "Why?"

The neglect of Blacks and of Black women by health psychology can be understood in the context of the problems that the discipline of psychology as a whole continues to face where cultural diversity is concerned. As noted in the introductory article, health psychology is not the only area of psychology that excludes and neglects Blacks, but instead is similar to clinical, social, personality, educational, developmental (Graham, 1992), and feminist (Landrine, 1995; Reid & Kelly, 1994) psychology in this regard. Because this exclusion of Blacks (and of other minorities) is a problem for psychology as a whole, debates regarding the value of a multicultural perspective and the need to study someone other than whites continue at this very moment (in June 1997) on the pages of psychology's official journal, the *American Psychologist* (e.g., Bernal & Castro, 1994; Ekstrom, 1997; Fowers & Richardson, 1996, 1997; Gaubatz, 1997; Graham, 1992; C. Hall, 1997; G. Hall, 1997; Teo & Febbraro, 1997; Yanchar & Slife, 1997). Likewise, because Blacks (more so than other minority groups) are particularly problematic for psychology (Yee, Fairchild, Weizmann, & Wyatt, 1993), debates regarding the extent to which race is a meaningless and harmful category and whether Blacks represent a racial or an ethnic group also continue on the pages of the *American Psychologist* (e.g., Betancourt & Lopez, 1993; Dole, 1995; Fairchild, Yee, Wyatt, & Weizmann, 1995; Fish, 1995; Levin, 1995; Phinney, 1996; Scarr, 1988; Sun,

1995; Yee et al., 1993; Zuckerman, 1990). Hence, "psychology's problems with race" (Yee et al., 1993, p. 1132)—with how to think about Blacks and with studying Blacks—are well known, characterize all areas of psychology, and are specific to psychology alone (Fish, 1995; Goodchilds, 1991; C. Hall, 1997; G. Hall, 1997; Jones, 1991; Landrine & Klonoff, 1996a). Health psychology's problems with Blacks simply reflect those of the discipline.

Consequently, however, that psychology needs to include Blacks and other ethnic and cultural minorities in its research is an obvious truism that has been stated again and again by all of the well-known scholars and researchers previously cited. That health psychology in particular needs to include Blacks and other minorities in its research similarly is an obvious truism that we stated previously in a now well-known article in *Health Psychology* (Landrine & Klonoff, 1992). That health psychology stands conspicuously apart from all other health disciplines (e.g., preventive and other areas of medicine, nursing, medical anthropology, and public health) in neglecting and excluding Blacks and Black women from its research is clear in this summary, and is stated here for perhaps the first time. Thus, more research on Black women's health is needed in health psychology and behavioral medicine.

In addition, however, and as noted repeatedly in the articles here, more research—and a different kind of research—on Black women's health is needed from the many other health disciplines (e.g., public health, preventive medicine) as well, to fully elucidate the causes of Black women's differential morbidity and mortality and improve their health. Although there is an abundance of studies on Black women's health in preventive medicine, public health, nursing, and related fields, the authors of the articles here each noted that important variables have been neglected in those studies, that the methodologies employed often were inadequate or ambiguous, and that specific studies crucial to clarifying the role of one variable (e.g., socioeconomic status) versus another variable (e.g., culture) have yet to be conducted. The question then is, "What kind of research on Black women's health is needed?", not only in health psychology, but in health research generally.

The articles in this special issue suggest that methodologically rigorous studies of cultural variables on the one hand, and of social–contextual variables on the other, are needed. Table 1 summarizes the cultural and social–contextual variables highlighted in the eight articles in this issue; only a few of these are discussed here.

CULTURAL VARIABLES

As shown in Table 1, several authors highlighted the need for research on the role that cultural health beliefs and practices might play in Black women's health behavior, morbidity, and mortality. That African Americans have their own cultural health beliefs, indigenous healers, and health practices (which came to the United

TABLE 1
Cultural and Social Variables in Black Women's Health

Variables	Noted By
Cultural	
Health beliefs (e.g., cancer is caused by injury to breast or impurities in the blood; fatalism; belief in luck; involvement in Black ethnomedicine)	Hoffman-Goetz & Mills, Paskett et al., Snowden et al.
Health-related norms and values	Hoffman-Goetz & Mills, Allison et al., Sikkema et al.
Black women's social networks	Hoffman-Goetz & Mills
Perceived risk for the disease/health problem	Paskett et al., Bowen et al., Sikkema et al.
Attitudes toward physicians	Bowen et al., Snowden et al.
Ethnic identity	Bowen et al., Allison et al.
Consumption of traditional cultural foods	McNabb et al.
Social-Contextual	
Age	Paskett et al., Bowen et al., McNabb et al., Snowden et al., Sikkema et al.
Health insurance	Paskett et al., Snowden et al.
Marital status	Paskett et al., Bowen et al., Snowden et al., Sikkema et al.
Residence (urbanization)	Paskett et al., McNabb et al., Snowden et al.
Socioeconomic status (education, income)	Bowen et al., Allison et al., McNabb et al., Snowden et al., Sikkema et al.
Dangerousness of immediate environment/violence against women	McNabb et al., Sikkema et al., Russo et al.
Racial discrimination	Allison et al., Snowden et al.

States with the slaves and persist) has been well documented by anthropologists, historians, and sociologists (e.g., Baer, 1985; Bailey, 1987, 1991; Brandon, 1991; Charatz-Litt, 1992; Cooke, 1984; Deas-Moore, 1987; Flaskerud & Rush, 1989; Goodson, 1987; Hall & Bourne, 1973; Hill & Matthews, 1981; Holloway, 1991; Jackson, 1981; Jacques, 1976; Johnson & Snow, 1982; Jordan, 1975, 1979; Laguerre, 1987; Mulira, 1991; Payne-Jackson & Lee, 1993; Sexton, 1992; Snow, 1974, 1977, 1978, 1983; Spector, 1979, 1996; Spicer, 1977; Tallant, 1946; Watson, 1984). These ethnomedical beliefs and practices rarely have been examined in the empirical studies of any health-related discipline, however (public health, preventive medicine, health psychology), and doing so may be beneficial (Landrine & Klonoff, in press).

For example, in a recent study of acculturation and cigarette smoking among Black adults, we found that African American ethnomedical beliefs and practices were a better predictor of smoking than age, gender, education, and income combined (Klonoff & Landrine, 1996). Similarly, Snowden et al. (this issue) found that Black women differed from White women in the use of ethnomedical home remedies, and that this in part predicted utilization of health services. Such a finding is consistent with anthropological studies indicating that up to 60% of Blacks rely on African American herbal medicine (e.g., Mathews, Kirkland, Sullevan, & Baldwin, 1992; Mitchell, 1978; Payne-Jackson & Lee, 1993), with its use most common among women, and specifically in poor communities where people lack health care, or where the ratio of physicians to patients is 1 to 3,550 (Payne-Jackson & Lee, 1993). Snowden et al.'s finding also is consistent with sociological studies demonstrating that the use of African American herbal medicine can be associated with noncompliance with treatment (e.g., Bailey, 1991). Likewise, Hoffman-Goetz and Mills (this issue) found that some Black women believe that breast cancer is caused by impurities in the blood. The belief that impurities in the body (particularly in the blood) cause illness is an ancient one in African American ethnomedicine, and such beliefs can play a role in Black women's health behavior (Bailey, 1987, 1991; Flaskerud & Rush, 1989; Hill & Matthews, 1981; Johnson & Snow, 1982; Landrine & Klonoff, 1996a, in press; Puckett, 1926; Snow, 1974, 1977, 1978, 1983; Watson, 1984). The belief that impurities in the blood cause cancer also has been found among Asian Americans and Hispanic Americans, and has been demonstrated to play a role in their seeking cancer screening and treatment as well (Garcia & Lee, 1989).

All of these findings suggest that African American ethnomedical beliefs and practices may play an important role in Blacks' (and particularly in Black women's) health behavior, and so warrant investigation in research conducted by any health-related discipline. Integrating African American ethnomedical beliefs into studies of health schema, causal attributions for illness, compliance with treatment, and seeking screening and treatment for illness may advance our understanding of the role of basic cultural variables in Blacks' and Black women's health.

An additional cultural variable noted in the articles here was ethnic identity. Allison et al. (this issue) hypothesized that ethnic identity might play a role in obesity, and Bowen et al. (this issue) found it to be strongly related to Black women's intentions to have mammograms. Although there is a large literature on Black ethnic identity (see Helms, 1990, for a review), this cultural variable also rarely has been addressed in the empirical studies of health in any health-related discipline. One of the only studies to do so, however, found that ethnic identity (i.e., use of the self-label Black vs. African American) was a strong predictor of hypertension (Scribner, Hohn, & Dwyer, 1995). Studies of the role of ethnic identity in Black women's health, and of the mechanism of that role, clearly would be useful. One possible mechanism is related to the definition of a race versus that of an ethnic group: Blacks who think of themselves as "Black" may regard themselves as members of a race (an ostensibly genetically distinct group), and thus intend to seek genetic testing, whereas those who think of themselves as African American may regard themselves as members of an ethnic group (a culturally distinct population), and thus intend to seek mammography, as Bowen et al. found. A variety of hypotheses regarding how, why, and the extent to which ethnic identity plays a role in the health of Black women and men must be tested, and are likely to reveal that this neglected cultural variable plays a powerful role.

An additional cultural variable noted by McNabb et al. (this issue) was the consumption of traditional cultural meals, prepared in the traditional manner. Such meals ("soul food") tend to be high in fat and salt (Landrine & Klonoff, 1996a) and so obviously might play a role in hypertension, obesity, and cancers. Our African American Acculturation Scale (Landrine & Klonoff, 1994, 1996a) includes a subscale assessing consumption of traditional cultural foods, as well as subscales assessing participation in African American ethnomedicine. In several studies using the African American Acculturation Scale, we found that the foods subscale was more strongly related than others to smoking and to hypertension, in a manner consistent with McNabb et al.'s hypothesis. The consumption of traditional cultural meals, however, has rarely received attention in any health discipline as a variable in the health of Blacks or of Black women.

Ethnic identity, consumption of traditional cultural foods, and participation in the beliefs and practices of African American ethnomedicine are just three of the many cultural variables that emerged as important in these eight articles. Empirical investigation of them may advance understanding of Black women's health and lead to new interventions to improve it.

SOCIAL–CONTEXTUAL VARIABLES

As noted in Table 1, several authors highlighted violence as an important social–contextual variable in Black (and in all) women's health, and as a variable that has yet to receive adequate research attention from any health discipline. In their article on this topic, Russo and her colleagues found that physical and sexual violence figures prominently in Black women's morbidity. Likewise, Sikkema and her colleagues found that community dangerousness and lack of cohesion (surrogates for violence and the threat of it) entered into the final regression as a variable that significantly increased Black women's risk for HIV. Similarly, in their article on beliefs about breast cancer, Hoffman-Goetz and Mills found that Black women's belief that intimate violence (injury to the breast) causes breast cancer plays a role in their avoidance and underutilization of mammography. These articles suggest three mechanisms through which violence plays a role in Black (and perhaps in all) women's health: directly, by causing physical and psychiatric symptoms; contextually, by creating dangerous, risky environments in which risky behaviors of a variety of types are more likely to occur; and indirectly, by eliciting shame, embarrassment, and similar cognitions and emotions that lead to avoidance of health care professionals. Only the first of these mechanisms has received research attention.

As indicated by the literature review in the Russo et al. article, a body of research on the direct role of violence in Black women's morbidity and mortality does exist. However, it is limited in number of studies and in scope, focusing more on immediate and long-term psychiatric rather than on physical outcomes, and it is often methodologically inadequate. The need for more research on the direct role of violence in Black women's health is clear, as is the need to improve measurement instruments and methodologies for studying the direct effects of violence.

In addition, studies on the indirect role of violence in Black and other women's health also are needed. Hoffman-Goetz and Mills found that Black women's belief that intimate violence (injury to the breast) causes breast cancer was related to their avoidance of cancer screening. In a recent study of Latinas' beliefs about breast and cervical cancer, Chavez, Hubbell, McMullin, Martinez, and Mishra (1995) found similar results. Trauma to the breast, in the form of blows, hits, bites, and bruises from accidents, beatings, breast feeding, and rough, brutal, or forced sexual relations was viewed as playing a major role in breast cancer: 74.4% of the Mexican American women mentioned such trauma as a cause of breast cancer, whereas only 15% of white women, and none of the physicians, mentioned this as a cause. Similarly, Latinas cited giving birth (vaginal deliveries), use of IUDs, abortions, miscarriages, surgical procedures, and blows to the vaginal area during forced or otherwise brutal intercourse as traumas that they believed to cause cervical cancer; 54% of the Latinas, but only 7% of the white women and none of the physicians, mentioned vaginal or genital trauma as a cause of cervical cancer. Thus, Chavez et al. (1995) found that many Latinas, like many of the Black women in the studies reviewed by Hoffman-Goetz & Mills (this issue) viewed violence against women as an etiology of cancers, and that such beliefs then played a role in their screening behavior. These beliefs unfortunately tend to be dismissed such that the possible etiologic role of violence in cancer among women has never been investigated. Ritenbaugh (1995), in a commentary on Chavez et al. (1995), noted that,

> A striking aspect of Chavez et al.'s work is the degree to which violence toward women figures prominently in the causative models for cancer reported by the women and the degree to which it is absent from the physicians' reports and the epidemiological research literature. Lack of a feminist perspective in ... cancer research may contribute to the dearth of studies. Given the growing interest in [the physical and sexual] abuse of girls and women, and the mounting evidence of its prevalence, a series of relevant questions comes to mind: Are women who have been abused more likely to get breast cancer? cervical cancer? ... Few of the risk factors for breast cancer identified by these women and glossed under the theme of physical trauma have been systematically studied.... Physical trauma may play no role in breast cancer etiology, but that conclusion should be based on careful epidemiological studies [that] have yet to be conducted. (pp. 77–78)

Violence may not, or it may indeed, play an etiologic role in cancers among women, and this possibility warrants empirical attention. There are several possible mechanisms through which violence could play a role in cancer prevalence or mortality. The first is a direct one in which injury to the breast, vagina, or cervix may indeed increase the probability of cancers through biologic mechanisms yet to be uncovered or examined; it is this possible direct role that Ritenbaugh (1995) argued must be investigated and empirically ruled out rather than summarily dismissed. Several indirect mechanisms also are possible. The first is that injury to the breast, vagina, or cervix as a result of intimate violence may lead to shame and efforts to hide one's injuries, and hence subsequently to avoiding cancer screening, as Hoffman-Goetz and Mills (this issue) and Chavez et al. (1995) suggested. The role of failure to receive screening in cancer mortality is clear in the articles here (e.g., Paskett et al.); in this manner, intimate violence could increase not the prevalence of cancer, but cancer mortality. Another possible indirect mechanism is suggested by stress research: Many studies have shown that stressful life events can suppress and compromise immunological functions and thereby render people more likely to succumb to disease, with this immunosuppression also linked to depression and the other negative affects associated with stress (Irwin, Daniels, Bloom, Smith, & Weiner, 1987; Kiecolt-Glaser et al., 1987; Kiecolt-Glaser, Garner, et al., 1984; Kiecolt-Glaser & Glaser, 1987, 1988; Kiecolt-Glaser et al., 1988; Kiecolt-Glaser et al., 1993; Kiecolt-Glaser et al., 1985; Kiecolt-Glaser, Speicher, et al., 1984; O'Leary, 1990). Intimate violence, like less brutal stressful life events, undoubtably (and indeed, necessarily) has similar immunological consequences for women, and hence could increase the probability of cancers. These are just a few of the many possible but neglected ways in which violence might play a role in cancer among Black and other women. As Ritenbaugh (1995) noted, women's belief that violence causes breast and cervical cancers may be the product of their observations of correlations, and hence must be examined seriously by a variety of health disciplines.

In addition to the direct and indirect roles that violence may play in Black women's health, there is a third mechanism that was suggested by the Sikkema et al. article here: High-risk environments or social contexts characterized by violence, disorganization, and lack of cohesion may be related to poor health and higher risk for disease among women, and specifically among low-income Black women. Several epidemiological studies support Sikkema et al.'s findings insofar as these studies have demonstrated that characteristics of the social context, including poor housing quality (e.g., Massey & Denton, 1993; Polednak, 1997; Wilson, 1987), segregation (e.g., Fix & Struyk, 1993; LaVeist, 1989; Massey & Denton, 1993; McCord & Freeman, 1990; Polednak, 1993, 1996, 1997), and community disorganization and violence (e.g., Lang & Polansky, 1994; Massey & Denton, 1993; Polednak, 1997; Wallace & Wallace, 1990; Wilson, 1987) are strongly associated with morbidity and mortality. Research on these social–contextual variables is virtually absent in health psychology and behavioral medicine, however, and is rare in preventive medicine and similar fields, but clearly is needed to understand and to improve Black women's health.

A second social–contextual variable noted by the authors here is racial discrimination. Despite the well-known prevalence of discrimination against Blacks (Bell,

1992; Fix & Struyk, 1993; Landrine & Klonoff, 1996b), there are only a handful of studies in any health discipline on its deleterious effects on Black health (Krieger, 1990; Krieger & Sidney, 1996; Landrine & Klonoff, 1996b). Discrimination undoubtably plays an important role in the poor health of Blacks and Black women, directly (as our study and Krieger's studies demonstrated) but also indirectly through the many mechanisms hypothesized in the Allison et al. and the Snowden et al. articles here. Examining the role of racial discrimination in the health of Blacks and Black women may be as important as examining the role of violence against women and of sexism in the health of Black and all other women. Violence against women and racial discrimination are just two of the many social–contextual variables highlighted by the articles here. Research on these and other social–contextual variables is needed to understand and improve the state of Black women's health and currently is virtually absent not only in health psychology, but in the other health-related disciplines such as public health and preventive medicine as well.

SUMMARY

The articles in this special issue have highlighted the nature of existing research on a few of Black women's most problematic health issues, and have underscored the need not only for more studies but also for studies with sounder methodologies. These articles call attention to a variety of cultural variables on the one hand and social–contextual variables on the other that must be examined to elucidate the many causes of Black women's differential morbidity and mortality. The cultural variables noted in the articles and further highlighted here have been particularly neglected by all of the health disciplines, no doubt because of our society's tradition of denying that African Americans have a culture at all (Harrison, 1994). Such cultural variables, including participation in African American ethnomedical and food practices, clearly are important, however, and so must be examined in careful, empirical studies that acknowledge and then investigate the influence of African American culture.

There are, however, two dangers inherent in focusing on African American culture and in regarding Blacks solely as African Americans—as a cultural population whose culture plays a role in their health. The first is that factors associated with Black's construction as a race can be overlooked. Although race is a meaningless and untenable concept from a genetic and biological—a scientific—perspective (Landrine & Klonoff, 1996a; Montagu, 1962, 1997; Polednak, 1989, 1997), race remains a social concept and construction associated with differential access to care, discrimination, and deprivations of a variety of types (Polednak, 1989, 1997). As Harrison (1994) put it:

> Regardless of its untenable status as a biological entity, race, especially in the ways
> it has been constructed ... is a *social* phenomenon, a marker of social location ... in

a racial hierarchy. Although ... races may indeed be ethnic [cultural] groups ... the privileging of cultural differences too often diverts analytic attention from the very issues of structural constraint and structural power that make the experiences, social location, and social relations of so-called races distinct. ... The assertion of African American ethnic identity ... represents one aspect and phase of the broader struggle against racist ideologies that ... negate black American cultural history. [But, simultaneously] notions of culture and cultural/ethnic diversity [that ignore] the *social* differences and inequalities that have come to be constituted in historically specific *racial orders* are inadequate. ... When race is merely subsumed under the rubric of cultural diversity ... racism is euphemized, denied, or negated. ... In light of ... the reality of racial stratification, the full ethnicization of African Americans as a group is contingent upon the demise of the U.S. racial order and the concomitant realization of social equality. (pp. 90–91)

Although African Americans are an ethnic (cultural) group whose culture has been denied and must now finally be examined as a variable in their health, Blacks also remain a socially defined race (not fully ethnicized) in a racially stratified society. Thus, although the concept of races may be our "most dangerous myth" and "fallacy" (Montagu, 1962, 1997), racial categorization nonetheless is a marker for a plethora of social, contextual, and structural inequalities, deprivations, and processes not similarly linked to ethnicity and strongly related to health. Hence, to fully elucidate the factors underlying Black women's differential morbidity and mortality, studies must address the interaction of ethnicity (African American culture), gender, and race (low status in a racial stratification system). Only by focusing on all of these factors can we "explain the subtle but insidious dissonances, incongruities, and contradictions that engender distinctive patterns of mortality and morbidity" among Black women (Harrison, 1994, p. 91). Long-neglected cultural variables in African American women's health should and indeed must be examined, but "in the context of families embedded in a wider societal context conditioned by federal policies that enable or constrain public health programs and community development" (Harrison, 1994, p. 93). To focus solely on cultural variables is to deny "that health and health care are situated in a wider social context structured and constrained by principles of racial hierarchy and forces of racism" (Harrison, 1994, p. 93).

The second related danger in focusing on the role of African American culture in Black women's health (or indeed, in focusing on the role of culture in the health of any ethnic minority group), is that research may take a "victim-blaming" turn (Hoff, 1994), in which the consequences of deprivation and exploitation are erroneously attributed to the culture or to the cultural or individual lifestyle of politically and economically subordinate groups. As Hoff argued, health research on Black women readily becomes racist and victim-blaming if it focuses on individual or cultural lifestyle variables and behaviors while ignoring the larger social and political context in which individual and cultural lifestyles are elicited and maintained. Studies of Black women's health that fail to embed and examine their health behavior within the context of their position at the very bottom of racial and gender stratification systems unwittingly portray Black women as promiscuous, deviant, knowledgeless women who have caused their own poor health—but cloak that ideological portrayal in the scientific language of "lifestyles" (Hoff, 1994), "risk-groups" (Schiller, 1992), and "cultural diversity" (Harrison, 1994; Schiller, 1992). Such research can be understood as "contemporary versions of the traditional racist gender constructions imposed on black women" (Harrison, 1994, p. 93) in which "victim-blaming is alive and well" (Hoff, 1994, p. 96).

Thus, the answer to our opening question, "What kind of research on Black women's health is needed?" is this: What is needed are studies that employ rigorous methodologies and use psychometrically sound instruments to test the model that aspects of African American culture are distal (indirect, diathesis) variables, whereas race-, gender-, and class-related social–contextual factors are proximal (direct, causal) variables in the health problems, health-related behaviors, health knowledge, morbidity, and mortality of Blacks and Black women (Landrine & Klonoff, in press). Such studies are needed in all of the health-related disciplines, and most particularly in health psychology. This is not simply because health psychology is far behind the other disciplines where conducting research on the health of Blacks and Black women is concerned. Rather, it is also because research in health psychology—precisely because it is psychology—in part can be differentiated from that in other health fields (e.g., medical anthropology, nursing, public health) by the psychometric integrity of its assessment instruments and the rigor of its experimental and laboratory methodologies. Thus, health psychology and behavioral medicine can make unique and valuable contributions (distinct from those of all other health-related disciplines) to efforts to understand and improve Black women's health.

The articles in this special issue represent merely the tip of the iceberg of the work that is needed, and thus did not attempt to address the multitude of problems and issues surrounding Black women's health. Instead, this special issue focused on only a few of Black women's health problems with the goal of providing information on intriguing and potentially powerful neglected cultural and social variables, and thereby encouraging future research on their role in Black women's health.

ACKNOWLEDGMENT

This research was supported by funds from National Institute of Mental Health Grant R03–MH54672 to Hope Landrine.

REFERENCES

Baer, H. (1985). Toward a systematic typology of Black folk healers. *Phylon, 43,* 327–343.

Bailey, E. J. (1987). Sociocultural factors and health care seeking among Black Americans. *Journal of the National Medical Association, 79,* 389–392.

Bailey, E. J. (1991). *Urban African American health care.* New York: University Press of America.

Bell, D. (1992). *Faces at the bottom of the well: The permanence of racism.* New York: Basic Books.

Bernal, M., & Castro, F. (1994). Are clinical psychologists prepared for service and research with ethnic minorities? *American Psychologist, 49,* 797–805.

Betancourt, H., & Lopez, S. (1993). The study of culture, ethnicity, and race in American psychology. *American Psychologist, 48,* 629–637.

Brandon, G. (1991). Sacrificial practices in Santeria, an African-Cuban religion in the United States. In J. E. Holloway (Ed.), *Africanisms in American culture* (pp. 119–147). Bloomington: Indiana University Press.

Charatz-Litt, C. (1992). A chronicle of racism: The effects of the White medical community on Black health. *Journal of the National Medical Association, 84,* 717–725.

Chavez, L. R., Hubbell, F. A., McMullin, J. M., Martinez, R. G., & Mishra, S. I. (1995). Structure and meaning in models of breast and cervical cancer risk factors: A comparison of perceptions among Latinas, Anglo women, and physicians. *Medical Anthropology Quarterly, 9,* 40–74.

Cooke, M. A. (1984). *The health of Blacks during reconstruction, 1862–1870.* Ann Arbor, MI: University Microfilms, Inc.

Deas-Moore, V. (1987). Medical adaptations of a culture relocated from Africa to the Sea Islands of South Carolina. *The World and I, 2,* 474–485.

Dole, A. A. (1995). Why not drop "race" as a term? *American Psychologist, 50,* 40.

Ekstrom, R. D. (1997). Compliments to Fowers and Richardson. *American Psychologist, 52,* 658.

Fairchild, H. H., Yee, A. H., Wyatt, G. E., & Weizmann, F. M. (1995). Readdressing psychology's problems with race. *American Psychologist, 50,* 46–47.

Fish, J. M. (1995). Why psychologists should learn some anthropology. *American Psychologist, 50,* 44–45.

Fix, M., & Struyk, R. J. (Eds.). (1993). *Clear and convincing evidence: Measurement of discrimination in America.* Latham, MD: Urban Institute Press.

Flaskerud, J. H., & Rush, C. (1989). AIDS and traditional health beliefs and practices of Black women. *Nursing Research, 38,* 210–215.

Fowers. B. J., & Richardson, F. C. (1996). Why is multiculturalism good? *American Psychologist, 51,* 609–621.

Fowers, B. J., & Richardson, F. C. (1997). A second invitation to dialogue: Multiculturalism and psychology. *American Psychologist, 52,* 659–661.

Garcia, H. B., & Lee, C. Y. (1989). Knowledge about cancer and use of health care services among Hispanic- and Asian-American older adults. *Journal of Psychosocial Oncology, 6,* 157–177.

Gaubatz, M. (1997). Subtle ethnocentrisms in the hermeneutic circle. *American Psychologist, 52,* 657–658.

Goodchilds, J. (1991). *Psychological perspectives on human diversity in America.* Washington, DC: American Psychological Association.

Goodson, M. (1987). Medical–botanical contributions of African slave women to American medicine. *The Western Journal of Black Studies, 2,* 198–203.

Graham, S. (1992). "Most of the subjects were white and middle class": Trends in published research on selected APA journals 1970–1989. *American Psychologist, 47,* 629–639.

Hall, A. L., & Bourne, P. G. (1973). Indigenous therapists in a Black urban community. *Archives of General Psychiatry, 28,* 137–142.

Hall, C. C. I. (1997). Cultural malpractice: The growing obsolescence of psychology with the changing U.S. population. *American Psychologist, 52,* 642–651.

Hall, G. C. N. (1997). Misunderstandings of multiculturalism: Shouting fire in crowded theaters. *American Psychologist, 52,* 654–655.

Harrison, F. V. (1994). Racial and gender inequalities in health and health care. *Medical Anthropology Quarterly, 8,* 90–95.

Helms, J. E. (1990). *Black and White racial identity.* New York: Greenwood.

Hill, C. E., & Matthews, H. (1981). Traditional health beliefs and practices among southern rural Blacks. In M. Black & J. S. Reed (Eds.), *Perspectives on the American South* (pp. 307–332). New York: Gordon & Breach Science.

Hoff, L. A. (1994). Comments on race, gender, and class bias in nursing. *Medical Anthropology Quarterly, 8,* 96–99.

Holloway, J. E. (1991). *Africanisms in American culture.* Bloomington: Indiana University Press.

Irwin, M., Daniels, M., Bloom, E., Smith, T. L., & Weiner, H. (1987). Life events, depressive symptoms, and immune function. *American Journal of Psychiatry, 144,* 437–441.

Jackson, J. J. (1981). Urban Black Americans. In A. Harwood (Ed.), *Ethnicity and medical care* (pp. 37–129). Cambridge, MA: Harvard University Press.

Jacques, G. (1976). Cultural health traditions: A Black perspective. In M. Branch & P. Paxton (Eds.), *Providing safe nursing care for ethnic people of color.* New York: Appleton-Century-Crofts.

Johnson, S. M., & Snow, L. F. (1982). Assessment of reproductive knowledge in an inner-city clinic. *Social Science and Medicine, 16,* 1657–1662.

Jones, J. M. (1991). Psychological models of race: What have they been and what should they be? In J. Goodchilds (Ed.), *Psychological perspectives on human diversity in America* (pp. 3–46). Washington, DC: American Psychological Association.

Jordan, W. (1975). Voodoo medicine. In R. Williams (Ed.), *Textbook of Black-related diseases* (pp. 716–738). New York: McGraw-Hill.

Jordan, W. (1979). The roots and practice of voodoo medicine. *Urban Health, 8,* 38–41.

Kiecolt-Glaser, J. K., Fisher, L., Ogrocki, P., Stout, J. C., Speicher, C. E., & Glaser, R. (1987). Marital quality, marital disruption, and immune function. *Psychosomatic Medicine, 49,* 13–34.

Kiecolt-Glaser, J. K., Garner, W., Speicher, C., Penn, G. M., Holliday, J., & Glaser, R. (1984). Psychosocial modifiers of immunocompetence in medical students. *Psychosomatic Medicine, 46,* 7–14.

Kiecolt-Glaser, J. K., & Glaser, R. (1987). Psychosocial influences on herpesvirus latency. In E. Kurstack, Z. J. Lipowski, & P. V. Morozov (Eds.), *Viruses, immunity, and mental disorders* (pp. 403–412). New York: Plenum.

Kiecolt-Glaser, J. K., & Glaser, R. (1988). Methodological issues in behavioral immunology research with humans. *Brain, Behavior, and Immunity, 2,* 67–78.

Kiecolt-Glaser, J. K., Glaser, R., Strain, E., Stout, J., Tarr, K., Holliday, J., & Speicher, C. (1986). Modulation of cellular immunity in medical students. *Journal of Behavioral Medicine, 9,* 5–21.

Kiecolt-Glaser, J. K., Kennedy, S., Malkoff, S., Fisher, L., Speicher, C. E., & Glaser, R. (1988). Marital discord and immunity in males. *Psychosomatic Medicine, 50,* 213–229.

Kiecolt-Glaser, J. K., Malarkey, W. B., Chee, M.-A., Newton, T., Cacioppo, J. T., Mao, H.-Y., & Glaser, R. (1993). Negative behavior during marital conflict is associated with immunological down-regulation. *Psychosomatic Medicine, 55,* 395–409.

Kiecolt-Glaser, J. K., Speicher, C., Holliday, J., & Glaser, R. (1984). Stress and the transformation of lymphocytes by Epstein–Barr virus. *Journal of Behavioral Medicine, 7,* 1–12.

Kiecolt-Glaser, J. K., Stephens, R. E., Lipetz, P. D., Speicher, C. E., & Glaser, R. (1985). Distress and DNA repair in human lymphocytes. *Journal of Behavioral Medicine, 8,* 311–320.

Klonoff, E. A., & Landrine, H. (1996). Acculturation and cigarette smoking among African American adults. *Journal of Behavioral Medicine, 19,* 501–514.

Krieger, N. (1990). Racial and gender discrimination: Risk factors for high blood pressure? *Social Science and Medicine, 30,* 1273–1281.

Krieger, N., & Sidney, S. (1996). Racial discrimination and blood pressure: The CARDIA study of young Black and White adults. *American Journal of Public Health, 86,* 1370–1378.

Laguerre, M. (1987). *Afro-Caribbean folk medicine.* New York: Bergin & Garvey.

Landrine, H. (1995). *Bringing cultural diversity to feminist psychology: Theory, research, practice.* Washington, DC: American Psychological Association.

Landrine, H., & Klonoff, E. A. (1992). Culture and health-related schema: Review and proposal for interdisciplinary integration. *Health Psychology, 11,* 267–276.

Landrine, H., & Klonoff, E. A. (1994). The African American Acculturation Scale. *Journal of Black Psychology, 20,* 104–127.

Landrine, H., & Klonoff, E. A. (1996a). *African-American acculturation: Deconstructing 'race' and reviving culture.* Thousand Oaks, CA: Sage.

Landrine, H., & Klonoff, E.A. (1996b). The Schedule of Racist Events: A measure of racial discrimination and a study of its negative physical and mental health consequences. *Journal of Black Psychology, 22,* 144–168.

Landrine, H., & Klonoff, E. A. (in press). Cultural diversity and health psychology. In A. Baum, T. Revenson, & J. Singer (Eds.), *Handbook of health psychology.* Mahwah, NJ: Lawrence Erlbaum Associates, Inc.

Lang, D. M., & Polansky, M. (1994). Pattern of asthma mortality in Philadelphia from 1969 to 1991. *New England Journal of Medicine, 331,* 1542–1546.

LaVeist, T. A. (1989). Linking residential segregation to the infant-mortality race disparity in U.S. cities. *Sociology and Social Research, 73,* 90–94.

Levin, M. (1995). Does race matter? *American Psychologist, 50,* 45–46.

Massey, D. S., & Denton, N. A. (1993). *American apartheid: Segregation and the making of the underclass.* Cambridge, MA: Harvard University Press.

Mathews, H., Kirkland, J., Sullevan, C., & Baldwin, K. (1992). *Herbal and magical medicine.* Durham, NC: Duke University Press.

McCord, C., & Freeman, H. P. (1990). Excess mortality in Harlem. *New England Journal of Medicine, 322,* 173–177.

Mitchell, F. (1978). *Hoodoo medicine: Sea Islands herbal remedies.* Berkeley, CA: Reed, Cannon, & Johnson.

Montagu, A. (1962). The concept of race. *American Anthropologist, 64,* 919–928.

Montagu, A. (1997). *The fallacy of race.* Thousand Oaks, CA: Sage.

Mulira, J. G. (1991). The case of voodoo in New Orleans. In J. E. Holloway (Ed.), *Africanisms in American culture* (pp. 34–68). Bloomington: Indiana University Press.

O'Leary, A. (1990). Stress, emotion, and human immune function. *Psychological Bulletin, 103,* 363–383.

Payne-Jackson, A., & Lee, J. (1993). *Folk wisdom and mother wit: John Lee—An American herbal healer.* Westport, CT: Greenwood.

Phinney, J. S. (1996). When we talk about American ethnic groups, what do we mean? *American Psychologist, 51,* 918–927.

Polednak, A. P. (1989). *Racial and ethnic differences in disease.* New York: Oxford University Press.

Polednak, A. P. (1993). Poverty, residential segregation, and black/white mortality rates in urban areas. *Journal of Health Care of the Poor and Underserved, 4,* 363–373.

Polednak, A. P. (1996). Trends in U.S. urban black infant mortality, by degree of segregation. *American Journal of Public Health, 86,* 723–726.

Polednak, A. P. (1997). *Segregation, poverty, and mortality in urban African Americans.* New York: Oxford University Press.

Puckett, N. (1926). *Folk beliefs of the southern negro.* Chapel Hill: University of North Carolina Press.

Reid, P. T., & Kelly, E. (1994). Research on women of color: From ignorance to awareness. *Psychology of Women Quarterly, 18,* 477–486.

Ritenbaugh, C. (1995). Commentary on "Models of cancer risk factors." *Medical Anthropology Quarterly, 9,* 77–79.

Scarr, S. (1988). Race and gender as psychological variables. *American Psychologist, 43,* 56–59.

Schiller, N. G. (1992). What's wrong with this picture? The hegemonic construction of culture in AIDS research in the United States. *Medical Anthropology Quarterly, 6,* 237–254.

Scribner, R., Hohn, A., & Dwyer, J. (1995). Blood pressure and self-concept among African-Americans. *Journal of the National Medical Association, 87,* 417–422.

Sexton, R. (1992). Cajun and Creole treaters: Magico–religious folk healing in French Louisiana. *Western Folklore, 51,* 237–248.

Snow, L. F. (1974). Folk medical beliefs and their implications for the care of patients. *Annals of Internal Medicine, 81,* 82–96.

Snow, L. F. (1977). Popular medicine in a Black neighborhood. In E. H. Spicer (Ed.), *Ethnic medicine in the Southwest* (pp. 19–95). Tucson: University of Arizona Press.

Snow, L. F. (1978). Sorcerers, saints, and charlatans: Black folk healers in urban America. *Culture, Medicine and Psychiatry, 2,* 69–106.

Snow, L. F. (1983). Traditional health beliefs and practices among lower class Black Americans. *Western Journal of Medicine, 139,* 820–828.

Spector, R. E. (1979). *Cultural diversity in health and illness.* New York: Appleton-Century-Crofts.

Spector, R. E. (1996). *Cultural diversity in health and illness* (2nd ed.). New York: Appleton-Century-Crofts.

Spicer, E. H. (1977). *Ethnic medicine in the Southwest.* Tucson: University of Arizona Press.

Sun, K. (1995). The definition of race. *American Psychologist, 50*(1), 43–44.

Tallant, R. (1946). *Voodoo in New Orleans.* New York: Macmillan.

Teo, T., & Febbraro, A. R. (1997). Norm, factuality, and power in multiculturalism. *American Psychologist, 52,* 656–657.

Wallace, R., & Wallace, D. (1990). Origins of public health collapse in New York City: The dynamics of planned shrinkage, contagious urban decay and social disintegration. *Bulletin of the New York Academy of Medicine, 66,* 391–434.

Watson, W. (1984). *Black folk healing.* New Brunswick, NJ: Transaction.

Wilson, W. J. (1987). *The truly disadvantaged.* Chicago: University of Chicago Press.

Yanchar, S. C., & Slife, B. D. (1997). Parallels between multiculturalism and disunity in psychology. *American Psychologist, 52,* 658–659.

Yee, A., Fairchild, H., Weizmann, F., & Wyatt, G. (1993). Addressing psychology's problems with race. *American Psychologist, 48,* 1132–1140.

Zuckerman, M. (1990). Some dubious premises in research and theory on racial differences. *American Psychologist, 45,* 1297–1303.

WOMEN'S HEALTH: RESEARCH ON GENDER, BEHAVIOR, AND POLICY, 3(3&4), 383–385

AUTHOR INDEX
Volume 3

WOMEN'S HEALTH: RESEARCH ON GENDER, BEHAVIOR, AND POLICY, *3*(3&4), 387–388
Copyright © 1997, Lawrence Erlbaum Associates, Inc.

SUBJECT INDEX
Volume 3

WOMEN'S HEALTH: RESEARCH ON GENDER, BEHAVIOR, AND POLICY, 3(3&4), 389–390
Copyright © 1997, Lawrence Erlbaum Associates, Inc.

EDITORIAL ACKNOWLEDGMENT OF
AD HOC REVIEWERS

In addition to the members of the Editorial Board, the following individuals reviewed one or more manuscripts for *Women's Health: Research on Gender, Behavior, and Policy* for Volumes 2 and 3. The editor is grateful for their wise counsel regarding manuscripts and would like to extend thanks for their valuable services.

Antonia Abbey
Dyanne D. Affonso
Leona S. Aiken
David Altman
Janet Audrain
Nancy E. Avis
Linda Beckman
Kathy Berra
Susan J. Blalock
Kim Blankenship
Niall Bolger
Virigina S. Cain
Patricia Campione
Joan C. Chrisler
Richard J. Contrada
Paul Costa
Faye J. Crosby
Robert T. Croyle
Lauren Daltroy
Sherri L. Darrow
Joanne DiPlacido
Michael Diefenbach
Lynn A. Durel
Anke Ehrhardt
Michelle Fine
Elizabeth Fries
Mindy Fullilove
Sheryle J. Gallant
Linda Gannon
Meg Gerrard

Jacqueline M. Golding
Melanie Greenberg
Judith A. Hall
Vicki Sue Helgeson
Jan L. Hitchcock
Marc Hochberg
Jeannette Ickovics
Christine Jackson
Susan R. Johnson
Anne S. Kasper
Patricia Katz
Jon Kerner
Janice Kiecolt-Glaser
Kathleen King
Carrie Klabunde
Robert C. Klesges
Elizabeth Klonoff
Mary P. Koss
David Livert
Marci Lobel
M. Cynthia Logsdon
Hyacinth Mason
Joni A. Mayer
Curtis Mettlin
Beth E. Meyerowitz
Sarah Moody-Thomas
Juana Mora
Kelly A. Morrow
Ana M. Navarro
Suzanne Ouelette